Procurement 4.0 and the Fourth Industrial Revolution

Bernardo Nicoletti

Procurement 4.0 and the Fourth Industrial Revolution

The Opportunities and Challenges of a Digital World

palgrave
macmillan

Bernardo Nicoletti
Temple University Rome Campus
Rome, Italy

Università di Tor Vergata
Rome, Italy

ISBN 978-3-030-35978-2 ISBN 978-3-030-35979-9 (eBook)
https://doi.org/10.1007/978-3-030-35979-9

This Palgrave Macmillan imprint is published by the registered company Springer Nature Switzerland AG.
The registered company address is: Gewerbestrasse 11, 6330 Cham, Switzerland

Contents

Abbreviations

ABI	Associazione Bancaria Italiana
AGV	Automated Guided Vehicle
AMA	American Marketing Association
API	Application Programming Interface(s)
ASC	Agile Supply Chain
B2B	Business to Business
B2C	Business to Consumer
BAS	Building Automation Systems
BAU	Business as Usual
BCG	Boston Consulting Group
BDAQ	Big Data Analytics Quality
BOL	Bill of Lading
BOM	Bill of Materials
BPaaS	Business Process as a Service
BPO	Business Process Outsourcing or Business Process Optimization
CAGR	Compounded Annual Growth Rate
Capex	Capital Expenditure
CBR	Case-Based Reasoning
CFFR	Collaborative Planning, Forecasting, and Replenishment
CFM	Cash Flow Management
CLM	Contract Lifecycle Management
CNC	Computer Numerical Control
COPIS	Customer, Output, Process, Input, Supplier
CPM	Critical Path Method
CPM	Corporate Performance Management or Critical Path Method
CPO	Chief Procurement Officer
CPS	Cyber-Physical System

CRM	Customer Relationship Management
CWL	Carlson Wagonlit Travel
DBA	Database Administration
DDLC	Document Development Lifecycle
DTC	Digital Trade Chain
E-Proc	e-Procurement
ECM	Enterprise Content Management
EDI	Electronic Data Interchange
EERP	Extended Enterprise Resource System
EMS	Small and Medium Enterprises
EOQ	Economic Order Quantity
EPC	Engineering, Procurement, and Construction
ERP	Enterprise Resource Planning
EVI	Early Partner Involvement
FMCG	Fast-Moving Consumer Goods
FTE	Full-Time Equivalent
GDPR	General Data Protection Regulation
GIS	Global Information Systems
GMS	Global Mobile System
GPO	Group-Purchasing Organization
GPP	Green Public Procurement
GRI	Global Reporting Institute
IaaS	Infrastructure as a Service
IBIN	Intelligent Bin
ICC	International Chamber of Commerce
ICT	Information and Communication Technology
IoE	Internet of Everything
IoO	Internet of Objects
IoP	Internet of People
IoS	Internet of Services
IoT	Internet of Things
ISO	International Standard Organization
ITS	Integrated Transport Management System
JiT	Just in Time
KPI	Key Performance (or Process) Indicator
KPO	Knowledge Process Outsourcing
KRI	Key Risk Indicator
KYC	Know Your Customer
LAN	Local Area Network
LGV	Laser Guided Vehicle
LMS	Logistics Manufacturing Services
MaaS	Mobility as a Service

MDM	Mobile Device Management
MMR	Mass Market Retailers
MMS	Managed Mobility Services
MMSP	Managed Mobility Services Provider
MOU	Memorandum of Understanding
MRO	Maintenance, Repair, Operations (Material)
MRP	Manufacturing and Material Requirement Planning
MSA	Master Service Agreement
MTO	Make to Order
MTS	Make to Stock
MWM	Mobile Workforce Management
NFC	Near Field Communication
NIST	National Institute of Standards and Technology
OBS	Organization Breakdown Structure
OEE	Overall Equipment Effectiveness
OEM	Original Equipment Manufacturer
OMP	Open Manufacturing Platform
Opex	Operating Expenditures
OT	Operations Technology
P2P	Purchase to Pay
PaaS	Platform as a Service
PBI	Process Business Intelligence
PLC	Programmable Logic Controller
PLM	Product Lifecycle Management
PROU	Perceived Ease of Use
R2P	Requisition to Pay
RACI	Responsibility-Accounting-Control-Information
RFB	Request for Bid
RFI	Request for Information
RFID	Radio-Frequency Identification
RFP	Request for Proposal
RFQ	Request for Quotation
RFX	Any Type of Request for Procurement
ROA	Return on Assets
ROI	Return on Investment
RPA	Robot Process Automation
RTLS	Real-time Locating System
S2P	Source to Pay
SaaS	Software as a Service
SCF	Supply Chain Finance
SCM	Supply Chain Management
SIM	Subscriber Identity Module

SIPOC	Partner, Input, Process, Output, Customer
SKU	Stock-Keeping Unit
SLA	Service Level Agreement
SMS	Short Message Service
SRM	Supplier Relationships Management
STP	Straight Through Processing
SWOT	Strengths-Weaknesses-Opportunities-Threats
TAM	Technology Acceptance Model
TCM	Total Cost Management
TCO	Total Cost of Ownership
TIM	Trust in Motion
TMS	Transportation Management System
TQM	Total Quality Management
UAV	Unmanned Aerial Vehicles
UMTS	Universal Mobile Telecommunications System
VA/NVA	Value-Added/Non-Value-Added
VoC	Voice of the Customer
WAN	Wide-Area Network
WBS	Work Breakdown Structure
WIP	Work in Process
WMS	Warehouse Management System
WSN	Wireless Sensor Networks
XML	Extended Messaging Language

List of Figures

CHAPTER 1

Introduction

The global recession has hit hard in many areas and all major functions of organizations have been impacted. Figure 1.1 summarizes some of the challenges organizations face in light of this situation. The importance of developing and managing innovative strategies in the field of procurement is clear. From a historical perspective, procurement has undergone huge transitions, especially in the last decades, in the sense that organizations have had to deal with pressures relating to cutting costs and increasing profits.[1]

It is essential to innovate through process improvement and automation management. To analyze how this can be done, a possible entry point is to scrutinize the implementation of innovations. This book presents such a new approach, calling it 'procurement 4.0.' This approach represents a set of solutions that can support managers and buyers at all stages of the procurement process, from strategic procurement to pre-negotiation (the search for new partners), up to the monitoring of expenditure and giving better estimates of future needs. These solutions are consistent with the approach of industry 4.0 initiative.

Procurement 4.0 can be seen as a component of the initiative industry 4.0.[2] But it is much more than this, too. It also offers a new and original

[1] Uusitalo, J. (2019). Strategic Procurement in the Face of Uncertainty. *Master's Thesis*. University of Jyväskylä, Finland.

[2] Lasi, H., Fettke, P., Kemper, H. G., Feld, T., & Hoffmann, M. (2014). Industry 4.0. *Business & information systems engineering*, *6*(4), 239–242.

B. Nicoletti, *Procurement 4.0 and the Fourth Industrial Revolution*,
https://doi.org/10.1007/978-3-030-35979-9_1

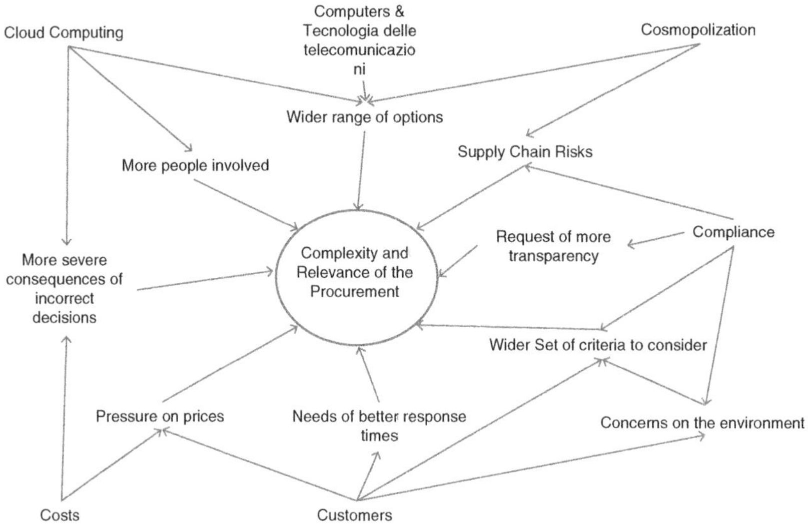

Fig. 1.1 Impact of the transformation on procurement

vision of procurement—one that is more agile, integrated, and responsive to the customers' and the organization's value-adding.

In terms of processes, this book explores problems and solutions in the definition of how procurement can add value for customers, inside and outside of an organization; and how it can help manage relationships, improve processes, and better management of resources, both internal and with partners.[3]

One of the major objectives of the procurement 4.0 initiative is to implement agile procurement. Agility is nowadays a much-used term in the management of organizations.[4] The topic is especially relevant because it is an interesting development: the concept of agile management derived from 'lean management,' which became a business mantra in recent years. The need to be lean is not—in and of itself—the goal that organizations

[3] In this book, the terms 'supplier' and 'vendor' are not used. These are replaced with 'partners,' because if the supply fails both the client and the supplier are damaged.

[4] Nicoletti, B. (2017), *Agile Procurement. Volume II: Designing and Implementing a Digital Transformation*, Springer International Publishing, London, UK, ISBN 978-3-319-61085-6.

must pursue; rather, it is a means to becoming more agile and flexible. In other words, agility is the objective for which leanness is the means.

This vital need for agility is a consequence of the turbulence of the current environment. An agile enterprise can respond quickly to changes in the economy, markets, and technology.

In order to be agile, organizations must be able to respond quickly to changes by adapting their configuration. Better organizational agility can be achieved by maintaining and adapting products and services to meet the needs of customers. This can be done by adjusting the organization and making the best use of available resources within the ecosystem in which the organization operates. Thanks to its agility, an organization can quickly adapt to market changes and the evolving environment in effective, efficient, and economical ways.

In a scenario of this type, it is important that the procurement function fits the organizational philosophy. To achieve this, there are essentially two approaches that should be followed simultaneously. One is to improve processes by adopting a lean approach, while at the same time management should be automated, to implement effective, efficient, and economical solutions. Procurement 4.0 is an extension of these concepts. It is based on the key principles of complex adaptive systems and complexity science. This approach creates the basis for success. One can say that the agility of procurement in an organization result of its intelligence.

Procurement 4.0 is geared to supporting the digital transformation of an organization. It aims to turn such responsiveness and change into a habit of an organization's life. It intends to reduce or eliminate the organizational trauma that paralyzes many organizations when they try to adapt to new markets, environments, and solutions. Change is perpetual: procurement 4.0 must be able to easily adapt and take advantage of emerging opportunities. Moreover, procurement 4.0 is an integral and essential component of a larger system within a given organization. Its activities produce and support digital processing chain effects both within procurement and in the wider organization.

This book delves deep into these methodologies and techniques, treating the field of procurement 4.0 as an agile business model and involving all its components.[5]

[5] Nicoletti, B. (2017), *Agile Procurement. Volume II: Designing and Implementing a Digital Transformation*, Springer International Publishing, London, UK, ISBN 978-3-319-61085-6.

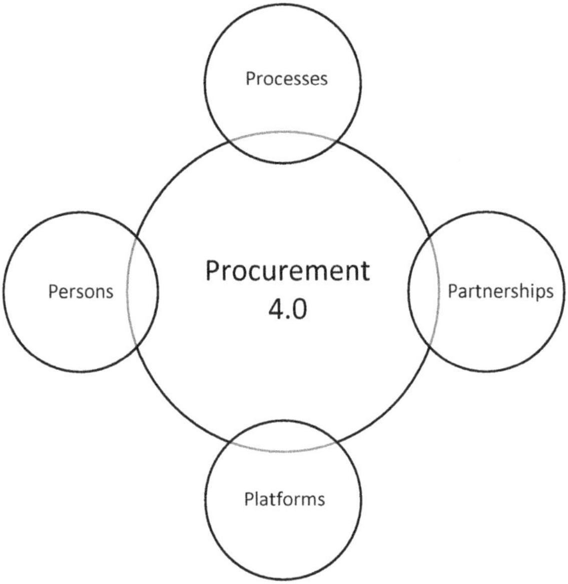

Fig. 1.2 Four Ps

The transformation of organizations must cover key success factors, which are summarized in this book as the four Ps (Fig. 1.2):

- Processes
- Platforms
- Persons
- Partnerships.

The central chapters in this book follow the sequence of these four Ps. The final part is a discussion of the future of procurement 4.0.

The core thesis that this book promulgates is that the function, discipline, and activity of procurement 4.0 can be a critical and strategic interface within operations management, supporting organizational efficiency, effectiveness, and economics as part of a long-term perspective. This is demonstrated through a number of references to real organizations in different sectors.

Nicoletti, B. (2017), *Agile Procurement. Volume I: Adding Value with Lean Processes*, Springer International Publishing, London, UK. ISBN 978-3-319-61082-5.

CHAPTER 2

Industry 4.0 and Procurement 4.0

2.1 Introduction

A saying attributed to Darwin argues that "[it] is not the strongest of the species that survives nor the most intelligent, but one best responsive to change."[1] This also applies to organizations. They need to renew themselves, otherwise they will be marginalized or bypassed.

This chapter discusses the increasing application of innovation in procurement. Such renewal can be labeled 'procurement 4.0.'

Industry 4.0 is the convergence of information and communication technology (ICT) and automation of machinery and infrastructure. The term refers to a Fourth Industrial Revolution. This is distinguished by advanced digitization within organizations, based on the integration of ICT solutions with operational technologies in the field of intelligent objects (machines and products).[2] This enables and transforms industrial production systems and services independently to control their production processes. In addition to the focus on digitization and automation, industry 4.0 provides support for the interaction of technology innovations whose quantitative effects allow organizations to create new products, processes, modes of production, and business models.

[1] Huxley, T. H. (2018). *The Darwinian hypothesis.* Amazon Digital Press LLC, Bellevue, WA.

[2] Piggin, R. (2014). Industrial systems: cyber-security's new battlefront [Information Technology Operational Technology]. *Engineering & Technology*, *9*(8), 70–74.

B. Nicoletti, *Procurement 4.0 and the Fourth Industrial Revolution*,
https://doi.org/10.1007/978-3-030-35979-9_2

Innovation is necessary for organizations to face new challenges. It is also essential to improving the effectiveness, efficiency, and economics of the procurement sector and to meet the growing need to add value and satisfy customers through all functions of an organization. There is a concomitant need to improve relations with the ecosystem of the organization and its partners. If the partners are not satisfied, an organization cannot create effective partnerships in an extended value network perspective. This book stresses the move from the concept of a value chain to a value network, and this term is used throughout.[3] The value for customers and the organizations is obtained through an ecosystem that combines vendors, customers, and public administration elements in a network organization.

The innovation goals can be summarized in three aspects[4]:

#1. Smarter sourcing (fewer transactions and more value in each of them). This involves:
- focusing on major spending areas
- consolidating vendors and turning them into partners
- delegating administration and focusing on high value-added activities
- managing critical and direct purchases
- governing a marketplace for indirect purchases with emphasis on self-service by the different functions of the organization.

#2. Making savings in the organization's resources:
- creating centers of excellence in procurement where it makes sense to do so
- optimizing the relationship with partners
- outsourcing where the benefits/cost ratio is bigger.

[3] The term value network has also been used with a different meaning. It was proposed by Stabell and Fjeldstad (Stabell, C.B., Fjeldstad, Ø. D. (1998) and refers there to Configuring value for competitive advantage on chains, shops, and networks: *Strategic Management Journal*, 19(5), 413–437). It is based on mediation technologies according to Thompson's typology (Thompson, J. D. (2017). *Organizations in action: Social science bases of administrative theory*. Routledge, London, UK). It connects clients and customers who are interested in creating mutual relations and interdependence. The mediating technologies support relations between actors scattered across time and space. This model is similar to what has been called the platform approach (Zhu, F., & Iansiti, M. (2007). *Dynamics of platform competition: Exploring the role of installed base, platform quality and consumer expectations*. Division of Research, Harvard Business School, Cambridge, MA).

[4] Hammer, M., & Champy, J. (2009). *Reengineering the Corporation: Manifesto for Business Revolution, A*. Zondervan, Grand Rapids. MI.

#3. Maximum utilization of the potential of new solutions:
- standardize
- Innovative use of new solutions such as cloud computing, the Internet of Things (IoT), mobile data, big data analytics, especially in the field of operations.

To move in these directions, it is important to push for better governance of procurement processes and to define a renewal plan to:

- better reflect the priorities of an organization;
- be more accessible to the entire organization;
- create efficiencies and commit to making savings for the organization.

Enel Global Procurement[5]

Enel S.p.A. is an Italian multinational energy company. Its business is in the sectors of electricity generation and distribution. It is also active in the distribution of natural gas. The organization of procurement in the Enel Group has been completely overhauled to increase the Group's economies of scale in terms of sourcing power and procurement intelligence. The objective is to ensure a competitive advantage for Enel in a challenging energy market that is in constant evolution. Particular attention was paid to training. Although part of the Central Procurement Directorate budget, this has been mostly directed to business users, due to the importance of internal customers' use of procurement and their involvement in procurement processes.

Similar care has been paid to partners. Enel organizes a 'supplier day' and webinars to illustrate the launch of new tenders. The main objective of these initiatives is to work in a more integrated way with partners. The supplier day promotes and strengthens relationships with Enel's best partners and, at the same time, creates an opportunity to get to know new partners. Webinars allow the organization to maintain and strengthen mutual understanding.

(*continued*)

[5] https://corporate.enel.it/it/storie/a/2018/02/open-innovation-meeting-ambrosetti-club-enel-roma. Accessed March 10, 2019.

(continued)

A supplier day begins with an update on the overall situation of the markets in which Enel operates, on the organizations within the Enel Group, as well as with detailed information on future short- and medium-term projects. The Enel Group's global procurement arm presents the work of its organization based on global and local categories of goods and services, and informs partners on the qualification processes and vendor evaluation—at the same time updating them about new products being introduced. For example, this has taken place alongside the adoption of a system of electronic tenders and the introduction of a portal for partner qualification.

These events are also an opportunity for an open and transparent discussion during a specific Questions & Answers session. The objective is to get feedback from partners on their overall experience of collaboration with the Enel Group. Each event ends with awards for the Best Partner for the previous year in different categories. This is another way to strengthen successful partnerships.

2.2 Industry 4.0

The term 'industry 4.0' was used for the first time in 2011 when an association of representatives from industry, politics, and academia promoted the idea as an approach to improve the competitiveness of German manufacturing.[6] The German government has supported the idea, announcing that industry 4.0 is an integral part of its initiative High-Tech Strategy 2020 Fuer Deutschland.[7] Subsequently, a working group on industry 4.0 developed the first recommendations for its implementation, published in April 2013.[8]

Industry 4.0 is a term that sets out a vision of the future: the so-called smart factory. It requires and facilitates also an agile and effective procurement 4.0. Industry 4.0 can be defined as the incorporation and manage-

[6] Schwab, K. (2017). *The fourth industrial revolution*. Currency. London, UK.

[7] Hermann, M., Pentek, T., & Otto, B. (2016, January). Design principles for industrie 4.0 scenarios. In *2016 49th Hawaii international conference on system sciences (HICSS)* (pp. 3928–3937). IEEE.

[8] Hermann, M., Pentek, T., & Otto, B. (2016, January). Design principles for industrie 4.0 scenarios. In *2016 49th Hawaii international conference on system sciences* (HICSS). IEEE, 3928–3937.

ment of intelligent products in the realm of physical processes, management, and information/digital. These physical processes in industry 4.0 interact with each other and across geographies and organizations.[9]

Industry 4.0 provides support in two basic directions of development. On the one hand, an application must be 'pulled' by the customer, inducing a change in operating conditions and in the model. This first aspect leads to changes not only in the organization but also social, economic, and political shifts. The most important of these are the following:

- A high capacity for innovation is an important success factor. The goal is customized sales. Over time, customers are granted an opportunity to define the terms of purchase. This trend leads to increasing customization of products. The final objective is a lot size of production of just one item.
- Because of market characteristics, agility is essential in all the operations of an organization, to allow flexibility and maximize the capacity to be adaptive.
- To meet the new requirements of the business model, faster decision-making procedures are needed. Organizational structure must therefore be as flat as possible.
- There should be a boost for economic and ecological efficiency for the production, in the management of costs associated with resources, as well as social awareness on sustainability issues.
- Industry 4.0 pushes the whole society toward innovation.

On the other hand, there is a push for new solutions—such as mobility, 3D printers, mobile computers, advanced computer applications, and so on. They are becoming more and more popular and accessible. In industrial practice, these innovative solutions are still not widely used, but these innovations allow:

- Reduction of human physical labor and the adoption of more automated solutions. Examples are automated guided vehicles (AGV) with the paths programmed in the factory or 'pulled' from another machine or from the product itself;
- New solutions such as simulation, artificial intelligence (AI), digital security, or virtual reality (VR) are guided by the increasing digitization of all production and the availability of advanced tools. Similarly, there

[9] Härting, RC, Schmidt, R., Möhring, M., Reichstein, C., Neumaier, P., & Jozinovic, P. (2015). *Nutzenpotenziale von Industries 4.0: Einblicke Aktuelle Studienergebnisse.* BOD-Books on Demand.

is now a more extensive network of technical and integrated components. Software allows organizations to collect and analyze data from sensors or tags attached to the goods, and then trace the goods within the factory. It is even possible for an organization to monitor, manage, and maintain its products at customer sites[10];

- Miniaturization to reduce the space necessary for computing devices, while devices with improved performance can be installed in a small space. Nanotechnology is becoming increasingly used.[11] This enables new fields of application, even in the procurement industry.

In short, industry 4.0 describes the integration of technology, ICT, and automation in support of developments in production systems and consequently in procurement processes. These developments have implications for technology and process, organization, and work.[12]

Investment in industry 4.0 is increasingly based on the value of the entire network. What becomes clear is that organizations from all sectors are focusing their investments in the optimization of procurement systems, emphasizing the importance of optimal management thereof in the Fourth Industrial Revolution.

Research on the development, application, and challenges of industry 4.0 was carried out in 2015. This involved 235 German companies in the field of manufacturing, engineering, the automobile industry, electronics, and ICT.[13] The study shows that surveyed companies will be investing an average of 3.3% of their revenues in industry 4.0 by 2020. These investments pertain to key areas in the value network: supply chains, product development, planning, production, services, and distribution. It is expected that 80% of the value network will be digitalized by 2020, with productivity increased by 18% and about €110 billion revenue generated per annum.[14]

[10] Nicoletti, B. (2009), Sintesi Seminario RFID per l'Impiantistica, *L'Impiantistica Italiana*, N. 6, November–December, 1–7.

[11] Porter, A. L., Youtie, J., Shapira, P., & Schoeneck, D. J. (2008). Refining search terms for nanotechnology. *Journal of nanoparticle research*, 10(5), 715–728.

[12] Lasi, H., Fettke, P., Kemper, HG, Feld, T., & Hoffmann, M. (2014). Industry 4.0. *Business & Information Systems Engineering*, 6 (4), 239.

[13] Geissbauer, R., Schrauf, S., Koch, V., & Kuge, S. (2014). Industry 4.0 – Opportunities and Challenges of the Industrial Internet, *PwCIL*, Germany. www.pwc.de/industry4.0. Accessed July 20, 2019.

[14] Geissbauer, R., Schrauf, S., Koch, V., & Kuge, S. (2014). Industry 4.0 – Opportunities and Challenges of the Industrial Internet, *PwCIL*, Germany. www.pwc.de/industry4.0. Accessed July 20, 2019.

Barilla[15]

Barilla, the premium Italian pasta company, built the largest automated warehouse in the world through the use of LGV (laser-guided vehicle) technology, in Pedrignano, Italy. The warehouse is on the historic site of the group, on the outskirts of Parma, Italy. It serves several Barilla factories and partners. With an area of 40,000 square meters, 80,000 pallets, 120 trucks loaded every day, and 54 wagons with the new LGV, the Barilla warehouse is an example of excellence in global logistics. Barilla aims to improve the services it offers customers (in particular, to large retails chain organizations) and then to be more competitive in its market.

This warehouse will handle a quarter of global material and components for Barilla and nearly half of all the pasta and sauces manufactured by the company and sold around the world, from Brazil to Japan. This structure relies heavily on LGV technology applied for trolleys used to move, store, and pick up goods, and for the supervision of the installation software. The vehicles move without the need for wires or traces. They use sophisticated software that identifies orders, looks for the location of the correct pallet store, or withdraws in real time, and interacts with the vehicles using a radio frequency network.

The structure—which required investment of nearly €15 million—is also a model of energy and environmental efficiency. It has eliminated about 3000 trips a year to external warehouses, reducing carbon dioxide emissions, as well as cutting 40% of lighting costs and 20% of heating and cooling costs.

[15] http://distribuzionemoderna.info/notizia-del-giorno/barilla-inaugura-a-pedrignano-il-piu-grande-magazzino-automatico-del-mondo. Accessed September 15, 2018.

Ocado[16]

Ocado is a British internet supermarket. It specializes in groceries, home essentials, and more delivered to the customer's home. It has a fully automated warehouse where autonomous robots collect products ordered by customers, then pack and pass them to drivers for delivery.[17] In the next step, a dedicated AI application recommends optimal delivery routes. The benefits include reduced labor costs, acceleration, and optimization of processes. There is also an improvement in stock turnover, increased effectiveness of warehouse space (there is no need to create paths for staff), and improved safety.

Figure 2.1 shows the industry 4.0 environment as a synthesis between ICT and automation. This section focuses on methods of procurement 4.0 to provide support.

2.2.1 The Main Components

Industry 4.0 includes a set of solutions enabling intelligent products and processes integrated with interconnected digital and physical components. All this is changing products, processes, business models, organizations, and procurement significantly.[18]

It is possible to define a model for industry 4.0. It consists of several components, which for mnemonic reasons are listed in this book under words with the initial C. The model considers a classification of the industry 4.0 components into 'hard' and 'soft.' Hard components are based on infrastructure; soft components are more oriented toward software. For each, it is possible to show a solution capable of supporting its implementation within an industry 4.0 initiative. All these components require strict management tools (or Command, to continue with words starting with C), which in turn should be supported by specific solutions.

[16] https://www.ocado.com/webshop/startWebshop.do. Accessed August 12, 2019.

[17] Wodecki, A. (2018). *Artificial intelligence in value creation: Improving competitive advantage*. Springer, Cham, Switzerland.

[18] Schmidt, R., Möhring, M., Härting, R. C., Reichstein, C., Neumaier, P., & Jozinović, P. (2015). Industry 4.0-potentials for creating smart products: empirical research results. In the *International Conference on Business Information Systems*. Springer, Cham, Switzerland: 16–27.

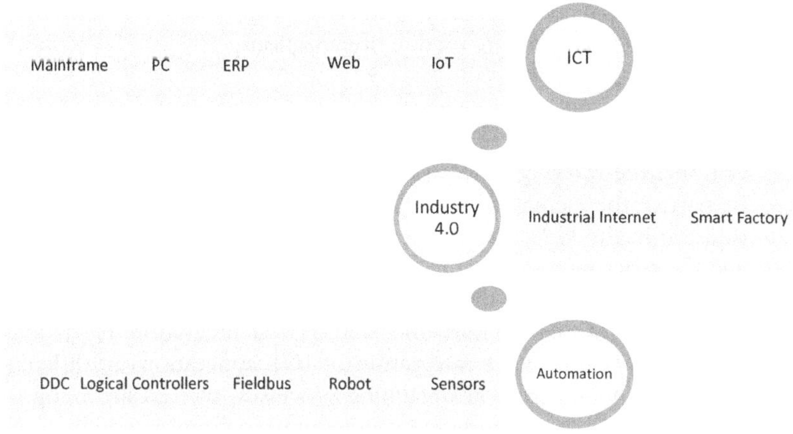

Fig. 2.1 Industry 4.0

Soft

- Collaboration refers to the need to have all machines, robots, and operators working together. Applications such as ERPs (enterprise resource planning) are useful to provide support that is as automated as possible to all management and operational processes. The cyber-physical system (CPS) includes automatic sensors and actuators used to collect and send data.
- Controllership refers to the numerical control machines. These are essential to make the system as independent as possible from the need of human operators. Halfway between cybernetics and control, are robots and AGVs. These advanced automated devices are critical to industry 4.0.
- Cybernetics refers to the use of computers, whether they are in a data center or distributed. The CPS describes the unification of the digital world with the real (physical) flows in the processes of procurement and production.[19] This means that the physical stages are accompanied by processes based on computers, using the concepts of digital twin,[20]

[19] Lee, J., Bagheri, B., & Kao, H. A. (2015). A cyber-physical systems architecture for industry 4.0-based manufacturing systems. *Manufacturing letters*, 3, 18–23.

[20] Schleich, B., Anwer, N., Mathieu, L., & Wartzack, S. (2017). Shaping the digital twin for design and production engineering. *CIRP Annals*, *66*(1), 141–144.

ubiquitous computing,[21] and pervasive computing.[22] Increasingly, robots and AI systems are used in organizations.

Hard

- Connection is essential to provide integration of all machines. The IoT, or rather the Internet of Everything (IoE), allows human operators to be part of the elements connected in the organization. The IoT is a solution in the CPS that enables communication with other systems and the cyber-physical system. The IoT makes it possible to create networks that incorporate the entire production process. In this way, it is possible to achieve both horizontal and vertical integration. Horizontal integration refers to the integration of ICT applications in different phases of an organization's planning processes, such as incoming or outgoing logistics, or production and commercialization, and between different organizations (value networks).[23] Procurement 4.0 pushes communication and cooperation into the distribution network (outbound logistics), internal organization (inbound logistics), as well as into the network of customers (output supplies). Vertical integration refers to the integration of different hierarchical levels, such as planning, production management, operations, quality control, and so on.
- Communication refers to the need to connect computing devices and all machines in a local area network (LAN) or a wide area network (WAN), normally via the internet, to support communication.
- Cognition is based on intelligent use of data. All information systems, sensors, and numerical controls (all thanks to the integrated connection tools) generate huge amounts of data, referred to as big data. These data should be analyzed and big data analytics is essential in industry 4.0.[24] Data analytics, data mining, and distribution of big data are critical supports for big data analytics. They must be characterized by the nine V characteristics—veracity, variety, velocity, volume, validity, variability, volatility, visualization, and value—needed to process data from

[21] Lyytinen, K., & Yoo, Y. (2002). Ubiquitous computing. *Communications of the ACM*, 45 (12): 63–96.

[22] Saha, D., & Mukherjee, A. (2003). Pervasive Computing: a paradigm for the 21st century. *Computer*, 36 (3): 25–31.

[23] Group, RF (2013). Acatech.mmendations-to-implement-the-strategic-initiative-Industrie-40-final-report-of-the-industr.html. Accessed December 28, 2018.

[24] Chiang, R. H., Grover, V., Liang, T. P., & Zhang, D. (2018). Strategic Value of Big Data and Business Analytics. *Journal of Management Information Systems*, 35: 2, 383–387, DOI: https://doi.org/10.1080/07421222.2018.1451950.

the CPS and add value to an organization.[25] Therefore, the software that manages this data is essential for the implementation of appropriate computing system applications. It is also very important to assess data quality. For this purpose, it possible to use a big data analytics quality (BDAQ), model. BDAQ is a hierarchical, multi-dimensional, and context-specific model. Perceived technology, talent, and information quality are significant determinants of BDAQ and company performance.[26]

Würth[27]

The Würth Group is a wholesaler of fasteners, screws and screw accessories, dowels, chemical products, electronic and electromechanical components, furniture and construction fittings, tools, and machines.[28] It is active worldwide.

Würth provides a good example of a CPS. It uses what it is called smart trash (IBIN, or intelligent bin),[29] which helps in the so-called C-parts management. This term originates from the Pareto Principle, also called ABC analysis.[30] C-parts are characterized by requiring a high sourcing effort, while concerning a low value of purchased products. The IBIN contains an infrared camera module integrated for C-parts management. This determines the number of parts necessary to replenish the IBIN. If the number is less than the safety stock, the IBIN automatically orders new parts using RFID (radio-frequency identification). This allows C-parts management based on consumption in real time.

[25] Owais, S. S., & Hussein, N. S. (2016). Extract five categories CPIVW from the 9V's characteristics of the big data. *International Journal of Advanced Computer Science and Applications*, *7*(3), 254–258.

[26] Fosso Wamba, S., Akter, S., & De Bourmont, M. (2018). Quality dominant logic in big data analytics and firm performance. *Business Process Management Journal*.

[27] https://www.wuerth-industrie.com/web/en/wuerthindustrie/ueberuns/unternehmen_wuerthindustrie/unternehmensportraet/profil_cteilepartner.php. Accessed March 22, 2019.

[28] http://www.wuerth.com/web/de/wuerthcom/portal/portalseite.php. Accessed September 24, 2018.

[29] https://www.wuerth-industrie.com/web/en/wuerthindustrie/cteile_management/kanban/ibin_intelligenterbehaelter/ibin.php, Accessed March 25, 2019.

[30] Ivanov, D., Tsipoulanidis, A., & Schönberger, J. (2019). Digital Supply Chain, Smart Operations and Industry 4.0. In *Global Supply Chain and Operations Management*. Springer, Cham, Switzerland, 481–526.

An important additional component is needed to ensure the governance (or Command) of systems, machines, and processes. This implies the need for Coordination, which can be ensured by proper design, management, and operation of all components included in a system.

The model should also include two further components that are examined in a later section:

- The Co-division or sharing of data and documents is important to support industry 4.0. There are traditional and advanced tools to ensure such sharing. These are effective not only within the internal organization but also externally, to connect with partners, distributors, and customers. The Internet of Services (IoS) enables partners to offer their services via the internet. It consists of participants, infrastructure services, business models, and the services themselves.[31]
- Confidence, or trust, must be the cornerstone of industry 4.0 solutions. In this case, the basis of trust is having a very strict security policy. Cyberattacks would be extremely dangerous for a system based primarily on non-human and highly integrated components, and therefore, fragile units.

2.2.2 Major Challenges

A characteristic of industry 4.0 is the increasing digitization and networking of products, processes, organization models, and value networks. It requires significant investment.

A study carried out by two organizations, PricewaterhouseCoopers and Strategy, in 2015 in the field of German engineering and manufacturing in the automotive industry, was based on surveys of 235 German organizations.[32] Respondents predict that the digital transformation will lead to a significant transformation of their organizations. They estimate that the share of investments in industry 4.0 initiatives will represent more than 50% of their capital investments planned for the next five years. Therefore, the foremost challenge of industry 4.0 is the funding of investment

[31] Schroth, C., & Janner, T. (2007). Web 2.0 and SOA: Converging concepts enabling the internet of services. *IT professional*, 9(3), 36–41.

[32] https://www.strategyand.pwc.com/cds. Accessed March 25, 2016.

required to deploy its solutions.[33] Other frequent challenges are the unclear business case for new internet and industrial applications, and the availability of sufficient talent to meet the needs of development, maintenance, and management of digital solutions. Moreover, organizations must define the rules and standards, while challenges in the field of ICT security should be addressed and resolved. Research centers, organizations, unions, and associations should cooperate to support the expansion of industry 4.0.[34]

To use other organizations in the field of procurement information systems, such as those in partner systems, it is essential to have access to the data but also to be able to process them. A solution in this respect is offered by the linked data—a method that allows aggregation and collection of large amounts of data from distributed sources.[35] To make this data accessible on the internet,[36] they must be published under the condition of 'open' use for a certain category of users. This allows organizations to browse and navigate the data by any media, through deep linking,[37] and the possibility of aggregation. Linked data is now a mature solution with great potential.[38]

2.3 Procurement 4.0

Industry 4.0 will change and improve traditional logistics and its self-perception. Procurement has become a core pillar in the value network for partners, operations, retailers, and customers. It is crucial for them to have

[33] Koch, V., Geissbauer, R., Kuge, S., & Schrauf, S. (2014), Industry 4.0. Opportunities and challenges of the Internet industry, http://www.strategyand.pwc.com/media/file/Industria-4-0.pdf. Accessed December 28, 2018.

[34] Zhong, R. Y., Xu, X., Klotz, E., & Newman, S. T. (2017). Intelligent manufacturing in the context of industry 4.0: a review. *Engineering*, 3(5), 616–630.

[35] Data, L. (2014). Connect data distributed across the Web. http://linkeddata.org. Accessed September 24, 2018.

[36] Tomassetti, F., Rizzo G., Glass, A., Hardy, L., Torchiano, M., & Morisio, M. (2011). Linked Data approach to the automation of the selection processes in systematic reviews. In *the assessment and evaluation in Software Engineering (EASE 2011), 15th Annual Conference. EIT*: 31–35.

[37] The term deep linking in the context of the internet is the use of hyperlinks to a specific, generally searchable or indexed, piece of content on a website (for example, "http://example.com/path/page"), rather than the website's home page (for example, http://example.com. Accessed March 22, 2019).

[38] Bizer, C., Heath, T., & Berners-Lee, T. (2011). *Linked data: The story so far. In Semantic services, interoperability and web applications: emerging concepts* IGI Global, Hershey, PA: 205–227.

the right goods in the right quantity at the right quality at the right time at the right place in the right condition and at right price (the seven Rs). These are the requirements for logistics, otherwise organizations cannot be competitive in the market.[39]

There has been continuous transformation of organizations over time. It is possible to divide the macro changes into four main periods, corresponding to the four industrial revolutions.[40] These changes have been substantial and have also led to economic and social change. Between subsequent disruptive changes, there has been continuous improvement. The following pages detail these four waves of innovation in the industrial sectors and in procurement (indicated as procurement x.0).[41]

2.3.1 *The First Industrial Revolution, Procurement 1.0*

Industry, as organized and systematic labor, was born a long time ago. The manufacture of bricks in ancient Rome provides an example. The first major change in industry can be traced back to the introduction of machines around the second half of the seventeenth century in the UK. Later this spread to Western Europe, North America, and then the rest of the world. Such change was momentous, as it allowed organizations to turn jobs based solely on manual tools and animal power into activities that use machines, infrastructure, and industrial production and transportation of both goods and people.[42]

This first Industrial Revolution was initiated thanks to the steam engine introduced by James Watt in 1782.[43] This innovation made possible a significant increase in production capacity. The development of naval transport, the railways, and later aircraft led to unprecedented changes, significantly improving transport capacity and speed of production.

This transformation also affected procurement, mainly due to the reduction of time needed to cover distance made possible by mechanized transport. Until then, procurement was done mainly with local partners. Small business owners or individual members handled the majority of pro-

[39] Uckelmann, D (2008). A definition approach to smart logistics, *Next Generation Teletraffic and Wired/Wireless Advanced Networking., 8th International Conference, NEW2AN and 1st Russian Conference on Smart Spaces, ruSMART 2008*, 273–84.

[40] Schwab, K. (2017). *The fourth industrial revolution*. Currency. London, UK.

[41] Domingo Galindo, L. (2016). The Challenges of Logistics 4.0 for the Supply Chain Management and the Information Technology, *Master Thesis, NTNU*, Trondheim, Norway.

[42] Revolution, I. (2009). History. Accessed December 28, 2018.

[43] McNabb, DE (2016). A Comparative History of Commerce and Industry, Palgrave Macmillan USA. New York, NY.

curement management, with owners acting as entrepreneurs but also as buyers and procurement agents.

The incoming and outgoing of supplies was based on a 'pull' approach; products were pushed to the markets, from the production side to the distributors. Producers set operations at a level based on historical trends of the demand. This situation resulted in a slow response to changes in demand. The consequences were excess inventory, bottlenecks, and delays, with unacceptable levels of service and product obsolescence.

The warehouse was simply a place in which to store materials or finished products. The intra-value network or the movement of goods within a factory was done with trucks driven manually by workers or in some cases by animals. Trains and steamships later allowed the procurement and transportation of materials and goods over longer distances.

2.3.2 *The Second Industrial Revolution, Procurement 2.0*

The Second Industrial Revolution was characterized by several discoveries, the most important of which was the introduction of electricity and the second being the invention of the telegraph. These innovations made possible huge advances in communication and transportation. Materials such as steel, copper, and aluminum became important in the construction of machines and products. The chemical industry was greatly expanded, too.[44]

The Second Industrial Revolution also witnessed other innovations, which helped substantially to reduce the purchase price of a large number of products. Frederick W. Taylor introduced the principle of the division of labor at the beginning of the twentieth century.[45] This meant a revolution in industry, now with the capability of mass production. It was the model for industrial plants for several decades. At around the same time, Henry Ford pushed the idea of the assembly line.[46]

Thanks to all these changes and the progress in transportation, procurement enjoyed an enlargement of the possible distances at which to choose partners. Procurement management began operating increasingly on a global or at least at a regional scale. Procurement began not necessarily to choose suppliers in the vicinity of factories. Enduring partnerships over greater distances were now often more common. New types of indus-

[44] Schwab, K. (2017). *The fourth industrial revolution*. Currency, London, UK.
[45] Taylor, FW (2004). *Scientific Management*. Routledge, London, UK.
[46] *The second industrial revolution*, ushistoryscene.com/. Accessed December 28, 2018.

try required expertise from buyers in mechanics, electricity, chemistry, and engineering. Organizations started to be supported by professional buyers with new skills and knowhow.

The 'push' delivery model of production was used to purchase materials in large batches, and warehouses began to be automated. The movement of goods within the plant was based on forklifts, normally with electric motors, driven by operators. Trains and ships transported finished products and materials even at large distances.

2.3.3 The Third Industrial Revolution, Procurement 3.0

The Third Industrial Revolution was marked by the introduction of the computer: a device with separate hardware and software.[47] This allowed great flexibility, technological innovations, and the introduction of completely new types of solution:

- Numerical control machines have the flexibility necessary for optimized mass production. These machines have computers with memory and are numerically controlled and programmable.
- Joseph F. Engelberger manufactured the first industrial robot in the USA in 1961.[48] In the 1970s, there was a leap forward with the introduction of the computers in robots. Their costs started to be drastically reduced, making it more profitable in many Western world situations to use robots in production rather than just relying on human labor and traditional machinery.
- Computer-based applications started to provide support to the organizations' functions.
- Container ships dramatically simplified the transportation of goods, reducing the need for labor and time to delivery, while improving security.[49]

[47] Rifkin, J. (2011). *The third industrial revolution: how lateral power is transforming energy, the economy, and the world.* Macmillan, London, UK.

[48] Engelberger, J. F. (2012). *Robotics in practice: management and applications of industrial robots.* Springer Science & Business Media. Berlin, Germany.

[49] Cudahy, B. J. (2006). *Box boats: How container ships changed the world.* Fordham University Press, New York, NY.

In procurement, several computer applications were developed to support its management. Examples of advanced software applications are ERP (enterprise resource planning), WMS (warehouse management system), TMS (transportation management systems), and other ICT solutions. Later, e-procurement began to spread, making possible an integrated ICT application support for procurement. All this progress was made possible by the use of computer applications for the management and control of procurement processes.

The automation in cargo handling was another big improvement in procurement.[50] The spread of door container ships innovated the automation of many port activities. The containers were now far more secure. They allowed an easy and fast switch from one mode of transport to another.

Procurement became increasingly global, with the selection of the best partners in a global market.

The application software allows planning of orders to partners, where the application can automatically receive orders through the network. In this way, incoming procurement is planned and controlled by software applications. Software-based systems and services platforms play an important role in production processes. They are the best way to facilitate connectivity, including analysis of data, to machines and components in production.[51]

Movement of goods within the factory is often done using automatic lines. Operators now used forklifts and they also increasingly programmed robot actions. The fleet of vehicles has a pre-plan and a program of optimized routes, computed by software applications. Product processing and delivery are managed according to defined plans and schedules before starting production.

2.3.4 The Fourth Industrial Revolution, Procurement 4.0!

The term 'industry 4.0' was used for the first time in 2011 when an association of representatives from industry, politics, and the academic world promoted the idea as an approach to improve German manufacturing

[50] Loose, D. R., & Walters, J. M. (2000). *Advanced cargo handling system concepts.* Battelle Memorial Institute, Columbus, OH.

[51] Bosch (2018), Industry 4.0 at Bosch – Connected Manufacturing, https://www.bosch-presse.de/pressportal/de/en/bosch-extends-its-industry-4-0-portfolio-144384.html. Accessed December 28, 2018.

competitiveness.[52] The German government has supported the idea, announcing that it was an integral part of its initiative High-Tech Strategy 2020 for Germany.[53] Later, the working group industry 4.0 developed the first recommendations for its implementation, published in April 2013.[54]

The widespread use of telecommunications networks (particularly the internet) marked the beginning of a new revolution. The introduction of the Internet of Things (IoT) and advanced software applications combined with the automation of machines in the production environment has introduced the Fourth Industrial Revolution.[55]

But this Fourth Industrial Revolution is not only about smart and connected machines and systems. It has a much wider scope. Occurring simultaneously there are waves of further breakthroughs in areas ranging from gene sequencing to nanotechnology, from renewables to quantum computing. It is the fusion of these technologies and their interaction across the physical, digital, and biological domain that makes the Fourth Industrial Revolution fundamentally different from the previous revolutions.

Industry 4.0 can be defined as the convergence of industrial production and ICT.[56] Industry 4.0 relates also to the convergence of the IoT, the Internet of People (IoP), and the Internet of Everything (IoE).[57] One of the basic paradigms of industry 4.0 is the use of modern ICT. ICT has in fact provided support to the management of procurement processes for a long time. The concept of electronic procurement (or e-procurement) is

[52] Schwab, K. (2017). *The Fourth Industrial Revolution*. Currency, London, UK.

[53] https://polen.diplo.de/pl-de/02-themen/02-5-wissenschaft-forschung/03-wissenschaft-innovation/hightech/485792. Accessed September 24, 2018.

[54] Hermann, M., Pentek, T., & Otto, B. (2016). Design principles for industrie 4.0 scenarios. In *System Sciences (HICSS), 2016 49th Hawaii International Conference*. IEEE, 3928–3937.

[55] Kagermann, H., Helbig, J., Hellinger, A., & Wahlster, W. (2013). Kagermann, H., Helbig, J., Hellinger, A., and Wahlster, W. (2013). *Recommendations for Implementing the Strategic Initiative INDUSTRIE 4.0: securing the future of German manufacturing industry; Final report of the Working Group 4.0 Industries*. Forschungsunion, Essen, Germany.

[56] Skilton, M., & Hovsepian, F. (2017). *The 4th Industrial Revolution: Responding to the Impact of Artificial Intelligence on Business*. Springer, Cham, Switzerland.

[57] Hermann, M., Pentek, T., & Otto, B. (2016). Design principles for industrie 4.0 scenarios. In *2016 49th Hawaii international conference on system sciences* (HICSS). IEEE, 3928–3937.

well defined,[58] and its architecture has been defined in detail.[59] Industry 4.0 further pushes the automation concept based on the characteristics of the initiative. The integration of industry 4.0 with operations technology requires a global and combined approach with re-engineering.[60]

Industry 4.0 is a disruptive innovation, as were the three previous industrial revolutions. They have in common that were initiated not by a single technology, but by the interaction of several solutions whose effects have created new modes of production but also influenced organizations, the environment, and social functions.[61]

Underlying the initiative of industry 4.0 is the internet. It allows communication among machines, humans, and digital applications in real time and very cheaply. This facilitates the use of what are known as 'smart products and smart services,' as well as advanced digitization within and between factories or service operations sites.[62] The industry 4.0 initiative is based on the convergence of ICT and automation of machinery and infrastructure. It is characterized by advanced digitization within organizations, in the form of a combination of internet technologies with technologies in the field of intelligent objects (machines and products). This enables and transforms industrial production systems in the direction of products that control their production processes. Besides the focus on digitization, industry 4.0 is supported by technological innovations whose quantitative effects together create new products, processes and modes of production, and business models, all strongly oriented to the personalization of the customer's products and services.[63]

[58] Brenner, W., & Wenger, R. (Eds.). (2007). *Elektronische Beschaffung: Stand und Entwicklungstendenzen*. Springer-Verlag, Heidelberg, Germany.

[59] Nicoletti, B., (2013), A Model and Best Practices of e-procurement in cloud computing, in-*Public procurement in Europe: public management, technologies and processes of change*, Amazon Books, Dedham, MA.

[60] Nicoletti, B. (2014), Lean and Digitize e-Procurement, proceedings of the *Public e-procurement in Europe: public management, technologies and processes of change*, Lisbon, Portugal, May 27.

[61] Schmidt, R., Möhring, M., Härting, R. C., Reichstein, C., Neumaier, P., & Jozinović, P. (2015). Industry 4.0-potentials for creating smart products: empirical research results. *In the International Conference on Business Information Systems*, 16–27. Springer, Cham, Switzerland.

[62] Stock, T., & Seliger, G. (2016). Opportunities of sustainable manufacturing industry in 4.0. *Procedia CIRP*, 40, 536–541.

[63] Riecken, D. (2000). Personalized views of personalization. *Communications of the ACM*, *43*(8), 26–28.

The intelligent factory (smart factory) allows the potential of connecting all elements involved in the production processes. It makes possible the application of such concepts as adaptability, interconnectivity, efficiency, and ergonomics.[64]

In today's fast-changing competitive environment, strategy is no longer a matter of positioning a fixed set of activities along with the industrial model of the value chain. Successful organizations increasingly do not just add value, they reinvent it. The key strategic task is to reconfigure roles and relationships among a constellation of actors (suppliers, partners, customers) to mobilize the creation of value by new combinations of players. This new organization paradigm has been called a 'value constellation.'[65] This new logic of value breaks down the distinction between products and services; it combines them into activity-based 'offerings' from which customers can create value for themselves. As potential offerings grow more complex, so do the relationships necessary to create them. As a result, an organization's strategic task becomes the ongoing reconfiguration and integration of its competencies, customers, and workers. An example of this type of organization is Ikea, which in a few years has become the world's largest retailers of home furnishings. Ikea has redefined the relationships and organizational practices of the furniture business.[66] This concept can be generalized: This book stresses the move from a value chain to a value network, and such terms are used throughout.[67] The value for customers and

[64] Lasi, H., Kemper, HG, Fettke, P., Feld, T., & Hoffmann, M. (2014). Industry 4.0. *Business & Information Systems Engineering* 6 (4): 239–242.

[65] Normann, R., & Ramirez, R. (1993). From value chain to value constellation: Designing interactive strategy. *Harvard Business Review*, 71(4), 65–77.

[66] Franke, N., Schreier, M., & Kaiser, U. (2010). The "I designed it myself" effect in mass customization. *Management Science*, 56(1), 125–140.

[67] The term value network has been used also with a different meaning. It was proposed by Stabell and Fjeldstad (Stabell, C.B., & Fjeldstad, Ø.D. (1998). Configuring value for competitive advantage: on chains, shops and networks, *Strategic Management Journal*, 19(5), 413–437). It is based on mediation technologies according to Thompson's typology (Thompson, J. D. (2017). Organizations in action: Social science bases of administrative theory. Routledge, London, UK). It connects clients and customers who are interested in creating mutual relations and interdependence. The mediating technologies support relations between actors scattered over time and space. This model is similar to what has been called the platform approach (Zhu, F., & Iansiti, M. (2007)). *Dynamics of platform competition: Exploring the role of installed base, platform quality and consumer expectations.* Division of Research, Harvard Business School, Cambridge, MA).

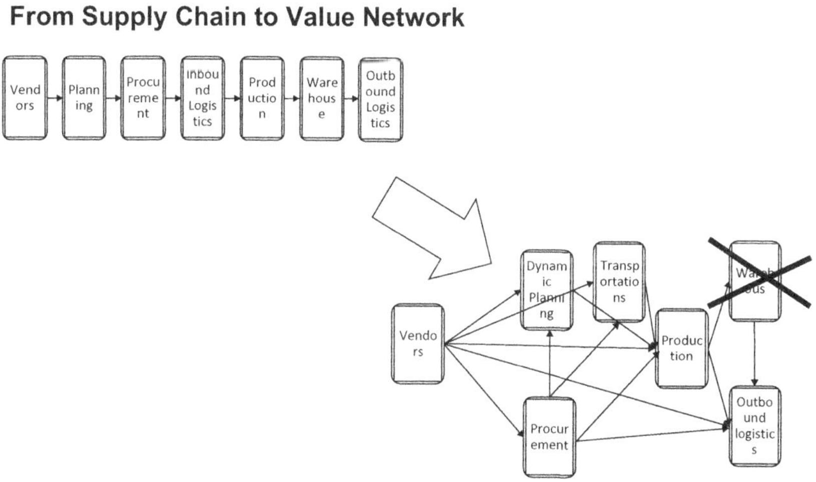

Fig. 2.2 From supply chain to value network

organizations is obtained by an ecosystem that combines in a network organization, vendors, customers, and public administrations (Fig. 2.2).[68]

The initiative of industry 4.0 involves a change not only in operations but also in the rest of an organization. A particularly important function here is procurement. The continual increase of global sourcing and outsourcing requires not only cross-functional integration but also sophisticated integrative processes across whole organizations.[69] The continuous shift toward industry 4.0 requires enhanced exchange of communication and information achieved through procurement systems. The solutions of industry 4.0 are intended to support this shift by collecting and processing relevant data over the whole value network while supporting intelligent decision-making.[70]

[68] Nicoletti, B. (2017), *Agile Procurement. Volume I: Adding Value with Lean Processes*, Springer International Publishing, London, UK. ISBN 978-3-319-61082-5.

[69] Castillo, F. (2016). *Managing information technology*. Springer International Publishing, Cham, Switzerland.

[70] CFB Bots. (2018). The Difference between Robotic Process Automation and Artificial Intelligence. https://medium.com/@cfb_bots/thedifference-between-robotic-process-automation-and-artificial-intelligence4a71b4834788. Accessed July 22, 2019.

The gradual movement of companies toward digitalization marks the era of the Fourth Industrial Revolution. In an industry 4.0 environment, organizations can increasingly connect and integrate with partners (upstream) and customers (downstream) in the network through the wireless IoE. Second, transparency of information can create virtual copies of the physical plant. Third, cyber-physical systems can enable decentralized decision-making. Finally, decision support systems (using mobile apps) can provide technical assistance. These principles can be used as a basis to design principles for digitalizing procurement function.[71]

Procurement 4.0 can benefit from the development of the IoO.[72] Technologies such as robots and AGVs allow the introduction of processes that do not require, or require much less, human intervention. The objective is integration between automation and ICT solutions. Implementation of these types of processing solutions in organizations will take place over a long time. They require large investments and special programs and training. The results are a substantial improvement in the performance and costs of procurement processes, better speed, but above all their flexibility, especially in support of product customization.

Equipment made available on the network, in terms of automatic storage and automatic production, is already widespread. Their further diffusion is limited because they are dedicated systems, in line with the shape and characteristics of the specific initiative for which they are used. The goal is to introduce new solutions that make labor savings in handling, save time in transport, and, in particular, increase flexibility and customization.

Procurement 4.0 impacts all components of procurement. For example, it impacts logistics through the utilization of warehouse robots that can transport goods from the warehouse to the final modes of transport. Even more radically, the movement of materials may be requested by the production machines themselves or even directly by the products.[73]

[71] Tham, C. K., Luo, T. (2013). Sensing-driven energy purchasing in smart grid cyber-physical system. IEEE *Trans. Syst. Man Cybern. Syst.*, 43 (4), 773–784.

Klötzer, C., Pflaum, A. (2015), Cyber-physical systems as the technical foundation for problem solutions in manufacturing, logistics and supply chain management. *October 2015 5th International Conference on the Internet of Things (IOT), IEEE.* 12–19.

[72] Domingo Galindo, L. (2016). The Challenges of Logistics 4.0 for the Supply Chain Management and the Information Technology, *Master's thesis, NTNU,* Trondheim, Norway.

[73] Hirano, H. (2016). *JIT Implementation Manual – The Complete Guide to Just-In-Time Manufacturing*: Volume 2 – Waste and the 5S's. Productivity Press. Boca Raton, FL.

Robert Bosch GmbH[74]

Bosch's connected industry unit aims to support customers in connecting the value network from end to end.[75] The portfolio of software allows organizations an entry point into the connected factory that is tailored to their needs. There are starter kits and retrofit solutions in the complete package. Individual lines can be combined. Factories and plant networks, including their internal and external logistics, can be interconnected. Several applications and solutions support workers and employees in their daily tasks. Relevant manufacturing data can be easily accessed using mobile devices and it is possible to get better machine availability in production. Internal transport processes and flows of goods outside the organization can be seamlessly monitored and traced back. Workers are kept permanently informed of the location, condition, and delivery time of goods and products. The result is an increase in productivity and agility in full support of competitiveness.

2.4 The Procurement 4.0 Model

In the area of procurement 4.0, there is not much literature. Henke and Schulte, for example, argue that the procurement of partners and production solutions interface layer provides the opportunity to position itself as a key factor for the development of industry 4.0. They postulate several opportunities.[76] Other publications have a more technical focus,[77] considering specific aspects such as logistics integration.[78]

[74] https://www.bloomberg.com/profile/company/RBOS:GR. Accessed July 2, 2019.

[75] https://www.bosch-presse.de/pressportal/de/en/bosch-extends-its-industry-4-0-portfolio-144384.html. Accessed July 2, 2019.

[76] Henke, M., & Schulte, A. T. (2015), Einkauf und die 4. Industrielle Revolution, *Beschaffung Aktuell*, 62 (3): 20–21.

[77] Sundermann, F. (2013), Einkauf 4.0: Einsparungen durch Zusammenarbeit von Einkauf und Technik, *Pool4Tool*, (11): 24–28.

[78] Aslanbas, M. (2014), Emporias Procurement Survey 4.0, in Emporias Management Consulting (Ed.), *Emporias, Quarterly 3* Munich, Germany: 10–14.

Alicke, K., Rachor, J., & Seyfert, A. (2016). Supply Chain 4.0–the next-generation digital supply chain. *McKinsey, available at* https://www.mckinsey.com/business-functions/operations/our-insights/supply-chain-40%2D%2Dthe-nextgeneration-digital-supply-chain. Accessed May 15, 2019.

Bubner, N., Bubner, N., Helbig, R., & Jeske, M. (2014). Logistics trend radar, Delivering insight today. *Creating value tomorrow*. DHL. (2013). Logistics trend radar–delivering insight today. Creating value tomorrow! *DHL document*.

This section examines in detail aspects of procurement 4.0 from the viewpoint of procurement processes and systems, what this book calls the six Cs related to the model of industry 4.0: cybernetics, communication, control, collaboration, connection, and cognition. There are two other Cs: Coordination requires strong governance of procurement 4.0. At the same time, confidence, that is mutual trust, is the basis for the success of this initiative.

The following pages examine each of the Cs in the case of procurement 4.0. Confidence is considered in Chap. 5.

2.4.1 Cybernetics

The base of the industry 4.0 revolution is the shift from a supply chain model to that of a value network. Intelligent machines and computer applications link all functions and allow an organization to share real-time information. At the same time, procurement processes need to be streamlined. Procurement 4.0 is the integration of ICT and automation in support of procurement to improve the added value to the customer and to the entire organization.

So-called smart factories share real-time information among all stakeholders. They make procurement processes optimized and transparent. With the use of cybernetics in the procurement sector, it is necessary to develop a secure system to ensure that data are protected and available at the right time and in the right place to support procurement activities.

Management of procurement 4.0 is based on a large network in which all parties involved in procurement (customers, distributors, and partners) have access. This is made possible by an internet platform that handles all orders from customers and partners in real time.

The intra-value network or the movement of goods within a factory is increasingly automated with AGVs. These are vehicles with paths programmed based on the prediction of procurement in entry/exit or at the request of processing machines. The basis of these forecasts is the information received from the internet platform used by all stakeholders.

Inventory costs are thus reduced. Customer orders and orders to partners are processed in real time. It must be possible to plan the dates of receipt of all materials and components needed for production, to provide the final products in the proper quantity and quality and on schedule.

The AGV fleet of vehicles have a planned route within the factory accessible via the internet platform. The platform provides the necessary information on their movements. Thus, management and partners can track vehicles using GPS to know their exact position in real time. Full automation has the main purpose of helping persons in their activities and to provide a safer working environment for workers.

2.4.2 Communication

An important aspect of the paradigms of industry 4.0 is the emphasis on ICT smart or intelligent systems.[79] This is different from the support to the operational work provided by e-procurement.[80] One might expect that the 'smart' adjective in the procurement sector is the basis for the automation of end-to-end procurement processes. But it means a lot more. Procurement 4.0 solutions automatically recognize the demand for a specific material or component. Hence, they can generate an order. This is transmitted to the respective partner without human intervention. In-depth automation is another difference between procurement 4.0 and e-procurement. In technical jargon, it can be defined as a system without the interruption of processing (straight-through processing, as it is known in financial systems).[81]

2.4.3 Control

The elements of the procurement 4.0 model imply a substantial change in the way procurement works today. They ask for a major rethinking regarding organization and skills. Both need to be remodeled over time. They accelerate communication in an ever-more tightly interconnected world. In the past, it was enough to be aware of some potential markets for low-cost procurement, such as some Asian countries and Eastern Europe. Procurement 4.0 requires the organization of procurement with a comprehensive and global approach. For example, having the procurement organization nucleus located in the main office may have worked in the past, but in future more and more buyers should be close (physically or virtually) to competitive procurement markets for each category.

[79] Schmidt, R., Möhring, M., Härting, R. C., Reichstein, C., Neumaier, P., & Jozinović, P. (2015). *Industry 4.0-potentials for creating smart products: empirical research results. In the International Conference on Business Information Systems,* 16–27. Springer, Cham Switzerland.

[80] Wisner JD, Keong Leong, G., & Keah-Choon, T. (2006), *Principles of Supply Chain Management*, Thomson Learning, Stamford, CT.

[81] Khanna, A. (2010). *Straight Through Processing for the Financial Services.* Academic Press. Cambridge, MA.

2.4.4 *Cooperation*

The paradigm in terms of a greater productive collaboration in industry 4.0 defines another difference between procurement 4.0 and the e-procurement approach.[82] Productivity benefits resulting from e-procurement initiatives being mainly connected with a reduction in transaction and process costs.[83] E-procurement allows an organization to turn paper documents into digital ICT applications. In this way, there is a transformation from a labor intensive activity to automated workflows and sustainable ICT processes. E-procurement also supports key activities such as the process of managing relationships with partners.[84] The driving factors of industry 4.0 collaborative productivity are improvements in terms of procurement, production, and engineering.[85] Industry 4.0 enables development processes of production to be radically shortened. An organization can activate new product-service functions and improve procurement.[86] E-procurement is focused on process efficiency, while the objectives of procurement 4.0 are increased productivity, flexibility, and performance that meet the highly tailored needs of customers.[87]

2.4.5 *Connection*

Handling operations define the efficiency of products in their movement along with the value network.[88] By optimizing external transport and

[82] Schuh, G., Powerful, T., Wesch-Powerful, C., Weber, AR, & Prote, JP (2014). Collaboration Mechanisms to increase to Productivity in the Context of Industries 4. 0, *Procedia CIRP*, 19 (2014) 51–56. DOI: https://doi.org/10.1016/j.procir.2014.05.016. Accessed March 9, 2019.

[83] Essig, M. (2006), Electronic Procurement – Konzeption und Anwendung, in: J. Zentes (Ed.), *Handbook* Handel, Gabler, Wiesbaden, Germany: 735–758.

[84] Essig, M. (2006), Electronic Procurement – Konzeption und Anwendung, in: J. Zentes (Ed.), *Handbook* Handel, Gabler, Wiesbaden, Germany: 735–758.

[85] Schuh, G., Powerful, T., Wesch-Powerful, C., Weber, A. R., & Prote, JP (2014). Collaboration Mechanisms to increase to Productivity in the Context of Industries 4. 0, *Procedia CIRP*, 19 (2014) 51–56. DOI: https://doi.org/10.1016/j.procir.2014.05.016. Accessed March 9, 2019.

[86] Schuh, G., Powerful, T., Wesch-Powerful, C., Weber, A. R., & Prote, JP (2014). Collaboration Mechanisms to increase to Productivity in the Context of Industries 4.0, *Procedia CIRP*, 19 (2014) 51–56.

[87] Kagermann, H. (2014), von Industries 4.0 Chancen nutzen, in Bauernhansl, T., Hompel, M. Ten, & Vogel-Heuser, B. (Eds.) (2014), Produktion Industries 4.0. *Automatisierung und Logistik*, Springer, Wiesbaden, Germany: 603–614.

[88] Sreenivas, M., & Srinivas, T. (2006). The role of transportation in logistics chain. *European Journal of Operational Research*, 95, 1–10.

internal handling processes, it is possible to impact on the structure of procurement costs.

Forklifts have been very important in physical processes of warehousing, storage, and order-picking. In industry 4.0, AGVs replace forklifts. If automatic operation, robots, and similar autonomous control solutions are introduced, they can solve some of the problems in traditional AGVs such as slowness. Intelligent autonomous vehicles in supply networks must be assessed for the integrated application of conceptualization, simulation, emulation, and physical application of testbeds for the effective design and *ex ante* evaluation of digitally enabled supply network operations.[89]

To implement automation of internal logistics, an organization needs to act in different parts of the transport process. It is necessary to implement an automatic path between workstations and warehouses. Organizations need to consider the legal and insurance aspects, beyond just the technical considerations. Even partial automation of these pathways can have a sizable impact on procurement costs, as it reduces the costs on truck drivers and increases overall safety of the workplace.

Another future implementation of procurement solutions is the use of drones. The largest logistics network organization in the world, DHL, is planning to use drones as emergency delivery means.[90]

Consorzio DAFNE[91]

The Consorzio DAFNE is an Italian consortium of pharmaceutical companies and intermediate distributors that aims to improve the management of procurement process and supply of pharmaceutical products. The Consorzio developed an interesting digital platform in the healthcare sector: the Condafne platform. In it, each actor in

[89] Tsolakis, N., Bechtsis, D., & Srai, J. S. (2018). Intelligent autonomous vehicles in digital supply chains: from conceptualisation, to simulation modelling, to real-world operations. *Business Process Management Journal.*

[90] Sreenivas, M., & Srinivas, T. (2006). The role of transportation in logistics chain. *European Journal of Operational Research*, 95, 1–10.

[91] https://www.consorziodafne.com/piattaforma-condafne-uno-schema-di-funzionamento/. Accessed March 4, 2019.

the supply chain has its own virtual space through which automatically to send and receive their administrative documents and electronic transmissions in a standard structured format. Each player can choose, independently, formats and channels used for communication. The platform takes care of any transcoding.
In terms of channels, all documents can be sent and/or received through Accountdafne (also known as the 'Mailbox' in a platform operated by OpenText GXS[92]), through direct transmission between the management of the organization and the Condafne platform. Alternatively, an organization can upload/download files generated by its management via the web by accessing the platform or using specific software. The platform can communicate with other ministerial and European systems involved in the process and with a digital storage system in a standard format.

NSO[93]
Italy is in the process of rolling out its e-ordering mandate within the healthcare sector. From October 1, 2019 all e-documents must have been issued according to the latest PEPPOL BIS 3.0 Italian extension. The NSO (Nodo Smistamento Ordini) is a separate instance of the same platform that SDI (Sistema de Interscambio), the internal review service e-invoicing system, is built on. NSO is intended to work similarly to SDI, but instead of e-invoices, the NSO will work with other document types, such as pre-agreed orders. The NSO will validate those that have been submitted.

[92] https://www.opentext.com/products-and-solutions/products/opentext-product-offerings-catalog/rebranded-products/gxs. Accessed July 21, 2019.

[93] https://www.pagero.com/news/more-information-upcoming-e-ordering-mandate-italy/. Accessed August 3, 2019.

There are multiple ways to connect to the NSO, such as Posta Elettronica Certificata (PEC) (a legal type of certified email), Secure-shell File Transfer Protocol (SFTP) and web services, either directly or via an intermediary accredited by the NSO. The NSO only supports PEPPOL BIS. The Italian Ministry of Economy and Finance has decided to approve usage of PEPPOL BIS 3.0 (business interoperability specifications) to ensure implementation of the mandate. PEPPOL BIS is a format maintained by OpenPEPPOL with formal requirements that ensure pan-European interoperability of procurement documents such as e-invoices, e-orders, dispatch advice, and so on. The Italian version of PEPPOL BIS, however, does not work outside of NSO e-document exchange, that is, it is not interoperable with other PEPPOL markets.

Besides orders and pre-agreed orders which are mandatory, the parties may (but are not obliged to) exchange order confirmations, order changes, and order cancellations.

2.4.6 *Cognition*

Data analytics is one of the most important enablers for procurement 4.0.[94] Intelligent (smart) technologies and related algorithms allow the aggregation, processing, and analysis of large volumes of data from many heterogeneous sources. Using all these big data analytics, an organization can improve its knowledge of partners, markets, and customers, forecast market trends, and take action to improve the shortcomings of processes and products. Big data analytics can allow managers to make better and more informed decisions. In a growing number of cases, big data analytics can automatically take operational decisions regarding procurement.[95]

Analysis of the data and their intelligent use is one of the key success factors for the organizations that want to exploit the potential of procure-

[94] Koch, V., Kuge, S., Geissbauer, R., & Schrauf, S. (2014). Industry 4.0: Opportunities and challenges of the industrial Internet. Strategy & PwC, http://www.strategyand.pwc.com/media/file/Industria-4-0.pdf. Accessed December 28, 2018.

[95] Nicoletti, B. (2014), Using Operational Analytics to Achieve to Digitized, Visible Supply Chain. *Inbound Logistics*, February.

ment 4.0. Data analytics tools can support an organization's partners in improving the design and performance of their components. Predictive analysis on where and when to expect the next defects offers the possibility to optimize maintenance and availability of spare parts.[96] It is the responsibility of an organization to ensure that all procurement opportunities are maximized through big data analytics. Procurement should work with partners to allow both the organization and its partners to benefit from the improvements resulting from a more effective, efficient, and economical extended value network.

McKesson[97]
McKesson is a $179 billion healthcare services and information technology organization with 70,000 employees and several partners. It uses a discovery and analytics platform to identify all of its procurement and sourcing contracts across the entire organization.[98] It stores all documents in a specific contract repository. In this repository, contracts can be searched for easily and quickly, saving staff time. The metadata from contracts analysis allows the organization to identify potential obligation risks as well as revenue opportunities and savings from otherwise hidden unfavorable payment and renewable terms.

2.4.7 Coordination

An implication of industry 4.0 for ICT procurement systems is a component of the organizational paradigm of industry 4.0. In the past, partners in e-procurement systems have provided considerable support for the exchange of information with the partners in the field of e-procurement applications.[99] Technology advances in an industry 4.0 initiative greatly

[96] Lee, J., Kao, H. A., & Yang, S. (2014). Service innovation and smart analytics for industry 4.0 and big data environment. Procedia CIRP, 16, 3–8.

[97] https://www.mckesson.com/. Accessed June 20, 2019.

[98] Burgess, A. (2017). *The Executive Guide to Artificial Intelligence: How to identify and implement applications for AI in your organization*. Springer, Cham, Switzerland.

[99] Kollmann, T (2011), *E-Business: Grundlagen elektronischer Geschäftsprozesse in der Net Economy*, Gabler, Wiesbaden, Germany.

increase the potential in this area. The key change is the transition from an exchange of information to the free flow of information in the value network between the products, services, and related organizations.[100] This exchange must be coordinated effectively.[101] Free movement implies a higher degree of exchangeability of the data, a higher degree of automation in the exchange of information, and possibly also an integrated use of the data in the approach of big data analytics,[102] or, in the future, based on the use of blockchain, as described in Chap. 4.

These implications can be used to distinguish e-procurement and procurement 4.0.[103] Procurement 4.0 improvements can be classified as:

- functional integration across the organization;
- use of systems that reduce manual labor in procurement tasks.

This can be done through a flexible procurement approach based on the digitization and automation of processes and infrastructure.

In procurement 4.0, both the depth of integration (especially among organizations) and the automation potential of the entire procurement process are much greater than those based on e-procurement. The latter is limited to facilitating tasks using computer applications, based on personalized information and exchange of documents. Automation processes and a higher degree of integration characterize procurement 4.0. Here, procurement is based on the digitization and advanced automation of partners within an organization and the function of the ecosystem. It is not limited to the use of new and improved solutions.

[100] Schlick, J., Stephan, P., Loskyll, M., & Lappe, D. (2014), Industries 4.0 in der praktischen Anwendung, in: Bauernhansl, T., Hompel, M. Ten; & Vogel-Heuser, B. (Eds.), *Industrie 4.0 to Produktion, Automatisierung und Logistik: Anwendung – Technology – Migration*, Springer, Wiesbaden, Germany: 57–84.

[101] Van Weele, AJ (2010). *Purchasing & Supply Chain Management: analysis, strategy, planning and practice*. Cengage Learning EMEA, Andover, UK.

[102] Lee, J., Kao, HA, & Yang, S. (2014). Service innovation and smart analytics for industry 4.0 and big data environment. *Procedia CIRP*, 16, 3–8.

[103] Glas, AH, & Kleemann, FC (2016). 4.0 The impact of industry on procurement and supply management: A conceptual and qualitative analysis. *International Journal of Business and Management Invention*, 5 (6), 55–66.

Next to the degree of integration, relations with partners may also differ in procurement 4.0 (for example around new goods and services in the field of procurement).[104] The impact of procurement 4.0 on organizations is extensive and pervasive.

All these elements of the model pose a substantial challenge and a potential change of the way of working in procurement. They require an important and holistic re-engineering of organizations and skills, both of which should evolve in a synergistic way.[105] Organizations need to create new professional profiles, for example both for buyers of new categories of products, contract experts in intellectual property, or data scientists to analyze relevant data, their management and their use. To find this talent, new sources must be opened with the help of partners in the field of procurement, such as partnership programs with universities and research centers. It is also useful to explore new channels such as social networks, social media, and similar. Larger organizations should consider establishing relationships with academia to conduct educational and informational activities, cross-functional training, and workshops for partners. Only if the professionals who work in procurement have digital competencies (also named e-competencies[106]), may an organization fully benefit from the opportunities offered by digitization.[107]

[104] Essig, M. (2006), Electronic Procurement – Konzeption und Anwendung, in: J. Zentes (Ed.), Handbook Handel, Gabler, Wiesbaden, Germany: 735–758.

[105] Geissbauer, R, Weissbarth, R & Wetzstein, J (2016) Procurement 4.0: Are the organization ready for the digital revolution? http://www.strategyand.pwc.com/reports/procurement-4-digital-revolution. Accessed December 18, 2018.

[106] Sternberg, R. J., Sternberg, R. J., & Grigorenko, E. L. (Eds.). (2003). *The psychology of abilities, competencies, and expertise*. Cambridge University Press, Cambridge, UK.

[107] Competence is a demonstrated ability to apply knowledge, skills and attitudes for achieving observable results. The European model of e-Competence (e-CF) provides a reference of 40 skills, as required and applied to the digital workplace transformation, using a common language for skills, abilities and levels of ability. For details, reference can be made to: Sanz, LF, Gómez-Pérez, J., & Castillo-Martinez, A. (2018). *Analysis of the European ICT Competence Frameworks. In Multidisciplinary Perspectives on Human Capital and Information Technology Professionals*, 225–245. IGI Global, Hershey, PA.

Amazon.com Inc.[108]

Amazon.com Inc. (Amazon) is the leading e-commerce business in the world. Starting in 2012 with the acquisition of Kiva Systems, a robot manufacturer, Amazon has promoted the automation of collection processes of ordered products.[109] Amazon uses a robot called Kiva, which reduces the manual interventions substantially. It supports improvement of the labor productivity of each distribution center.

Amazon has seven fully automated logistics systems in Europe (three in the UK, two in Poland, one in Spain, and one in Italy). Their automation has provided a 15% increase in the volumes processed.[110]

They are robotic centers that use a proprietary system that moves the robot stock in a working day of 20 hours, with four hours per shift to allow for minor maintenance. The 24,000 UK employees have a workday of 10 hours, four days a week. An automated logistics system improves the working and safety conditions of the workers in the warehouses.[111]

[108] https://www.amazon.com/. Accessed July 21, 2019.

[109] https://www.designboom.com/technology/amazon-kiva-robots-generation-fulfillment-12-02-2014/. Accessed September 15, 2018.

[110] Eppner, C., Höfer, S., Jonschkowski, R., Martin, RM, Sieverling, A., Wall, V., & Brock, O. (2016, June). Lessons from the Amazon picking challenge: Four aspects of building robotic systems. In *Robotics: Science and Systems*: 4831–4835.

[111] Culey, S. (2012). Transformers: 4.0 supply chain and how automation will transform the rules of the global supply chain. *European Business Review*, 40–45.

BMW Group[112]

BMW is a large car manufacturer based in Germany. Customers can choose their preferred car on the BMW Online site by customizing templates with several options. Hence the need for detailed production planning. This covers not just the next few months, but the next few hours. Advanced automation helps in this sort of situation, but it is essential to be more agile and have a streamlined procurement process.

For BMW, this transformation is set to start from the customer orders, received online, and move through the supply base, flexible factory lines, and straight out to dealers and customers.

BMW is convinced that it cannot work alone in implementation of the industry 4.0 model; 70% of the value creation in its vehicles is implemented through partners. BMW relies on their expertise to maximize the use of the system planned to fit the industry 4.0 model. The company is moving fast in the implementation of procurement 4.0. The objective is to remove the so-called yellow line, which refers to the point where the car components are supplied to the assembly line. Traditionally, this separates procurement from production at BMW.

To implement procurement 4.0, BMW is moving toward a management system for controlling its value network and digital support. It is reorganizing production processes, connecting all the workflows in the procurement sector. The objective is an improvement in the visibility of the entire value network, thanks to digitization.

In the long term, BMW intends to abandon a central unit of procurement and distribute its own procurement professionals on site with major partners. BMW sees that these new solutions rely heavily on secure data interfaces and standards. They allow the original equipment manufacturer, first-tier partners, and the materials and equipment involved in procurement to be directly digitally integrated via networks in cloud computing and without the intervention of human operators.

[112] https://rctom.hbs.org/submission/procurement-4-0-full-integration/. Accessed September 15, 2018.

2.5 Innovation in Procurement Processes

For innovation in procurement to be effective, it is important to adopt an open innovation structure in the organization. This is achieved through several stages:[113]

- innovating or redefining the organization's structure;
- clarifying roles and responsibilities;
- making sure that innovation is diffused;
- quickly reaching a steady state (routine) for the innovations introduced.

This redefinition of innovation consists of adjustment rather than an entirely new approach. This adjustment is related not only to how procurement can meet the needs of an organization. The organization must also take into account the increasing importance given to partners and relationships. To achieve this, some organizations have tried not only to meet their own needs but to achieve a high degree of flexibility with their partners through increased visibility into their procurement flows and administrative aspects.

There are three different fields associated with the redefinition of innovation: namely, simplification and digitization at the level of transactions, the assignment of benefits, and the degree of use by partners.[114]

The restructuring process consists of complete organizational change. In a globalized ecosystem, there is the need of new partnerships between the different areas of an organization, particularly between financial sectors and procurement. This is necessary to make effective innovations in procurement. It is vital to have a breakthrough upstream of the organizations

[113] Zafar, A., & Kantola, J. (2018). Relationship Between Firm's Performance and Factors Involved in the Innovation Selection of Providers. *In International Conference on Applied Human Factors and Ergonomics*, 194–205. Springer, Cham, Switzerland. Wuttke, DA, Blome, C., Foerstl, K., & Henke, M. (2013). Managing the innovation adoption of supply chain finance – Empirical evidence from six European case studies. *Journal of Business Logistics*, 34 (2), 148–166.

[114] Wuttke, DA, Blome, C., Foerstl, K., & Henke, M. (2013). Managing the innovation adoption of supply chain finance-Empirical evidence from six European case studies. *Journal of Business Logistics*, 34 (2), 148–166.

in which partners take an important role. This kind of innovation requires cooperation and strong communication with partners. Restructuring of procurement is important because these new partnerships bring procurement professionals into a position where they perform tasks that they did not do in the past. In particular, they need to 'sell' procurement 4.0 solutions upstream of the organization and to partners. These tasks are traditionally performed by marketing personnel to downstream customers.

Redefinition and restructuring in procurement 4.0 can be beneficial for the partners and customers of organizations.[115] The internal restructuring of an organization is not enough without the close involvement of partners. Considering the redefinition of procurement, this is only possible with a proper restructuring of the organization. The latter is only possible with solutions based on a redefinition of innovation. For example, in some organizations, the adjustment of performance evaluations and new collaboration between procurement and finance functions allow both the redefinition and restructuring of procurement processes. The functions must be aligned toward the same goal: effective adoption of procurement 4.0. At the same time, this alignment is possible with the restructuring process. The functions of an organization should consider the adoption of procurement 4.0 as a tool to improve the performance of organizations. On the other hand, the managers of the several functions of the organization in question must evaluate potential challenges before deciding how to implement procurement 4.0.

As for the involvement of partners, some organizations have realized that besides alignment on objectives, the involvement of the partners is also necessary to redefine an organization considering the needs of partners. This involvement not only enables a simpler process redesign, it also facilitates the alignment of different functions, thanks to communication with different partners. Some surveys have confirmed that this involvement has facilitated a link between restructuring and redefinition and not directly enhanced the effectiveness of procurement 4.0.[116]

[115] Wuttke, DA, Blome, C., Foerstl, K., & Henke, M. (2013). Managing the innovation adoption of supply chain finance-Empirical evidence from six European case studies. *Journal of Business Logistics*, 34 (2), 148–166.

[116] Wuttke, D. A., Blome, C., Foerstl, K., & Henke, M. (2013). Managing the innovation adoption of supply chain finance-Empirical evidence from six European case studies. *Journal of Business Logistics*, 34 (2), 148–166.

After the redefinition and restructuring process, the adoption of procurement 4.0 can become routine for an organization. Some organizations have put this innovation in place and now they are working to make it routine. To do so, organizations need to convince all those responsible for the effectiveness of an organization to adopt procurement 4.0 gradually, but ultimately entirely.

Another important phase of innovation diffusion is to apply it upstream as well. This phase makes the increasingly rapid dissemination of innovation throughout an organization move upstream too, through the dissemination of innovation among partners. Functional managers play an important role in this spreading action of procurement 4.0. These actors should be in direct communication with the procurement organization network operators to get better awareness of the decisions in order to involve more partners.

The benefits that an organization can provide to the partners are various; they represent a tool to be used as a lever for the adoption by partners of the procurement 4.0 approach. This diffusion depends on an important element: trust. Through trust, partners can accept adoption of procurement 4.0. Thus, some organizations have tried to create strong trust with partners.

Another important factor in the spread of procurement 4.0 is the power of procurement organizations in respect to partners. Some organizations have the power to impose the adoption of a procurement 4.0 approach directly on their partners. The power of the buyer–seller relationship thus becomes particularly important. The procurement leverage of the power of relationships and trust are important elements for organizations that want to adopt procurement 4.0.

Organizations are well placed to promote the sustainability of procurement 4.0. The value of this innovation often revolves around the initiative of an organization that has chosen to innovate. Innovation not only optimizes the relationship between partners and customers but also facilitates the continuity of partners. If large organizations expand the perspective of the members of a value network, the benefits are risk-sharing in exchange for more reliable income and stabler supplies.

2.6 Technology Acceptance Model

In the introduction of procurement 4.0, it is worthwhile to analyze a model developed to assess the acceptance of new technology solutions (TAM, the technology acceptance model).[117] Some studies have used this model to assess acceptance of the internet and mobility technologies,[118] and of the supply chain.[119]

The TAM is based on the hypothesis that the important determinants for the adoption and use of new technologies are[120]:

- perceived usefulness, which is the degree to which persons think that using a particular innovation allows their organization to improve its performance. Perceived usefulness measures include the increase in performance, productivity, and efficiency, overall usefulness, time savings, and an increase in work performance;
- the perceived ease of use, which is the degree to which a person believes that the use of a new solution requires little effort. The perceived ease of use measures include the ease of control, ease of use, simplicity, clarity, and flexibility of use.

Both these factors have a significant and direct effect on an organization planning to adopt procurement 4.0 and its tools. These two beliefs create a favorable disposition or intention toward the use of technology and consequently influence its use.

[117] Davis, F. D. (1989). Perceived usefulness, perceived ease of use, and user acceptance of information technology. *MIS Quarterly*, 13 (3): 319–340.

[118] Kim, Y., Park Y. J., & Choi, J. (2016). The Adoption of Mobile Payment Services for Fintech. *International Journal of Applied Engineering Research*, 11 (2): 1058–1061.

Chen, M. C., Chen, S. S., Yeh, H. M., & Tsaur, W. G. (2016). The Key Factors Influencing Internet Services Finances Satisfaction: An Empirical Study in Taiwan. *American Journal of Industrial and Business Management*, 6 (06): 748–762.

[119] Kamble, S., Gunasekaran, A. & Arha. H. (2019) Understanding the Blockchain technology adoption in supply chains-Indian context, *International Journal of Production Research*, 57(7), 2009–2033.

[120] Song, Y. W. (2019). *User acceptance of an artificial intelligence (AI) virtual assistant: an extension of the technology acceptance mode*. Doctoral dissertation. The University of Texas at Austin, Austin TX.

There are other factors to take into account when considering the procurement 4.0 approach from the TAM. Despite the benefits of procurement 4.0, to overcome trust issues, for example, is a major challenge for its wider adoption. In the case of organizations, especially of SMEs, research has extended the TAM model to include the theory of planned behavior,[121] examining the influence of several potential factors.[122] Considering this and other studies, it is possible to generalize the TAM model.[123] A comprehensive model for TAM should include (Fig. 2.3)[124]:

- behavioral intentions arising from the adoption of procurement 4.0, namely the propensity to adopt a new solution;
- perceived economic factor, which has a significant and direct effect for SMEs in adopting procurement 4.0;
- perceived usefulness, which has a significant and direct effect on the intention of an organization to adopt an innovation. It is determined by the level of convenience and by the affordability arising from adopting procurement 4.0;
- perceived trust, which has a significant and direct effect on the intention of an organization to adopt procurement 4.0;
- characteristics of the digital operation;
- non-quality of service provided by the vendor of the new solutions;
- awareness and knowledge shown, or the realization, perception, and knowledge of a situation or facts;

[121] Ajzen, I. (1991). The Theory of Planned Behavior. *Organizational Behavior and Human Decision Processes*, 50 (2), 179–211.

[122] Bin, MA, Pyeman, JB, Ali, NB, Abdul, NB, & Khai, KG (2018). Determinants of Supply Chain Finance Adoption Among Malaysian Manufacturing Companies: A Proposed Conceptual Framework, *International Journal of Education and Research*, 6 (4), 237–248.

[123] Nicoletti, B. (2017). *The Future of FinTech*. Palgrave Macmillan, Cham, Switzerland.

Bin, MA, Pyeman, JB, Ali, NB, Abdul, NB, & Khai, KG (2018). Determinants of Supply Chain Finance Adoption Among Malaysian Manufacturing Companies: A Proposed Conceptual Framework, *International Journal of Education and Research*, 6 (4), 237–248.

[124] Schierz, PG et al. (2010). Understanding customer acceptance of mobile payment services: an empirical analysis, *Electronic Commerce Research and Applications*. 9 (3): May–June: 209–216.

Nicoletti, B. (2014). *Mobile Banking*, Palgrave Macmillan, Houndmills, UK.

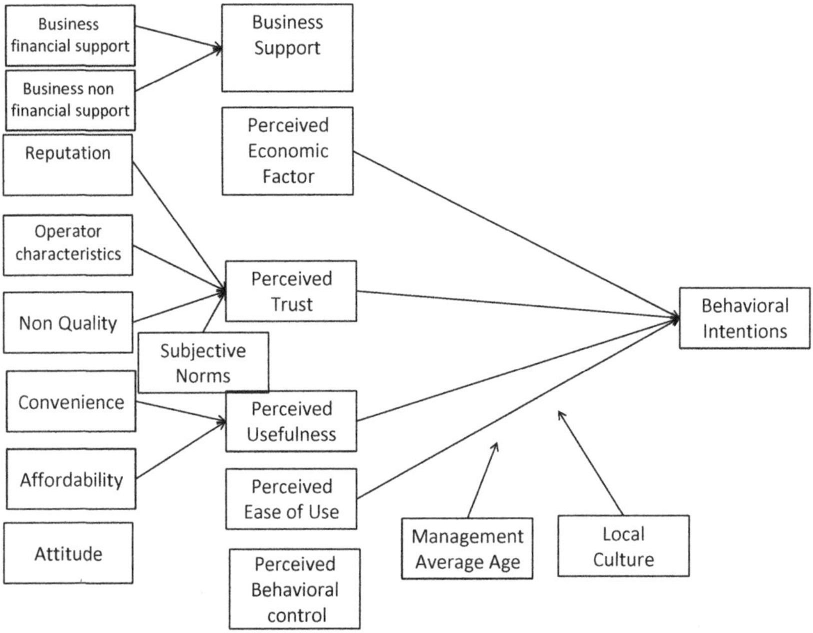

Fig. 2.3 Technology acceptance model

- potential support organizations can be divided into two parts: 1) financial assistance, such as the availability of subsidies, working capital, and concessions; 2) non-financial support, such as courses, consulting, management, distribution, research and development;[125]
- reputation based on the perception of reliability, credibility, social responsibility, and reliability of organizations offering procurement 4.0;[126]

[125] Yusoff. MNH & Yaacob, MR (2010). The Government Business Support in the New Economic Model, *International Journal of Business and Management*, 5 (9), 60–7.

[126] Fombrun, CJ (1996). *Reputation: Realizing Value for the Corporate Image*: Harvard Business School Press, Cambridge, MA.

- attitude toward procurement 4.0 refers to the favorable or unfavorable evaluations of the organization to innovation (attitude toward innovation);[127]
- subjective norms that relate to perceived social pressures that also influence behavioral intention of an organization (social pressures);[128]
- perceived behavioral control refers to the perception of ease or difficulty of performing the behavior associated with a specific innovation.[129]

2.7 Successful Transformation

In a successful enterprise-wide digital transformation, there are several different ways in which the elements can be combined and sequenced. There are three major transformation archetypes[130]:

1. Step-wise—transforming to a procurement 4.0 organization can appear as a step into the dark for senior management. The most common transformation model shows a distinction between the aspiring, designing, and piloting phase and the scale and improve phase. Many organizations run multiple rounds of pilots and iterations before fully committing to scaling up across a large part of the organization. Often, this process takes one to two years, as managers and the organization become familiar with the procurement 4.0 approach and prove that ways of working can bring value to their organization. Organizations may well go through several subsequent rounds of aspiring, designing, and piloting before scaling up elsewhere.

[127] Ajzen, I. & Fishbein, M. (1980). *Attitude Understanding and Predicting Social Behavior*, Prentice- Hall, Englewood Cliffs, NJ.

[128] Ajzen, I. & Fishbein, M. (1980). *Attitude Understanding and Predicting Social Behavior*, Prentice- Hall, Englewood Cliffs, NJ.

[129] Ajzen, I. (1991). The Theory of Planned Behavior. *Organizational Behavior and Human Decision Processes*, 50 (2), 179–211.

[130] https://www.mckinsey.com/business-functions/digital-mckinsey/our-insights/five-moves-to-make-during-a-digital-transformation. Accessed May 20, 2019.

2. All-in—although less common, increasing numbers of organizations have a strong conviction early on and fully commit upfront to move the whole organization to a procurement 4.0 model. Managers from such organizations plan the execution of all steps of the transformation as quickly as possible. In these types of transformation, it is not common for the entire organization to shift to a procurement 4.0 model in one fell swoop. It is more common for the transformation to proceed through several planned waves.
3. Emergent—it is impossible to plan out a procurement 4.0 transformation in detail from the start. Most procurement 4.0 roadmaps have emergent elements. Some organizations have chosen to progress their entire agile transformation through an emergent, bottom-up approach. In this sort of approach, aspiration from the top managers sets a clear direction. Significant effort is spent building procurement 4.0 mindsets and capabilities among the management.

It is helpful to look at the structure of digital and analytics transformation points for some key moves at particular stages of a transition that set successful change efforts apart.[131] These actions suggest ways in which other organizations can plan and execute digital transformations successfully.

For starters, looking at those who report the greatest levels of success in pursuing digital transformations, their organizations ruthlessly focus on a handful of digital themes tied to performance outcomes.[132] In defining their transformations' scope, these successful organizations boldly establish enterprise-wide efforts and build new organizations. They also create an adaptive design that allows the transformation strategy and resource allocation to adjust over time. They adopt procurement 4.0 execution practices and mindsets by encouraging risk-taking and collaboration across several parts of the organization. In the successful efforts, leadership and accountability are clear for each step of the transformation.

[131] https://www.mckinsey.com/business-functions/digital-mckinsey/our-insights/five-moves-to-make-during-a-digital-transformation. Accessed May 19, 2019.

[132] https://www.mckinsey.com/business-functions/digital-mckinsey/our-insights/five-moves-to-make-during-a-digital-transformation. Accessed May 19, 2019.

2.8 Conclusions

This chapter shows which variables affect the adoption of procurement 4.0 and how procurement organizations can spread it. The adoption of procurement 4.0 is different from adoption of traditional innovations. In this new kind of innovation, redefining procurement 4.0 for the organization needs the involvement of the upstream partners. This is made possible through a process of restructuring able to align different sectors, such as procurement and production. The reorganization of these two sectors should push toward the same goal, that is, the effective adoption of procurement 4.0. This is a new concept for many organizations. And the challenge of this innovation is not only internal; it is also external since it also requires the involvement of partners in the initial stages of the procurement process. This involvement is necessary so that more partners adopt procurement 4.0. Over time, this adoption should become routine.

Yet, few organizations are achieving the results expected. A McKinsey Global Survey on the topic confirms that the rate of success is alarmingly low.[133] About eight out of ten respondents say their organizations have begun digital transformations in recent years, but just 14% say their efforts have reached sustained performance improvements. Only 3% of respondents report complete success in sustaining their change.

The implementation of procurement 4.0 requires a strategy and an integrated design for the various aspects of procurement. It is a vision which should cover the four Ps:

- Processes
- Platforms
- Persons
- Partnerships.

This book looks at all four aspects and analyzes the changes necessary to effect the overall design of procurement 4.0. This is the subject of the following chapters, where discussion of the four aspects follows the components of the model of procurement 4.0 presented in this chapter.

[133] https://www.mckinsey.com/business-functions/digital-mckinsey/our-insights/five-moves-to-make-during-a-digital-transformation. Accessed May 19, 2019.

Appendix: Results of a Survey on the Digitization of Procurement: Challenges and Opportunities

Introduction

The Italian journal *Procurement* created a survey on "Digitization: Challenges and Opportunities."[134] The responses received were almost twice the expected amount—a sure signal that interest in the subject is remarkable, a reflection of the ongoing and hastening digital transformation. The latter is impacting all areas and functions of organizations. This appendix shares some interesting results of this survey.

Responses received came from a wide range of industries. This shows that the results are quite general. Respondents were primarily from organizations of a certain size (with an annual turnover of more than €250 million). There was also participation by some smaller organizations.

The employment status of respondents was something of a surprise in some cases, as the positions of respondents corresponded to roughly 50 different denominations. On the one hand, there were also persons not belonging to the procurement function in the strict sense—a multitude of denominations characterizes a lack of standardization. In the English-speaking world, on the other hand, the job description of the person in charge of procurement is pretty well standardized as chief procurement officer (CPO).

The most interesting part of the survey consists of the answers to four questions:

- Which areas have been digitized in the organization concerning procurement processes?
- Which applications is the organization using?
- What are the benefits achieved?
- What are the expected digitization plans for procurement processes?

[134] Nicoletti, B. (2017). The Digitization and its opportunities. https://tesisquare.com/wp-content/uploads/2018/01/WP_Procurement.pdf. Accessed March 30, 2019.

The following pages examine in detail the answers to these questions.

Which Areas Have Been Digitized in the Organization, with Reference to Procurement Processes?

The survey results show that the qualification of partners and their internal management is the most digitized sector, with 63% of responses. A similar percentage of responses (55.8%) is related to the collection and approval of requirements for sourcing of the business areas and invoice checking/ordering processes. The area following these two is that of issuing orders, with 51%.

The impression is that priority has been given to automation of processes of partner selection and approval/control of purchases. This is confirmed by the low percentage (36.4%) of collaborative management of the Procure to Pay process. The latter would be an important aspect for strategic partner management and for critical supplies.

Which Applications Does the Organization Use?

The administrative application (ERP) is by far the most widely used computer application (82.9% of responses). The workflow for the requirements follows this (60.5% of responses).

These answers confirm what is apparent in the previous question: automation priority is assigned to control and accounting processes. It also appears that there has been little focus on specific procurement applications. The automation of this sector has been drowned in a more general context (ERP) and therefore is not responsive to the specific needs of procurement but much more oriented to administrative aspects.

What Are the Benefits Obtained?

This is probably the most interesting part of this survey. It appears that reduction in the duration of the contract-invoice-payment cycle has been reached in most cases. As many as 34% responses show a decrease of more than four days. At the other extreme, 31.6% of the participants in the survey indicate that there have not been any improvements.

The answers to this question highlight the reduction in the cost of maverick sourcing (without control by procurement) as a result of greater spending control; 14.3% of participants in the survey showed a reduction of more than 15% in maverick sourcing, while 31.4% responded that there had been some improvement. The digitization of procurement affects maverick sourcing because there is stricter control of costs. The answer to this hypothesis is probably in the fact that 31.4% of respondents' organizations do not monitor this KPI. At least that percentage of organizations have no knowledge of the costs of maverick sourcing. It is understandable then why in the selection process for being automated in many cases the organization has chosen control of purchases. The organization probably felt that these purchases were not under its control.

In terms of reduction of administrative costs for each purchase order issued, the survey reports that as many as 68.7% responses reported that there were cost savings of between 5% and 15%. Only 24.3% said they had no reduction in administrative costs per order.

Unfortunately, a question was not included on the digitization benefits associated with the improvement of relationships with partners or on the improvement of relationships with internal customers who require the supply.

What Are the Procurement Processes Planned for Digitization?

Partners in contract management (proactive monitoring of deadlines) is the item that received the highest score in the responses in terms of digitization plans. Anyone who is familiar with procurement knows that this aspect is one of the most neglected, and is often scattered between procurement and the department that requires the supplies. Unfortunately, it determines costs for lack of contract renewals or determines non-compliance with internal and external regulations. The process that follows in terms of digitization priority, with 31.7%, is the qualification of partners and internal management of this aspect. As seen from the answers to the first question, this process has been one of the priorities of digitization in many organizations. Many organizations have already implemented the automation of this process and more will do so.

Workflow management for goods and services and authorization requests for billing and issuing of orders have a low value in the context of digitization plans, based on this survey. The reason is that these processes in many cases have already been automated or are not considered part of procurement but fall under the management of operations.

The timeframe for implementation of automation priorities, as indicated by the majority of respondents to the survey, is in many cases longer than nine months (65.6%). Only in 31.3% of cases is this time shown as between three and nine months. In short, in many organizations procurement is not part of the digitization priority. This situation affects (and debases) the contrasts through the fact that in many cases the purchases represented between 40% and 80% of operational costs.[135] So in times of spending review, better digitization of procurement processes should be a priority for many organizations. It is striking that even when people are talking about industry 4.0, thinking to achieve it without advanced procurement digitization is quite surprising.

Conclusions

The results of the survey confirm the model presented in this book. Implementation of the components of procurement 4.0, at least in the Italian organizations, advances—although slowly. It will be good if organizations start accelerating in dealing with an environment, both Italian and global, that is increasingly challenging.

[135] Day, M. (2002), *Handbook of Purchasing Management*, 3rd ed., Gower, Hants.

CHAPTER 3

Processes in Procurement 4.0

3.1 Introduction

The global recession has hit hard in many areas and continues to exert a significant effect. All the main functions of organizations in every industry are impacted. In this situation, there is a growing convergence between the objectives of management and those of the chief procurement officer (CPO) of a company (called in some organizations, 'head of procurement,' or 'supply chain/sourcing manager,' or similar). CPOs must develop and manage appropriate strategies to deal with these issues. These findings are based on the results of a survey conducted by the Aberdeen Group.[1] The survey involved more than 220 managers close to procurement processes. It was also based on in-depth interviews with more than 20 CPOs of leading global organizations.

The global crisis financial is a challenge but it also an opportunity, wherein the Aberdeen Group analyzed the priorities that the CPOs consider. According to the survey, 50% of them indicate that the budget earmarked for procurement has been reduced in recent years, more or less significantly. This has led in many cases to the cancellation of planned major projects. There have been also some positive developments for

[1] Bartolini A. (2009), The CPO's Agenda 2009, *Second CPO Global Business International Forum*, Milan, Italy, June 17 and 18. https://slideplayer.com/slide/9276671/. Accessed May 13, 2019.

B. Nicoletti, *Procurement 4.0 and the Fourth Industrial Revolution*,
https://doi.org/10.1007/978-3-030-35979-9_3

CPOs: 63% of those who responded to the survey state that global economic trends will impact the role of a procurement organization by giving greater visibility to the CPO and increasing their importance in organization strategies. In the face of these new challenges, CPOs must respond by emphasizing their role as providers of value in an organization. Gone are the days when the procurement function was considered a service function or simply an 'order processor.' On the contrary, it is a crucial function, as the commercial department adds value to the organization through increased revenues. CPOs add value through a reduction in costs and improvement in the services provided to the rest of the organization. Procurement costs are always relevant as they can go from 40% to 80% of the operational costs of the organization depending on the type of organization.[2]

The CPOs surveyed perceive four main priorities:

- attention to the effectiveness, efficiency, and economics of the procurement processes;
- willingness to invest in the upgrading of skills and capabilities of staff of the procurement function;
- ability to analyze and better manage spending;
- ability to strengthen and improve collaboration and partnerships.

The Aberdeen Group provides some recommendations to CPOs willing to improve the performance of their function, following the behaviors of the best organizations identified during their research. Thus, CPOs should focus on[3]:

- punctually defining the sourcing processes, to increase their effectiveness, efficiency, and economy;
- improving risk management capabilities in the sourcing process;
- monitoring the application of the contract terms by the partners and collaborating with the finance and control executives to jointly develop strategies for optimizing the financial management of procurement.

[2] https://assets.kpmg/content/dam/kpmg/pdf/2012/07/the-power-of-procurement-a-global-survey-of-procurement-functions.pdf. Accessed May 13, 2019.

[3] Bartolini A. (2009), The CPO's Agenda 2009, *Second CPO Global Business International Forum*, Milan, Italy, June 17 and 18. https://slideplayer.com/slide/9276671/. Accessed May 13, 2019.

Bayer Italy[4]

Bayer Italy is the Italian subsidiary of Bayer. Bayer focuses its activities in the areas of life sciences, health, and agriculture. It has a turnover of €1.02 billion, three production sites on the national territory with some of the most advanced plants in the world, about 2000 employees (data from December 2018).

Bayer Italy has annual storage costs of €10 million and transportation costs of €14 million (€10 million in Italy and €4 million abroad). Bayer Italy has many offices, factories, logistics partners, and about 20,000 customers (that is, points of destination to be served, often every day), in very different fields: wholesalers, pharmacies, hospitals, pet shops, garden centers, and mass retailers.

The organization has set itself the problem of how to re-engineer the management of the transport system. The first phase was focused on processes and the second on collaboration along the value network. The main focus here was on:

- contract management systems, and
- pre-invoicing systems.

It was necessary automatically to compute 100% of the costs of transportation (without considering human resources costs) to notify the partners of the numbers to be invoiced.

This first phase took about six months of work to cope with the complexity and variability of transportation in Italy, where there are many determinants of costs, tariff systems, and types of contract. The system can compute the number due to the logistics providers using special algorithms that combine all these elements.

Once the pre-billing system was finalized, Bayer Italy tackled the next problem and turned it into an opportunity. The organization has designed an integrated transport management system, going beyond the concept of interfaces. This is based on a collaborative platform that can communicate with several transport organizations.

(*continued*)

[4] https://emiliocogliani.wordpress.com/2018/01/08/bayer-italia-controlla-costi-di-trasporto-e-consegne-in-tempo-reale-il-miglior-tms-di-tutto-il- group/. Accessed March 4, 2019.

(continued)

The success of this collaborative process has gone far beyond expectations, moving from exchange of just delivery notes (transport documents), whose data in the past had to be entered manually into the system, to a system based on a cloud computing platform that tracks delivery documentation (proof-of-delivery) in real time. It can collect information from all partners involved and through a multitude of data sources.

Advanced cybersecurity solutions assure that the opening to external systems does not impact the organization: In general, the process is much more efficient than one based on emails. Every actor is involved and every step of the product delivery process is tracked. Potentially, the system is also open being accessed by customers with a suitable profile.

The core benefits come from four areas:

- Automatic computation of 100% of the transport costs. The system handles 20,000 customers and about 250,000–300,000 shipments per year with only one operator. In this way, Bayer Italy can avoid the costs and errors associated with manual entries and can check the correctness of invoices received.
- The system allows not only the monitoring and tracking of deliveries but also the booking of time slots, detection of exceptions, and automatic alerts to the operator.
- The system is multi-channel and multi-organization; Bayer Group has many subsidiaries that operate in very different areas.
- A business intelligence dashboard supports monitoring performance but also simulation of potential distribution rearrangements, for example destinations or movements to distribution centers and the warehouses, with the associated impacts in terms of costs.

Procurement 4.0 requires a re-engineering of the processes of an organization.[5] This is the main subject of this chapter. It is necessary to consider all processes and their associated activities. The objective must be agility, hence leanness of processes and their digitization.

[5] Hennelly, P., Srai, J., Graham, G., & Wamba, S. F. (2019). Reconfiguring business processes in the new political and technological landscape. *Business Process Management Journal*, 25(3), 386–390.

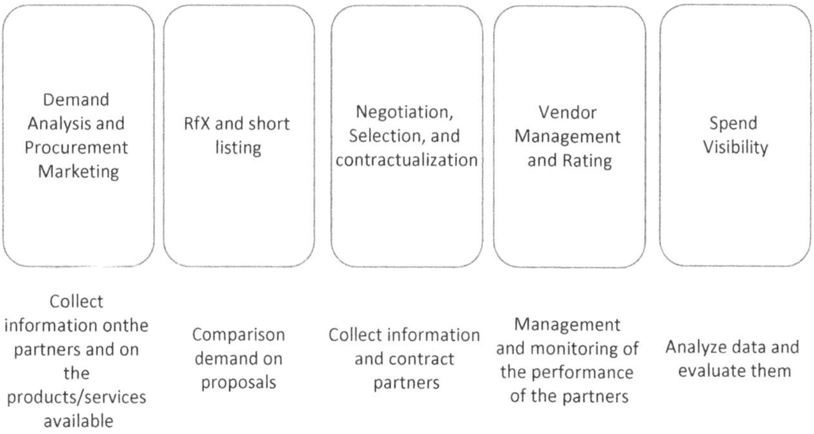

Fig. 3.1 Procurement processes

End-to-end procurement involves a series of processes as well as providing support on strategic choices (Fig. 3.1):

1. It must start with an assessment of the current situation. It is necessary to analyze the processes of an organization and understand what to outsource (make, buy, or partner). For most small and medium-sized organizations, the process of buying and managing the network of partners are processed so as to be entrusted to specialized e-procurement platforms, provided by external organizations.[8] Large organizations typically prefer investing in an internal platform for e-procurement, but more and more organizations are switching to applications provided by external specialized organizations.
2. It continues with the definition of the supply network through a process of searching for new partners (scouting) and the selection of partners.
3. The next step is the definition of rules and a system of management of the value network, with classification and clustering of partners.
4. The organization needs to improve its procurement decisions.

Process business intelligence, analyzed at the end of this chapter, can provide special benefits in the implementation of procurement 4.0.

3.2 Structure and Activities of Procurement Processes

The processes involved in procurement are complex. They include many activities at three different levels: strategic, tactical, and operational. The overall process is sometimes referred to as P2P: procure-to-pay, or S2P: source-to-pay, to show that it is end-to-end—from the requirements received from internal customers to the final payment for the acquisition of the goods and services.[6]

The goal of procurement processes is to ensure efficient communication between the users, the staff of the procurement organization, its partners, and the financial and accounting departments. Once the information flows to partners, the processes must ensure an efficient flow of supplies from the partners to the end-user. In parallel, there is a financial flow to consider, including orders and partners' invoices to administration and accounting departments. In synthesis, procurement implies three flows[7]:

- informational/digital
- physical
- financial.

Procurement processes must be effective, efficient, and economical. They must also comply with an additional E: They must be ethical, in the sense that there must be an effective control to prevent abuses, avoid frauds, and assure the compliance to internal regulations and applicable laws.

Many functions are involved in the processes of procurement, engineering, sourcing, logistics, warehousing, operations, quality, finance, administration, and project management. All these entities must work together according to the procedures and specific characteristics of end customers of the relevant organization/s.

[6] Zenzaro, S. (2015, April). An ASM model for the procure to pay case study. In *Proceedings of the 7th International Conference on Subject-Oriented Business Process Management* ACM: 19.

[7] Nicoletti, B. (2017). *Agile Procurement: Volume I: Adding Value with Lean Processes.* Springer, Cham, Switzerland

In procurement processes, it is useful to distinguish the following main activities:

- issuing a request for acquisition (the so-called acquisition request)
- choosing a partner
- issuing an order
- receiving the goods or services
- managing invoices (controlling, approving, and accounting)
- paying invoices
- evaluating partners (partner rating).

Each of these macro activities can be further broken down into other micro activities. For instance, procurement processes include the sourcing process. In the first stage of this process, there is a definition of requirements. At that point, the organization needs to decide whether to make, buy, or partner. For each good or service, it is necessary to decide whether to produce them inside the organization, or to buy in, or to find partners to provide them. If the decision is to buy, buyers, with the support of the users, should select the right partner and start the negotiation phase. During and after delivery, the organization should evaluate its partners (vendor or partner rating) to create over time a valid set of competent partners (vendor register). The vendor register can also be created through a specific process of certification or qualification before admitting partners to tender.

Clear description of the activities carried out by every single function of the organization during procurement is important. The study of these activities can highlight areas with low benefits, which can be outsourced or, if possible, eliminated or reduced substantially.[8]

Procurement 4.0 requires digital transformation of all procurement processes. The following pages consider some critical processes that support procurement 4.0:

- procurement process intelligence
- logistics
- risk management
- procurement finance.

[8]These areas are called waste (or *muda* in Japanese) in the lean and digitize approach. Nicoletti, B., (2012), *Lean and Digitize: An Integrated Approach to Process Improvement*. Gower Publishing, Farnham, UK. ISBN-10: 1409441946.

3.3 Command: Procurement Process Intelligence

It is important to maximize the value provided by procurement 4.0 to organizations and to end customers. In the current state of market volatility, there is a danger that certain variables will come into play and disrupt programs. It is essential to increase organizational agility. To achieve this, it is important to act on processes and platforms. This means:

- modernizing and improving the efficiency of procurement processes (online auctions, orders via the internet, and so on);
- optimizing price/quality ratio, ensuring the quality standard of supplies and ancillary services;
- rationalizing spending on goods and services;
- creating a network of communication with the supply ecosystem.

To achieve all these objectives with procurement 4.0, it is necessary to adopt a model of business process intelligence, also referred to as procurement process intelligence. This is business intelligence focused on the optimal management of procurement processes. It has a major innovative aspect: Business intelligence is designed primarily to analyze information and in some cases allow simulations (what-if analysis).[9] Procurement process intelligence adds also the management of workflows connected with these processes.[10] The next sections detail this approach.

3.3.1 Digitize and Lean Procurement

Procurement 4.0 aims to optimize the value provided by the procurement function. The information is sometimes uncertain in this area, though: In the current times of volatility and flux, there is a difficulty in forecasting some variables that can come into play and distort programs. It thus becomes important to increase agility.

Many organizations have process improvement projects. For example, Novartis has a Process Lifecycle Management Team for the implementation

[9] Turban, E., Sharda, R., & Delen, D. (2010). *Decision Support and Business Intelligence Systems*. Google Scholar.

[10] Nicoletti, B. (2018). Processes in Agile Procurement. In *Agile Procurement*, 113–147. Palgrave Macmillan, Cham, Switzerland.

of internal processes and a research team which focuses on opportunities in procurement.[11] A consultancy supports this endeavor by working in the organization in a cross-functional level.

This chapter goes further and proposes a procurement 4.0 approach based on a methodology described as 'lean and digitize'.[12] Unlike traditional methods that focus on organizational and operational aspects, this methodology argues that the transformation project must include two phases:

- process improvements through the use of Lean Six Sigma methodology (see below), with the realization of aspects that do not require automation, such as new organizational and operational models, elimination of unnecessary activities, layout optimization, and so forth;
- automation of management and operational processes which lend themselves to digitization.

Based on research and experiences, the lean and digitize methodology can be summarized as follows (Fig. 3.2). It can be divided into six macro phases and 20 + 1 steps.[13] At the end of each macro phase, there is a progress control indicated, according to Six Sigma terminology, by tollgates (exit control).

To achieve this approach in the case of procurement 4.0, it is important to adopt an attitude of business process intelligence applied to procurement. This is an innovative approach focused on measuring and managing procurement processes optimally.

Traditional business intelligence undoubtedly has a strategic value within procurement. The ability to manage and use excellent information assets is the real key to defining successful strategies and improve their competitiveness. The analysis of data, obtained through the use of

[11] https://www.novartis.com/careers/career-search/job-details/257932BR. Accessed February 24, 2019.

[12] Nicoletti, B., (2012), *Lean and Digitize: An Integrated Approach to Process Improvement*. Gower Publishing, Farnham, UK. ISBN-10: 1409441946.

[13] Nicoletti, B., (2012), *Lean and Digitize: An Integrated Approach to Process Improvement*. Gower Publishing, Farnham, UK. ISBN-10: 1409441946.

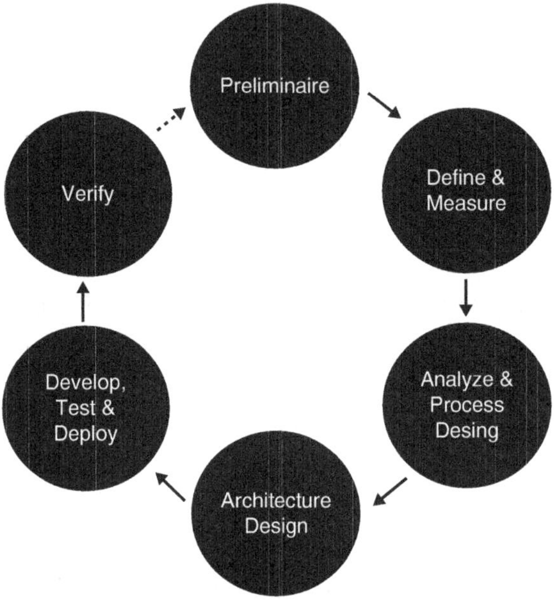

Fig. 3.2 Lean and digitize methodology

business intelligence solutions is not sufficient. To really improve performance, organizations should:

- discover indicative trends;
- describe possible scenarios;
- check the effect of actions that might be undertaken;
- make operational decisions based on detailed information provided by business intelligence;
- proceed accordingly, involving and coordinating with all parties and persons involved;
- closely monitor progress and, if necessary, take corrective actions.

Traditional business intelligence allows an organization to make decisions consciously and quickly, increasing the capacity to react in critical situations. The use of business intelligence, made possible by advanced analysis, allows being able to act promptly upon the occurrence of a critical condition and prevent any inefficiencies.

Procurement process intelligence is business intelligence focused on optimal management of procurement processes. The innovative aspect is the fact that the traditional approach of business intelligence is aimed primarily at analyzing information, and in some cases performs simulations ('what if' analysis). In the case of procurement process intelligence, the process also provides for the possible direct action through:

- expert systems
- actions appropriately guided by persons or automated
- use of collaboration tools.

The emphasis is thus on systems that can act in continuity (real time) and direct actions, in a quick sequence that is focused on processes.

The main components of procurement process intelligence are (Fig. 3.3):

- forecasting
- procurement strategy

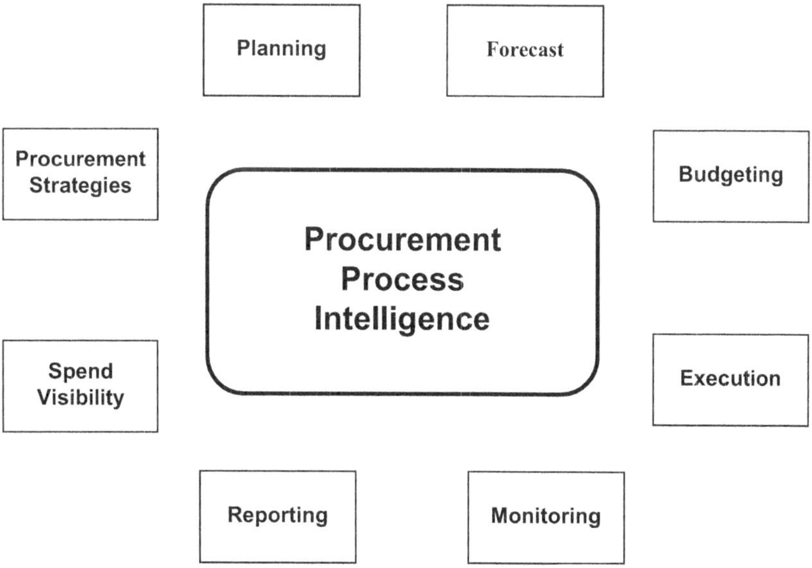

Fig. 3.3 Procurement process intelligence

- planning
- budgeting
- cooperation
- execution
- monitoring
- analysis of expenses.

Thanks to the rapidity of implementation, ease of use, high flexibility, and the main characteristics of the system, it should be possible to:

- increase levels of reactivity;
- identify and analyze critical indicators in real time;
- support decisions at all levels of the organizational structure;
- act on processes, monitor and take corrective action.

Development of procurement process intelligence should include the following steps:

- record activities—a process of analyzing, identifying a start and an end, repetition in time, and length of run with the support of computer tools that record occurrence;
- make processes transparent to ascertain immediately the status and the progress of a procedure;
- process the data and produce statistics, taking into consideration a set of activities and returning a dashboard with synthesized and summary information concerning one or more dimensions (timing, amount, distribution over time, resources, and anomalies);
- compare data and measure variations visually, by transposing the statistical measure in a structured and visual form and as easily interpretable in results (pie chart, histogram, table, graph, and so forth) with time comparison;
- control in an active manner, by continuously monitoring and analyzing the organization's performance or functions, and signaling when these fall below set thresholds;
- define what actions to take and perform them as automatically as possible;
- monitor process performance and take action to remediate and/or improve;
- replicate successes in other areas of the organization or, possibly, in other organizations of the same group.

Solutions of this type can increase the value that the procurement function brings to an organization.

In the realization of a business process intelligence system, it is important to start with a thorough analysis of the system and a definition of the objectives to be achieved. It is necessary to define the architecture of whatever procurement business intelligence solution is to be adopted. The last step in the scheme is the spending analysis. This underlies the whole cycle and represents the most important ingredient for success.

The rest of this section describes in detail the main components of a procurement process intelligence system.

All systems that help improve processes are essential for transforming procurement entities from a 'factory that issues orders' to a valued partner of a given organization. Some organizations have succeeded in saving up to 60% on previous costs using such business intelligence applications. With this approach, Bayer has been able to optimize its travel expenses by analyzing its travel behavior. Through this, it was possible to define more precise traveling rules for employees. Carlson Wagonlit Travel (CWT) has provided an ICT tool that allowed Bayer to optimize expenses in this area.[14]

3.3.2 *Procurement Process Intelligence Components*

Procurement process intelligence has several components, which are summarized in the following pages.

Forecasting, Procurement Strategy, Planning, and Budgeting

With the integration in a single solution of the world of strategy, planning, and monitoring with that of business intelligence it is important to have a collaborative platform that can provide analytical and planning features simultaneously. It is therefore essential to design and implement processes and systems to support, facilitate, and make consistent—in a flexible way—all the planning processes (long, medium, and short term) that an organization intends to use and put under its control.

[14] https://www.carlsonwagonlit.com/it/it/why-choose-us/our-company/our-history/. Accessed March 30, 2019.

The forecasting modules, strategy, planning, and budgeting, through collaborative management of scenarios and other features targeted to the analysis of the consequences of decisions, are intended to:

- analyze and share future results;
- simulate alternative hypotheses;
- prepare and validate more targeted planning.

These modules must be complemented by a performance management component which supports the planning and control processes, both in strategies and operations, in line with an organization's needs.

The platform must innovatively support the following activities while providing unique flexibility thanks to its fundamental integration with business intelligence:

- forecast the flow of processes over time;
- plan and control of both strategy and operations;
- plan from an economic and financial point of view;
- budget;
- simulate the consequences of possible choices;
- manage profitability and costs;
- produce summary dashboards on activities' progress.

The solution must be flexible, permitting:

- adaption to any need or requests from the procurement scheduling function;
- provision of a workflow aimed at collecting required approvals as stated in the organization's procedures.

The finance and control department using the platform must be able to:

- communicate the organization's strategy;
- implement and monitor performance;
- feel its influence in all organizational levels necessary to ensure that what is planned is then effectively executed.

Collaboration

The collaboration process must allow the organization in question to adopt new ways of collaboration inside and outside to support procurement 4.0. The traditional procurement support applications (ERP, manufacturing and material requirement planning, product lifecycle management, and so forth) provide access to structured information but do not allow activation of unstructured collaborative ('data-driven') mechanisms where persons, including the partners, interact, negotiate, decide, and finally execute a plan.[15]

An important difference between a procurement process intelligence system and all other collaboration platforms is that traditional collaborative systems are centered on persons, while the system must allow the organization to center collaboration on data, documents, and especially processes. The key objective is to have a platform that can provide collaborative capabilities and execution of the processes of procurement 4.0 through contextual information and relevant documents. It should allow procurement 4.0 to become more agile. This agility then allows organizations to seize any opportunities that the market offers and to ensure procurement processes become flexible, preventing the organization from failing to adapt to increasingly rapid changes in markets and supply.

The collaborative platform must be able to integrate structured and unstructured data and provide collaborative capabilities and performance transactional capabilities to connect internal actors with partners outside the organization. The system must provide the following collaboration features:

- workflow (automatic management of workflows)
- instant messaging
- remarks
- alert signals
- exchange of documents (such as RFX, orders, invoices, and so forth)
- joint work
- unified search and if possible semantic searches[16]
- mobility tools (SMS, tablet, and similar).

[15] Anderson, C. (2015). *Creating a data-driven organization: Practical advice from the trenches.* O'Reilly Media, Inc., Sebastopol, CA.

Execution

With the support for executing processes, the procurement business process should allow procurement 4.0 professionals to integrate information, decisions, and actions. It should be possible to execute a collaborative decision (for example, the issuance of order) with a single mouse click or a mobile app, and contextually to record the information directly in the same analysis system that has generated the decision. These features allow an organization to:

- integrate processes, monitoring in real time all key performance indicators (KPI) of procurement, that is, the critical variables placed under observation, and correlating them so as to generate intelligence;
- use intelligence, inherent in the system, to handle unplanned events collaboratively by providing all actors in the ecosystem of the organization (including partners and distributors) with optimal guidelines to maximize KPIs defined for that specific process;
- close the loop by running or triggering actions necessary to implement the decision taken by procurement 4.0 professionals or by the system itself.

Monitoring and Spend Analysis (Visibility of Expenses)

Managing this delicate process becomes less complex if procurement 4.0 professionals use specialized tools. Proper spending analysis enables organizations to gain insight on spending and gather data on their partners, both for the internal market and for key performance parameters. In this way, an organization can come to know the volume purchased and assess the breakdown by department, product category, or other taxonomies. This facilitates checking of any deviations from budgets and objectives. This solution should be available in any management system, allowing an organization to turn data into information, then into decisions, the latter into actions, and finally to keep track of any activity of procurement processes.

Procurement process intelligence capabilities should include all typical analysis of the procurement world, from spending on partners to delivery punctuality. It should also be able to assign scores to partners based on the quality of their supplies. In this way, it will increase the bargaining power of an organization which, as it comes into possession of all the necessary evaluation criteria, can identify more effective procurement procedures. These applications offer valuable support in containing spending on goods and services. KPIs simplify the analysis, allowing an organization to get a concise and immediate view of procurement trends. With these systems, procurement professionals should be able to quickly check progress on the main objectives of their particular function and the state of the budget. It must be possible to create measurement systems or spending through thematic sets of indicators of procurement. These indicators should measure and analyze any deviations from optimal values, creating an intuitive and immediate snapshot of the current and historical situation of the area.

Any such systems must also support the rationalization of spending on goods and services organizations through the use of advanced statistical analysis tools able to monitor sourcing economies and optimal service levels, with capabilities for:

- interfacing electronic market instruments for the purchase of goods and services, such as electronic catalogs, online auctions, and marketplaces, to allow procurement 4.0 to be used effectively, efficiently, and economically for new solutions;
- displaying the chain of procurement processes resulting in measurable benefits in terms of purchased quality and resource recovery to focus on other value-added activities and on external and internal customer satisfaction;
- knowing the potential of partners and its procurement professionals;
- analyzing historical spending over time.

Procurement process intelligence solutions must offer concrete and timely decision support. They should provide not only a magnifying glass on the data assets of an organization but also a way to maximize returns from its utilization through integrated collaborative mechanisms.

Procurement business intelligence systems must provide opportunities for all persons and institutions involved to make collaborative decisions based on the information and to propagate decisions on processes directly using available functionality in the systems.

3.3.3 *Technology for Business Process Intelligence*

From a technology point of view, a business process intelligence system must be an integrated platform that through the use of a single development environment, unified security management, processes description, and their administration, should allow the managing and support of analysis activities, planning, knowledge sharing, and process execution, all using a collaborative environment. This integration allows an organization to drive the execution of decisions, to optimize them, and, above all, to be able to consider its overall objectives at every step of the decision-making process.

There are technologies and vendors of application software packages with powerful integrated collaborative analytical engines. They can produce dashboards, reports, evaluation grids, alert signals with short deadlines, and, when necessary, modes of collaborative work needed for information sharing.[17]

3.4 Collaboration: Logistics 4.0

In a nutshell, industry 4.0 can be described as a completely automated process with interconnected operations. To get to this involves a series of changes in organizational management. Procurement 4.0 also implies support and therefore a change in logistics. The logistics processes must become faster, more interconnected, and more agile. Thus, organizations should move toward logistics 4.0. In the case of logistics, successive phases have already been introduced and indicated with numbers.

- Logistics 1.0 supports the basic functions of logistics, in which an organization search manually to get the right product, at the right place, at the right time, and under the right conditions.
- Logistics 2.0 indicates the development of integrated logistics services.
- Some logistics organizations have begun to enter collaborative supply chain logistics, Logistics 3.0.
- Logistics 4.0 is the topic of this chapter, which considers several important aspects, especially in terms of better integration within the business ecosystem.

Logistics 4.0 should support the processes of procurement 4.0, from processing market requirements and production planning to delivery of

[16] Guha, R., McCool, R., & Miller, E. (2003). Semantic search. In *Proceedings of the 12th international conference on World Wide Web*, 700–709. ACM, New York City, NY.

products to an organization.[18] The solutions to these challenges lie in the digitalization of logistics activities and processes: that is, the application of digital logistics.

Logistics 4.0 should provide powerful support in terms of collaboration inside and particularly outside organizations. The following fields need action:

- Data collection, including especially use of the IoT. This should provide support to the interaction through the web not only of persons, but also of objects, machines, and work-in-progress products thanks to the increasing diffusion of sensors.
- Classification and storing of data as a tool to create value, because movement of data can exploit machine computing power. This aspect includes all issues related to big data,[19] to open data,[20] and so forth. That is, once the data are collected, they must be cleaned, categorized, and stored.
- Analytics—once the data are stored, they should be used for analysis and management of an organization with appropriate tools to 'instruct' the machines and monetize the data.[21]
- Mobility, understood as the use of mobile phones and tablets, facilitates interactions within systems and with other operators at any time and location within the ecosystem.

Cloud computing allows organization to move from a supply chain to a value network. In other words, cloud computing substantially facilitates coordination and collaboration between organizations and their partners

[17] Commercial packages are available to cover all or part of business process intelligence. An example is Jaggaer, with its Jaggaer Spend Visibility solutions. This is an analysis tool that enables organizations to have real-time, and in usable form, up-to-date purchase dates that are complete and consistent, in different information systems, and decision solutions that cover many aspects of business process intelligence.

[18] Radivojević, G., & Milosavljević, L. (2019). The Concept of Logistics 4.0. *4th Logistics International Conference,* May 23–25. Belgrade, Serbia.

[19] Accenture (2014), Big Data Analytics in Supply Chain: Hype or Here to Stay?, *Accenture Global Operations Study Megatrends.*

[20] Kitchin, R. (2014). *The data revolution: Big Data, Open Data, data infrastructures and their Consequences.* Sage, New York, NY.

[21] Woerner, S. L., & Wixom, B. H. (2015). Big data: extending the business strategy toolbox. *Journal of Information Technology,* 30 (1), 60–62.

and/or other groups of dispersed organizations, and potentially globally. At the same time, it allows the flexibility and agility characteristic of procurement 4.0.

When an organization starts a procurement 4.0 development path, it should do the same for logistics. This would mean that the organization has to face in two directions at the same time, using:

- innovation in technology to meet the needs that arise both from the market and customers for digital solutions and the requirements of a supply of digitized services;
- innovation in logistics processes, structures, platforms, partners, and in employees to meet the challenges and opportunities of digital transformation.

In future, procurement portfolios will change more and more rapidly, thanks to the shift from mass production to production in smaller batches, even down to the scale of a product being created one unit at a time.[22] In this way, an organization can assure maximum product customization. In turn, logistics must respond more quickly and readily.

Logistics 4.0 impacts on the entire logistics cycle:

- the logistics of the value network, allowing open and flexible operations;
- inbound logistics, with the support of big data analytics, enabling predictive logistics;
- warehouses and storage management to support the management of inventories and a reduction in storage costs in the value network;
- intralogistics: AGVs driven by the production machines, which in turn are heavily robotized;
- outbound logistics to support the management of autonomous deliveries and a predictive management;
- logistics routing based on autonomous transport (for instance, drones and driverless vehicles) and real-time connections for re-routing.
- this will go even further in the future with 3D printing, and logistics will face new challenges, finding new ways and tools to manage materials and goods.

[22] DHL. (2013). Logistics trend radar–delivering insight today. Creating value tomorrow! *DHL document.*

The solutions of procurement 4.0 in terms of supporting material-handling equipment are several[23]:

- semi-automatic trilateral trucks
- hybrid trucks
- AGVs
- RFID readers
- sensors—fleet management
- safety for sensors
- automatic braking systems
- interaction between machines and AGVs
- autonomous intelligent vehicles
- automatic trilateral trucks.

It also offers solutions in preparing orders in the form of better ergonomics for the workplace and the employment of cobots (collaborative robots).[24]

Procurement 4.0 also acts at the storage level. Used to store products and manage inventory levels, stores are a key part of the value network in procurement 4.0. Proper inventory management can lead to a reduction in costs and can improve customer satisfaction. Traditional models of stock management have become less efficient and unable react sufficiently to rising market requirements. Now, there are modern devices such as smart pallets and smart warehouses that can help in logistics 4.0.[25]

ICT is now used for most inventory management; procurement 4.0 can substantially improve such management using the IoT.[26] This allows the connection of multiple objects and humans in real-time data sharing. The resulting information can then be used to support an automatic decision-making process.

[23] Tappia, E. & Moretti, E. (2019). La Ricerca dell'Osservatorio Contract Logistics "Gino Marchet". *Euromerci*, no 4–5, 34–37.

[24] Peshkin, M. A., Colgate, J. E., Wannasuphoprasit, W., Moore, C. A., Gillespie, R. B., & Akella, P. (2001). Cobot architecture. *IEEE Transactions on Robotics and Automation*, 17(4), 377–390.

[25] Tappia, E. & Moretti, E. (2019). La Ricerca dell'Osservatorio Contract Logistics "Gino Marchet". *Euromerci*, no 4–5, 34–37.

[26] McFarlane, D., & Sheffi, Y. (2003). The impact of automatic identification on supply chain operations. *The international journal of logistics management*, 14 (1), 1–17.

This approach to inventory management can help provide real-time visibility of the warehouse, to increase the speed and efficiency of the system, preventing shortages and inventory counterfeits.

The challenges of logistics 4.0 are primarily the consequence of high-level requests related to organizational, technical, and software solutions.[27] An organization needs to change the way it operates, its management, and so applies the latest ICT solutions so that it can meet the preconditions for introducing a new concept of smart logistics.[28] Thus, challenges facing logistics 4.0 are high in terms of introduction and implementation costs, strict requirements because of hardware infrastructure, requirements for the application of process-oriented management methods, and so on. The solutions to these challenges are good implementation, commitment of the whole organization to change, motivation of employees for additional training and development of their intellectual resources to support change.[29]

The Osservatorio Gino Marchet at the Politecnico di Milano carried out a survey on the progress of logistics and, in particular, on its outsourcing.[30] This research reveals that the main positive effect of industry 4.0 is the ability to integrate different systems, not only within the warehouse but along the entire value network. Nearly one operator in two (48%) expects an increase in productivity. Over one-third (37%) expect increased visibility on processes, while 27% envisage improved traceability of products, and 23% improvements in security. The main problems identified in the survey are linked to payback times of 4.0 solutions (35%), complexity of the communication between information systems (23%), and lack of adequate skills (21%).

[27] Radivojević, G., & Milosavljević, L. (2019). The Concept of Logistics 4.0. *4th Logistics International Conference,* May 23–25. Belgrade, Serbia

[28] Mousheimish, R. Taher, Y. &. Finance, B. (2015), Towards smart logistics processes: A predictive monitoring and proactive adaptation approach, *ACM International Conference Proceeding Series,* v August 2015 24–26, 169–170, August 24.

[29] Olegków-Szlapka J., & Stachowiak A. (2019). The Framework of Logistics 4.0 Maturity Model. In: Intelligent Systems in Production Engineering and Maintenance. *ISPEM 2018. Advances in Intelligent Systems and Computing,* 835. Springer, Cham, Switzerland.

[30] (2018). Logistics: a dynamic sector that seeks innovation. *Euromerci,* December 28–30.

Barilla[31]

Barilla Group, the premium Italian pasta producer, is committed to improvement of procurement processes. It uses new solutions provided by the industry 4.0 model and through these Barilla has created a split between strategic and operational processes to better understand how different solutions can be implemented. This distinction makes it possible to perform a quantitative analysis of operational processes, in particular, with detailed mapping of the activities of issuing a purchase order and contract management to identify standard and repetitive tasks that can be automated. In this way, it is possible to free employees from low value-added activities.

DB Schenker[32]

DB Schenker is an active player in global logistics and the management of value networks. It has a turnover of €15 billion and 66,327 employees.[33] Thanks to its effectiveness in road and rail transport, DB Schenker has managed to become an important carrier in over 40 European countries.[34] DB Schenker is also active in transporting goods by air and beyond Europe. The company is committed to following a logistics strategy that prioritizes investing in digitization and other automation innovations. In cooperation with the Fraunhofer Institute, the organization has created the DB Schenker Logistics and Digitization Enterprise Lab, headquartered in Dortmund, Germany. The lab researches possible solutions for the management of logistics through robots and automated packaging systems. These solutions are based on cyber-physical industry 4.0 characteristics.

(*continued*)

[31] Riva, A. (2018). The Impact of Industry 4.0 on procurement and supply management: a multinational food company houses. *Thesis Politecnico di Milano*, Milan, Italy.

[32] Horenberg, D. (2017). Applications Within Logistics 4.0: A research conducted on the visions of 3PL service providers, *Bachelor's thesis, University of Twente*, Enschede, Netherlands

[33] Deutsche Bahn Group. 2015. Deutsche Bahn Fact & Figures 2015.https://www.deutschebahn.com/file/en/11887746/dawl4KJk_JtwAPsVq8PIk6DPUU/10948124/data/2015_duf_en.pdf. Accessed March 10, 2019.

[34] Schenker, AG (2017). "Global Leading Logistics Provider | DB Schenker". https://www.dbschenker.com/global/about/profile. Accessed March 10, 2019.

(continued)

Furthermore, DB Schenker has developed two platforms: the Drive4Schenker platform was made possible by the collaboration of DB Schenker with uShip, and the Transporeon platform is used by Kuehne + Nagel. These platforms allow the organization to optimize truck loads and improve transport services by providing carriers with advanced solutions. The organization can now even participate in small procurement activities thanks to the digitization of its entire logistics chain.

DHL[35]

DHL offers international transportation of goods and manages logistics contracts.[36] It is also active in developing the use of autonomous vehicles. In the report "Vehicles in Logistics" DHL says: "these systems may find the quickest route to avoid traffic congestion, reduce handling costs with cars, and minimizing the environmental impacts, resulting in a total experience more environmentally friendly and safe for all."[37] Besides investigating the possibility of innovative road transport, DHL also focuses on air transport. With the use of autonomous drones or unmanned aerial vehicles (UAV—an aircraft piloted by remote control or onboard computers), goods delivery can be quickly done even in places difficult to reach. Tests are already being performed with a 'Parcelcopter' that can grasp a parcel and deliver it at a speed of 70 km/h over a distance of 8.3 km.[38]

[35] Horenberg, D. (2017). Applications Within Logistics 4.0: A research conducted on the visions of 3PL service providers, *Bachelor's thesis, University of Twente*, Enschede, Netherlands

[36] https://www.dhl.com/en.html. Accessed July 21, 2019.

[37] Niezgoda. 2016. "DHL Customer Solutions & Innovation Represented by Matthias Heutger Senior Vice President Strategy, Marketing & Innovation." DHL Trend Research. http://www.dhl.com/content/dam/downloads/g0/abo ut_us / logistics_insights / dhl_trendreport_robotics.pdf. Accessed March 10, 2019.

[38] Palermo, E., S. & Writer. 2017. "Delivery Drones Become a Reality in Germany." Live Science. Accessed June 6, 2018. http://www.livescience.com/48032-dhl-dronedelivery-service.html. Accessed March 10, 2019. Franco, M. 2017. DHL Uses Completely Autonomous System to Deliver Consumer Goods by Drone. http://newatlas.com/dhl-drone-delivery/43248/ Accessed March 10, 2019.

3.5 Cybernetics: Risk Management in Procurement

The risk management process is an important aspect to consider in procurement 4.0. The definition of 'risk' given by CIPS (the Chartered Institute of Procurement and Supply) is "likelihood of an undesired result."[39] A more specific definition in the case of procurement is that risk is potential disruption in procurement processes in dealing with services, products, and/or resources. Common types of risk in procurement are fraud, excessive costs, partner quality, and delivery times.[40]

Risk management is an integral part of an efficient strategy in a company's supply chain management, given the possible implications of poor risk management.[41] Organizations need to consider any risks that they may incur.[42] One could cite some quite extreme examples. Think of what happened as a result of the disaster at the Fukushima nuclear power plant in Japan[43]; many organizations lost their supplies for a long time.[44] Or consider the case of hard drives for personal computers: A disaster in a factory in Thailand reduced availability of components for these products for a long time.[45] Events such as these are not uncommon—an integrated approach implemented enterprise-wide can be the deciding factor between just avoiding calamities to suffering the full extent of their ramifications.[46]

[39] https://www.cips.org/en/cips-for-business/knowledge-for-business/cips-risk-index/. Accessed 10 March 2019.

[40] Trkman, P., & McCormack, K. (2009). Supply chain risk in turbulent environments—A conceptual model for managing supply chain network risk. *International Journal of Production Economics*, *119*(2), 247–258.

[41] Shi, D. (2004). A review of enterprise supply chain risk management. *Journal of systems science and systems engineering*, 13(2), 219–244

[42] Nicoletti, B., (2012), Global sourcing and risk management, *Procurement & Strategies*, 10 (1), February 18–19.

[43] Ogawa, Y., Akiyama, Y., Yokomatsu, M., Sekimoto, Y., & Shibasaki, R. (2019). Estimation of Supply Chain Network Disruption of Companies Across the Country Affected by the Nankai Trough Earthquake Tsunami in Kochi City. *Journal of Disaster Research*, *14*(3), 508–520.

[44] Icelandic volcano eruption halts all air freight over Europe for six days (April 2010).

[45] Randewich, N. (2011). Thai floods boost PC hard drive prices, http://www.reuters.com/article/2011/10/28/us-thai-floods-drives-idUSTRE79R66220111028, Accessed March 6, 2017.

[46] Shi, D. (2004). A review of enterprise supply chain risk management. *Journal of systems science and systems engineering*, 13(2), 219–244.

It is also important to consider reputational risks, which can impact organizations' procurement. These are connected with improper operations in the partner organizations.[47]

Much has been written about the risks inherent in procurement and it is very much worthwhile to examine how to protect an organization from these risks, which may be very different in nature. Risks can be analyzed and classified as 'operational risks,' 'technical risks,' financial risks,' and so forth.[48] One form of risk that unfortunately is very much present is that of corruption in partners. This is a big and important topic that this book does not have space to deal with, although procurement 4.0 introduces several technologies that can be very useful in this area.[49]

In the Basel II Accord for financial services, operational risks are defined as the risk of losses due to inadequacy or failures of processes, human resources, and internal systems, or from external events.[50]

Risk management comprises five key activities: analysis, assessment, mitigation, monitoring, and lessons learned. These actions provide a structured and effective way to address the issues of risk management. These actions are important since prevention is always better than cure. The rest of this chapter goes into detail on these aspects.

3.5.1 Risk Analysis

Risk analysis is the process of identifying all potential activities that can create problems.[51] It should be part of any process of procurement management and is an important activity, for example, in determining

[47] Supplies of palm oil to Unilever alleged to contribute to destruction of Indonesia's rainforests (April 2008). Mattel forced to recall children's toys due to safety issue following sourcing of components from China (August 2007).

[48] Chege, L. W., & Rwelamila, P. D. (2000). Risk Management and Procurement Systems-an Imperative Approach. *CIB REPORT*, 373–386.

[49] Obanda, W. P. (2010). Fighting corruption in tactical procurement. *Doctoral dissertation*, PHD dissertation.

[50] Remains, A., & Sironi, A. (2011). The financial crisis and Basel 3: origins, aims and structure of the new regulatory framework (No. 1). Carefin Working Paper.https://www.bis.org/publ/bcbs195.pdf. Accessed March 10, 2019.

[51] Hallikas, J., Karvonen, I., Pulkkinen, U., Virolainen, V. M., & Tuominen, M. (2004). Risk management processes in supplier networks. *International Journal of Production Economics*, *90*(1), 47–58.

procurement strategy, plans for individual categories of expenditure, procurement itself, and, where appropriate, extemporaneous procurement outside the procurement office (maverick sourcing).[52]

Risk analysis can be a simple or very formal process. The latter approach is more appropriate for projects or procurement initiatives of high value and high risk, such as moving to a new data center or a new partner solution. Analysis can also be informal, using an iterative or intuitive process, less or more significant for procurement, or it can be reactive, such as in response to a crisis.

3.5.2 Risk Assessment

Risk assessment refers to estimation of the probability of the occurrence of a risk, the potential impact that this risk may have on processes, and the ways to try to anticipate or forecast their occurrence.[53] Such evaluation is not an easy task, considering that procurement is a complex system. Highly predictable risks may have a reduced impact; therefore, it might not be worth taking any action to control or avoid these risks. On the other hand, low-probability risks can have a significant impact and may require some form of action. The cost of control and reduction or elimination of risks needs to be carefully assessed.

3.5.3 Mitigation of Risks

To mitigate risks, organizations needs to take action in the areas of:

- probability
- impact
- predictability.

After assessing all the risks identified and those requiring intervention, it is necessary to draw up plans and lists responsibilities to control

[52] Bakar, N. A., Peszynski, K., Azizan, N., Sundram, K., & Pandiyan, V. (2016). Abridgment of Traditional Procurement and E-Procurement: Definitions, Tools and Benefits. *Journal of Emerging Economies & Islamic Research*, 4(1).

[53] Baird, I. S., & Thomas, H. (1985). Toward a contingency model of strategic risk taking. *Academy of Management Review*, *10*(2), 230–243.

and mitigate such risks. Dangerous risks should be assigned to a person responsible for their management, possibly with the help of other team members. Risk allocation should depend on assessment of the probability and consequences of these risks. It should include identification of who is better able to control or manage the risks. This is an important aspect of any procurement process. Procurement, value network management, and relevant professionals should be involved. Moreover, as risks change over time, risk assessment should be iterative.

Some risks might not be controllable or manageable in a simple manner. In such cases, an organization can resort to two other ways to mitigate risks:

- Insurance. Some risks can be insured against. This is the case, for instance, with risks of cybersecurity attacks.[54] It should be noted that any risk assessment process is not all encompassing, because there is always a degree of uncertainty.
- Transfer them to partners. This aspect should be treated with caution as the transfer of risks to a partner will lead to a sure increase in costs, since partners should include in their pricing the costs of eliminating risks and covering their consequences.

There is a need of different policies for different types of procurement. An even more effective way to prevent risks is based on increasing the resilience of procurement. This is discussed in section 4.4.8 in this chapter.

3.5.4 Monitoring of Risks and Lessons Learned

As with most skills, effective risk management improves with experience and with practice. It is thus important to monitor trends in risks. At the end of a project or periodically, it is necessary to review what happened. Evaluation should focus on what the organization can learn and implement as improvements in working processes. Monitoring and measurement are not a single task but parts of a structured process.

[54] Drew, J. (2012). Managing cybersecurity risks. *Journal of Accountancy*, 214 (2): 44–48.

3.5.5 *Digital Transformation and Risk Management in Procurement*

Digital transformation can provide effective, efficient, and cost-effective risk management in procurement too.[55]

Thanks to customized procedures, an organization can access, combine, purify, and compare all relevant data, whether structured and unstructured, from internal and external sources, including third parties. Based on these data, it is possible to carry out a series of actions:

- Develop automatic rules for controlling and monitoring as new risks are identified, using a closed-loop learning system.
- Through advanced study, analyze the procurement data model, including specific scenarios for procurement, and an extensive set of predefined rules can be developed using the experience and expertise of professionals.
- Monitor transactions in real time with an online scoring engine that uses a hybrid analytical approach (including organizational rules, anomaly detection, predictive modeling, and analysis of associative links) to detect suspicious activity.
- Combine alerts and more monitoring systems alarms. This action may be associated with common data and provide a more complete view of the procurement risks.
- Analyze social networks beyond the processing of individual invoices, payments, and purchase orders, to evaluate all activities and related relationships in the ecosystem.
- Promote collaboration, compliance, and efficiency with easy-to-use interfaces that provide search and interactive visualization components.

Figure 3.4 shows an integrated scheme for ICT support to risk management in procurement 4.0.

[55] Rigby, D., & Bilodeau, B. (2011). *Management tools & trends 2013*. Bain & Company, London, UK.

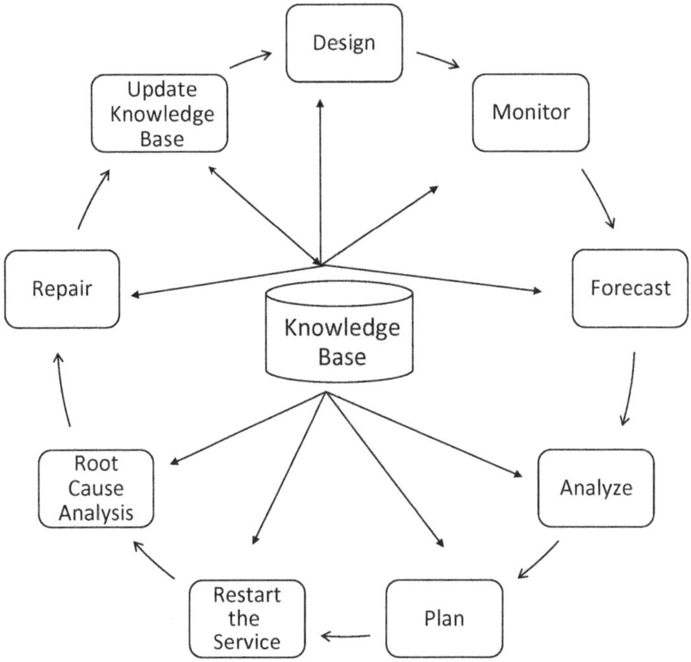

Fig. 3.4 ICT support to risks management

3.5.6 *Skills for Risk Management*

Addressing risks in procurement requires the right processes and platforms. Persons are also very important. The role of professional procurement management must also take into account the risks in procurement management. It is necessary to:

- promote the organization's needs for risk management in procurement;
- identify who in the organization is/should be responsible for each critical risk;
- work with them in the analysis and assessment of risks;
- inquire about the organization/partners and the persons involved, to assess the chances that partners might create problems within their supply;

- bring added value to the organization's decisions by conducting careful assessment of risks in procurement connected with commercial strategies;
- be fully aware of a series of contractual strategies and tactics that can be applied when the organization defines and negotiates contracts to avoid or mitigate risks.

Several methodologies and procurement management techniques can make a substantial contribution to this process. For example, evaluation of partners (partner rating or partner evaluation) or evaluation of tenders may reduce the risk of relying on an unreliable partner.[56]

Where there is a clear identification of the persons responsible for management of a specific critical risk, the relevant procurement professional should communicate the likely risks to his/her colleagues—such as partner managers who deal with the internal or external clients, the holders of the budget, or financial managers.

To address risk management in an effective, efficient, and economical way, a procurement professional should have the following skills:

- knowledge of business processes and market characteristics
- management of priorities
- knowledge of the methodologies and risk management techniques
- analytical and open mind
- an objective approach.

3.5.7 *Global Procurement and Risk Management*

Procurement 4.0 tends to involve global ecosystems of partners. Such a situation will always encounter risks. Many organizations that were late in considering such risks have taken the plunge headlong into working in low-cost countries. Often, they did not properly consider or mitigate many potential risks that might have been associated with global procurement.

[56] Muralidharan, C., Anantharaman, N., & Deshmukh, S. G. (2001). Vendor rating in purchasing scenario: a confidence interval approach. *International Journal of Operations & Production Management*, 21(10), 1305–1326.

For instance in 2011 of hard drives on the market almost doubled.[57] The reason is very simple: A flood in Thailand damaged a large factory that produced hard drives. Thus, this is a problem of globalization, which represents a great opportunity but can bring organizations to situations that involve significant risks. It is therefore helpful to analyze these risks and especially their potential remedies.

There are many reasons why organizations might choose a global procurement strategy—lower production costs are perhaps the primary factor. But there are many uncertainties and challenges in global procurement. The difficulty is to assess the risks of such decisions as fully as possible.

Taxonomy of Costs Related to Global Procurement

A few models provide comprehensive assessment of risks and their costs, to guide managerial decision-making. M. Holweg et al. have described the risks and opportunities of one potential solution.[58] They present a model to illustrate the differences between possible procurement strategies. They define three basic elements of costs in a procurement strategy:

- static
- dynamic
- hidden.

This chapter follows this approach and tries to generalize about the evaluation of the costs of risks related to global procurement scenarios.

Static Costs

Static costs are the most obvious factor. They include costs such as those for transport and customs clearance and, if appropriate, insurance and management. In detail this involves:

- purchase price at the factory;
- transport costs per unit, assuming that there are no unexpected delays or quality problems;

[57] Randewich, N. (2011). Thai floods boost PC hard drive prices, http://www.reuters.com/article/2011/10/28/us-thai-floods-drives-idUSTRE79R66220111028. Accessed March 6, 2017.

[58] Holweg, M., Reichhart, A., & Hong, E. (2011). On Risk and Cost in global sourcing. International *Journal of Production Economics*, 131 (1), 333–341.

- customs costs and related taxes for shipments and export;
- insurance transaction costs;
- quality control costs and compliance, taking into account environmental and local safety regulations which might be higher than those of the supplying country;
- research and development costs and agency fees to identify and interact with local partners.

Dynamic Costs

Dynamic procurement costs depend on a dynamic assessment related to the size of a procurement decision in global supply. This refers to the fact that supply and demand can vary widely and are not always controllable by the buyer. Some examples are:

- The increase in the pipeline and security stocks, which are amplified by the volatility of demand and product variety. This risk is closely aligned with delivery time. The key question is: will the product sell at the time of its availability?
- The possible obsolescence of inventories because of logistics with long refueling times and quality problems.
- The cost of lost sales and stock breakouts in procurement processes when they are not able to promptly respond to changes in demand.
- The possible need for expedited shipping, for example by air, to ensure speedy delivery.
- The actual realization of expected savings from offshoring.

Hidden Costs

Static and dynamic costs are undoubtedly of great relevance, but it can also be interesting to assess hidden costs. Several factors can have a significant impact on dynamic, distribution, and partially hidden costs and, therefore, on the overall risks associated with the economic success of global procurement decisions:

- time difference between supply of domestic and international deliveries. Often, time is a key strategic variable. This occurs in a system of production and logistics structured around the 'just in time' mode or based on fashion dynamics;
- the organization needs the flexibility to take into account uncertainty and variability in the demand for products;

- the importance of the level of service (or the cost of lost sales and obsolescence);
- logistics costs;
- objective quality and/or complexity of a product (in terms of technological sophistication or production according to a customer's specifications);
- stability of the country/region of the foreign partner.

Hidden costs are not only directly related to the operations of procurement processes. They can impact on the environment of the broader organization in various ways:

- There can be unexpected inflation in labor costs, particularly in countries that start from a very low wage level (as happened, for example, in India, with its huge quantity of human resources).
- Besides financial risks arising from basic operations, global procurement involves other financial risks that differ from those encountered in domestic procurement. These include currency fluctuations (especially in the case of some currencies), cancellation/delay expenses, and solvency/risk balance of the partner continuity.
- Delivery times for investments or developments are often long. A lot can change from design to marketing. Time is money in these situations.
- There can be an increase in transport costs, for instance due to variability in oil prices or possible delays due to several factors such as strikes or natural disasters.
- Overheads associated with using international procurement can be high. These include expenses for travel and staff, or local agencies in the procurement markets for partner selection, management, and supply.
- The possible loss of intellectual property through unreliable partners—this is a growing concern for many countries, such as some in the Far East. It refers to the potential loss of intellectual property regarding the design, engineering, materials, and other items in the products of an organization.
- The need to manage cultural differences and languages, with complications in general in terms of negotiations and relationships.

- Political instability and changes in economic or political systems.
- Some partners may not always be up to date and reliable in their technology. The basic question is whether the partner can deliver the product in an acceptable manner. Challenges range from scale-up problems with quality, to service problems when the component deliveries are at an early stage.
- Regulations may change over time and be more difficult to meet than expected, with consequent delays. This aspect refers to the technical regulations (building permits, integration of infrastructure, and so forth) and organization rules (duties, dumping, and political embargoes).
- Offshoring can lead to quality problems that, if not well managed, can damage the brand, as well as potentially leading to huge fines.
- Poor working and environmental conditions can also damage a brand. For example, it was discovered that some leading companies were selling t-shirts produced by a particular company in the Far East, which, in turn, was using a textile manufacturer that polluted local rivers.[59] Another issue is that partners may not meet the standards for health and safety of their employees.[60]
- Other factors include the degree of exclusivity for the buyer organization, whether it is a single strategic source/single plant, volume commitments/partner capabilities, pre-emption rights for more capacity, plans inventory (startup and in progress), construction/startup schedules, and execution logistics.

To evaluate all these factors, an organization can develop a simplified decision-making framework for an initial grasp of the risks associated with a global procurement decision. This framework should classify each factor on a five-point Likert scale.[61] This can be achieved using a spider

[59] https://www.theguardian.com/sustainable-business/2017/jun/13/hm-zara-marks-spencer-linked-polluting-viscose-factories-asia-fashion. Accessed April 21, 2019.

[60] Sethi, S. P. (2002). Standards for corporate conduct in the international arena: Challenges and opportunities for multinational corporations. *Business and Society review*, 107(1), 20–40.

[61] Allen, I. E., & Seaman, C. A. (2007). Likert scales and data analyses. *Quality progress*, *40*(7), 64–65.

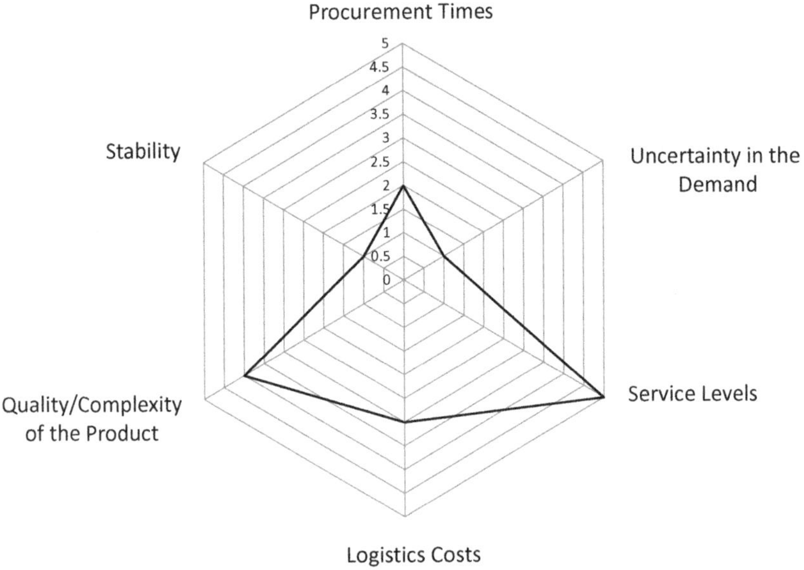

Fig. 3.5 Spider chart

chart like the one shown in Fig. 3.5. In this way, it is possible to compare different scenarios of procurement and the risks associated with each. The result is a decision support evaluation that is more quantitative than qualitative.

From a lean thinking approach, any transport or storage must be seen as a possible waste of resources. Before accepting these as necessary costs, they must be carefully considered.

The problem is that some organizations ignore the hidden costs involved in global procurement. Many global procurement initiatives tend to bring fewer benefits than expected. In reality, they are not economically viable compared to what was anticipated in the original evaluation because of the hidden and dynamic costs. Normally, the initial evaluation only takes into account static costs. Each global procurement instance must therefore be critically assessed according to specific situations. The model examined here can help. Often the best solution is a mix of local and global procurement.

Zara[62]

Zara is a Spanish producer and distributor of fashion goods. The company is an example of logistics and procurement 4.0 that needs to face global risk management. In fact, Zara is more than a fashion organization; it is also a logistical transport manager and has completely redesigned its logistics, internalizing some production. Logistics is a competitive process for Zara.[63] The benefits of having a short procurement chain are:

- speed of response to new trends and cost containment;
- reduction of safety stock;
- constant supply throughout the year, from several internal and external partners. Zara can vary fabrics and patterns, with shipments going to stores twice a week, in contrast to competitors with much higher re-feeding times.

In the fashion industry, rationalization of the production cycle is important. The competitive advantage that an organization can have is in the timing (faster response) and the supply chain model. It must be efficient in its use of these characteristics:

- agility
- reduction of time to market
- ability to quickly change according to new fashions.

For these reasons, Zara has chosen a hybrid approach: internal production and at the same time relying on certain partners. It maintains production capacity in both Europe and in Asia, even though offshore costs are significantly lower. In this way, Zara allocates the production of products with uncertain demand to European producers. On the other hand, it leaves the production of products with predictable demand to Asian manufacturers. The result is that approximately 60% of production is carried out in Europe (mostly in Spain).

(*continued*)

[62] Fernie, J., & Sparks, L. (Eds.). (2018). *Logistics and retail management: emerging issues and new challenges in the retail supply chain*. Kogan Page Publishers, London, UK.

[63] Bevilacqua, M., Ciarapica, F. E., & Giacchetta, G. (2012). *Design for Environment as a Tool for the Development of a Sustainable Supply Chain*. Springer Science & Business Media.

(continued)

The "Living Collection" by Zara is produced, distributed, and sold in direct response to the choices and desires of its customers. With local production, Zara can supply its stores twice a week compared to a week or more as with its competitors. Fresh offers are planned and completed daily. It takes less than two weeks for a designed object from the company's La Coruna design team to get into one of its shops around the world. Zara can thus be 12 times faster than the competition. Customers know that Zara renews its special offers every week and so often visit its shops 11 times a year, compared to four in the case of the competition (corresponding to the traditional four seasons).[64]

This situation is not limited to Zara. General Electric (GE) surveyed various UK manufacturing organizations, revealing that 27% of them have increased their domestic purchases compared with 13% that had reduced them. An extreme case is that of the Rhodes Group, which increased purchases of iron castings from domestic organizations from 40% to 90%.[65]

These cases must be considered as it is clear that organizations can continue to buy on a global basis, but with a more mature and careful approach.

Buyer Tools for Managing Global Procurement Risks

Given the complexity, uncertainty, and cross-functional interactions required in these scenarios of risk management, a structured model for managing risk is essential. This process includes several areas of interest and several tools that help to strengthen relevant capabilities.[66]

- Deepen and understand: Think through the different types of risks, their likelihood, impacts, and potential interdependence. It should be a process of 'devil's advocate,' subjecting the projects to a 'what if' analysis and then finding possible outcomes.

[64] Burt, S., Dawson, J., & Larke, R. (2006). Inditex-Zara: re-writing the rules in apparel retailing. In *Strategic issues in international retailing*, 83–102. Routledge, Abingdon, UK.

[65] Nicoletti, B. (2018). Partnerships in Agile Procurement. In *Agile Procurement*, 105–140. Palgrave Macmillan, Cham, Switzerland.

[66] SCDigest editors. Understand the risks of Global Procurement.http://www.scdigest.com/assets/newsviews/08-06-04-2.pdf. Accessed March 6, 2019.

- Quantify: Whenever possible, quantify several risk scenarios with their probability of occurrence and financial impacts. The reality is that doing this quantification well can lead to canceling of some of the procurement initiatives in low-cost countries with marginal returns but with great potential consequences.
- Plan: Beyond understanding and quantification, there is a need to create mitigation and contingency plans by considering technical, physical, and financial implications, and to handle the communication of these risks. How can serious risks be mitigated? And if something goes wrong, who needs to know and what action should be taken?
- Share: The theory of classical risk management includes sharing risks with multiple recipients. The problem is to understand how risks can be shared with partners. One possibility is a joint venture with a partner. This venture may be shared with other parties.
- Properties: Managing the investments of partners as if they were their own. If something happens, communicate quickly to avoid wasteful investment by the partner, as well as within the organization. Think, for example, about how the organization could maintain its ability to handle setbacks in sales without unduly decreasing the supply of partners. It is important to take into account the possible sequence of events and use them to improve results in both selling and buying organizations.
- Manage portfolios: Risk can be seen in two ways: in individual projects and across several projects. It is important to consider a portfolio view of projects. Too few organizations take the broader perspective of managing portfolio risks and build it into balancing of risks.

In the case of procurements for projects, there are three possible things that may happen: cancellation of a project, the project suffering a loss, or obsolescence of the project. However, the risk portfolio requires four data views[67]:

- Total commitments—the organization or branch of the organization must take into account all its projects.

[67] SCDigest editors. Understand the risks of Global Procurement.http://www.scdigest.com/assets/newsviews/08-06-04-2.pdf. Accessed March 6, 2019.

- Competing commitments—does it make sense to have two or more projects with parallel commitments that might cancel each other out or delay each other?
- Sequential commitments—is there a next-generation project that will make commitments obsolete until they have paid off?
- Aggregate projects—how many projects have a single source and what impact will they have on the provider and the client organization's reputation if there are failures or successes? Does the provider have the resources to manage many projects and are the organization's priorities clear enough?

These views should be submitted regularly the organization's management. Over time, they should be updated so that all the changes in the timetable, priorities, or feasibility are taken into account. The implications for the rest of the portfolio and any partners should be communicated and managed. Any financial implications should be identified and declared well in advance.

Conclusions
Risks are inherent in any organizational setup, and especially in global value networks. Organizations can significantly reduce their exposure to risks by fully analyzing all the major categories of risk in their global procurement initiatives, by considering potential mitigation actions, and by visualizing risks across their entire portfolio of projects and products.

3.5.8 Resilience and Procurement 4.0

The global economic and business environment is increasingly turbulent and difficult to predict. On the other hand, more and more organizations use external partners to perform even basic functions and processes for their operations. The reasons are simple:

- they add value for the customer;
- this enables them to focus on the core business of the organization;
- such an approach represents gains in flexibility.

An interesting case is represented by procurement 4.0 and its intense utilization of outsourcing or externalization. This term refers to organizations that use external partners to perform their processes or sub-processes.[68] For example, organizations can outsource the management of a data center, maintenance of computer applications, and the like. There is growing interest in this business model, which marks the transition from a vertical to a network ecosystem. The result is some highly integrated network organizations.

This section examines how procurement can help in the management of operational risks particularly associated with outsourcing. Resilience is a very important aspect to consider here.[69] The resilience of the system is its ability to withstand a significant break in degradation within acceptable parameters and to recover within an acceptable timeframe.[70]

Research on Resilience in Procurement

Several studies have emphasized the importance of resilience, especially in the case of physical delivery networks. It has been pointed out that the provision of basic services such as energy, transport, and healthcare takes place through complex infrastructures where procurement methods and organization play a key role.[71] These issues, if not properly governed, due to the occurrence of events of varying severity and origin, can cause instability in the supply of essential services and products. The potential consequences can have a very big impact on the organizations and, in some cases, on the whole community. Studies highlight the key drivers and best practices for procurement for the correct governance of business continuity and the maintaining of service in critical infrastructure, with particular reference to the protection of critical information infrastructure.[72]

Some authors have highlighted the importance of resilience in the risk management of projects.[73] They analyze questions such as what should be considered over the horizon of risk, how to interpret events that can-

[68] http://www.isfol.it/pubblicazioni/archivio-immagini-editoria/12M0334_paratesto.pdf. Accessed March 15, 2019.

[69] Haimes, Y. Y. (2009). On the definition of resilience in systems. *Risk Analysis: An International Journal*, 29 (4), 498–501.

[70] https://www.igi-global.com/dictionary/system-resilience/51260. Accessed March 26, 2019.

[71] Carrozzi, L. (2009), Procurement Management for the Protection of Critical Infrastructure, *Master Thesis in Procurement Management,* University of Tor Vergata, Rome, Italy.

[72] White House (2013). *Critical infrastructure security and resilience.* White House, Washington, DC.

[73] Turner, N. & Kutsch, E. (2015), Project Resilience: Moving beyond traditional risk management, PM World Journal, 4 (11): 1:8.

not be quantified or qualified with confidence, how to better prepare for the effects of what is unknown. This section discusses how to contain the unknown in a timely and appropriate way. It describes some practices that can be used to achieve a state of effective—although not perfect—resilience. These practices should make it possible to deal with risks, uncertainties, and complexities in an effective, efficient, and economical way.

The ability to recover and to develop a shared understanding of the definition, theory, and managerial implications, in particular, of cyber-risks and the related resilience of the solutions is very important.[74] In the future targeted solutions have to be provided to the challenges in developing cyber-resilience in procurement strategy and tools, and better methods offered for responding to security breaches in procurement along with some best practice guidelines.

It is important to analyze the role of procurement in identifying problems and managing intra- and inter-organization problems generated by pursuing organizational resilience.[75] Ensuring resilience in procurement processes in a turbulent environment requires the engagement of both internal and external elements of the entire ecosystem connected with an organization. Some studies have revealed that procurement activities can contribute significantly to the creation of resilience in an organization's processes. From the literature, some intra- and inter-organizational issues have been identified. They could have an impact on the wider resilience of procurement. It is possible to identify possible actions that procurement should take to reinforce resilience connected with procurement.

An important principle is that the design of a value network has an important effect on the risks inherent to procurement.[76] Managers should work in teams to design networks that are as flexible as possible. Several standard principles apply to the design of resilient value networks. It is

[74] '- (2015), Cyber-Resilience in the Supply Chains, *Technology Innovation Management Review*, Apr.

[75] Pereira, RC, Christopher, M., and Lake Da Silva, A. (2014). Achieving supply chain resilience: the role of procurement. *Supply Chain Management: An International Journal*, 19 (5/6), 626–642.

[76] Waters, D. (2011), *Supply chain risk management: vulnerability and resilience in logistics*, Kogan Page Publishers, London, UK.

vital to adopt a strategic vision, with a better understanding of the concept of risks in the value network and value network design, keeping in mind the potential risks, the search for collaborative solutions, and so on.

Value networks vary in detail, but there are some common characteristics in flexible networks. Some of these are the physical characteristics, the presence of the resilient network being short, wide, and agile, with spare capacity, and so forth. Other features include those centered on relationships, with a flexible network that evinces cooperation, trust in partners, visibility, process integration, and so on, to enable a common solution for mutual problems. Even the best risk management witnesses unexpected events. When they are serious, they are generally described as crises, disasters, or emergencies. The way to deal with these events is to make contingency plans that potentially can be used to address any crisis.

The literature raises some questions about the role of procurement in building resilience. Yet, this aspect has not been well explored in the current literature. Most studies focus on the resilience of physical value networks. These tasks are concentrated on sealing capacity, from the outsourcing of procurement procedures. The subject is particularly relevant because of the increased spread of such organizations. Solutions for outsourcing have evolved in recent decades, going from acting on tenders, working in partnership, commissioning strategic services, acting with prime contractor, and, more recently, insourcing (that is, bringing back into the organization some or all outsourced processes).[77]

Outsourcing has different risks. Despite the growth of outsourcing, especially in information systems in recent years, this trend is still subject to strong criticism. Some of the literature shows that outsourcing is one of the main sources of information and communication systems risks, based on the results of a survey of 357 organizations.[78] The main concern with outsourcing ICT is the excessive dependence of the seller, which this type of contract tends to generate. In some characteristics of organizations (particularly their size), there are significant risks connected with outsourcing. The findings also show that full outsourcing could prove to be a

[77] Bovaird, T. (2016), The ins and outs of outsourcing and procurement: what have we-learned from the past 30 years?, *Public Money and Management*, 36: 1, 67–74.

[78] Gonzalez, R., Gasco, J., & Llopis, J. (2005), Information systems outsourcing risks: a study of large providers. *Industrial Management & Data Systems*, 105 (1), 45–62.

risky strategy, especially because of the dependence it creates. The outsourcing of activities of information systems is a complex issue that has significant implications for the procurement of an organization (an important mechanism for managing the performance of outsourcing partners is incentive/penalty clauses). A responsible ICT outsourcing contract should quantify all the risks and benefits. The methods and tools for analysis and quantification of outsourcing risks that ICT managers use are often rudimentary. It is vital to employ methods and mathematical models for risk analysis and construction of incentive/penalty clauses in contracts for outsourcing ICT.[79]

There are few studies on how to manage risks in full outsourcing.[80]

Agility

In general, resilience refers to the ability of a material to deform elastically, to bend under stress without being permanently changed. This is the behavior that organizations need to have in meeting the growing challenges of today's socioeconomic environments. Resilience in the case of outsourcing is the ability of a service provider to adapt to the conditions of use and to withstand external events so as to ensure continuous availability of the services to be provided.

All the previous resiliency characteristics can be summarized in one word: agility. This is the basic feature necessary to increase the flexibility of an organization to deal with unexpected events.[81] All risk is based on uncertainty and it exists in all operations. Despite the best plans, any organization is always susceptible to unpredictable events, and so organizations must have the flexibility to manage these risks. The best way to cope with them is to increase flexibility and to maintain an agile organization. Agility means that the operations are sufficiently flexible to address the risks occurrences effectively, efficiently, economically with conditions of

[79] Osei-Bryson, K. M., & Ngwenyama, O. K. (2006). Managing risks in information systems outsourcing: An approach to analyzing outsourcing risks and structuring incentive contracts. *European Journal of Operational Research*, 174 (1), 245–264.

[80] Sullivan, W. E., & Ngwenyama, O. K. (2005), How are public sector organizations managing risks IS outsourcing? An analysis of outsourcing guidelines from three jurisdictions. *Journal of Computer Information Systems*, 45 (3), 73–87.

[81] Waters, D. (2011), *Supply chain risk management: vulnerability and resilience in logistics*, Kogan Page Publishers, London, UK.

rapid response, and, if necessary, by implementing remediation changes. For example, instead of increasing the number of available resources in an outsourcing deal to cope with unexpected strong increases in demand, an organization can use flexible operations to increase the distribution and provision of services with short lead times.

In practice, it is often difficult to predict the details of dangerous events. Agility is often the best answer. This can be achieved in several ways, such as the ability to achieve short delivery times, so that all the changes are completed quickly, making possible a rapid recovery from outages. Standardization can help a lot, too. Standardized processes can be used interchangeably in different outsourcing operations if necessary. An organization can thus reduce resource use, solving delivery problems, reducing the impact on ongoing work to consolidate the number of partners, and so on.

The important point for agility is that operations can switch from one service to another without waiting for the availability of new resources. Operations must be standardized to the maximum possible extent, so that they can easily switch between products, with:

- wildcard collaborators trained to move toward areas of deficiency through rapid reprogramming of operations;
- diversion of work and resources away from areas of surplus to areas with shortages;
- operations that can move between different positions when there is an urgent need of capacity increase, for example by moving ICT services from one data processing center to another (this is possible with cloud computing);
- simultaneous development to accelerate new methods and products. Flexible partners, use of multiple sources with different characteristics to meet the different needs, different types of contracts, and the possibility to use the spot market.

Studies on the effects of standardization show that there are benefits, at least in the case of the BPO (business process outsourcing).[82] These studies prove that the process standards have a positive impact on reducing the

[82] Wüllenweber, K., & Weitzel, T. (2007). An empirical exploration of h240c-240cow Reduces standardization process outsourcing risks. *System Sciences*, IEEE 2007, January, 240–250.

risks of outsourcing of business processes. The perceived risk theory and the theory of reasoned actions allow the development of a BPO risk model.[83] The model shows empirically that perceived risk is higher for less standardized processes. Using data from 126 German banks, one study reveals that the financial risks and benefits are significantly different between high and low standardization processes. Risks are consistently higher for less standardized processes.

Basic Features of Resilience

Some features are important to ensure the resilience of outsourcing. They seem distinct, but in reality, they are very interconnected. Some authors have considered them in the case of resilience in general.[84] To benefit from resilience in the case of procurement outsourcing, there are nine key actions. These are the nine Cs (Fig. 3.6):

- Contracting: This feature refers to the need of a precise agreement with partners, or more precisely to their commitments for the supply of a service. It is at the base of all the other features, which must be clearly stated and defined in contracts.
- Commanding: This feature is very important for risk management. An organization must have effective leadership of outsourcing, both internally and from the partner side. The leadership must be able to make decisions before, during, and after a disaster, attack, or emergency. It must also be efficient, and therefore able to intervene in a timely and cost-effective way. Risks and potential disasters should be managed in line with the objectives of ensuring continuity in the organization's profitability.
- Checking: The control system is connected with the ability to have good outsourcing governance. It implies a strong and detailed plan. It must also take into account the unpredictable. It should include the 'what if' and consider management of what might happen.

[83] Sheppard, B. H., Hartwick, J., & Warshaw, P. R. (1988). The theory of reasoned action: A meta-analysis of past research with recommendations for modifications and future research. *Journal of consumer research*, *15*(3), 325–343.

[84] Gulati, R. (2010). *Reorganize for Resilience: Putting customers at the center of your business.* Harvard Business Press, Cambridge, MA.

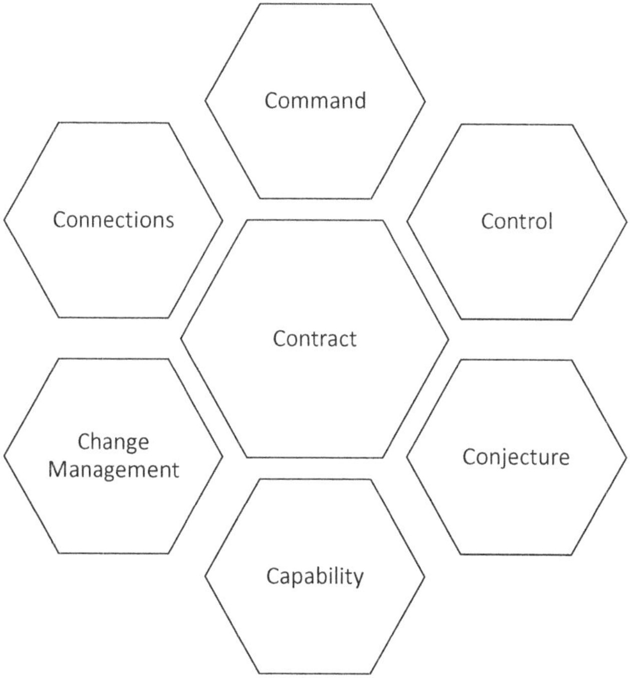

Fig. 3.6 Nine Cs in resilience

- Conjecture: This implies the ability to predict or anticipate the occurrence of a disaster. It is important to consider the risks, starting with the very design of a solution. Prevention is better than cure.[85] Conjecture must be based on trying to prevent a damaging event from occurring, thereby reducing the consequences if it does happen, and finally getting compensation if necessary. To be more precise, it is necessary to evaluate carefully the best options for mitigating damage from a risk after it occurs. Customers and outsourcers should explicitly include the effects of risks in their decisions. It is necessary to consider the risks associated with pushing too hard on the organization's leanness, on excessive efficiency, or on some other objectives that inadvertently increase vulnerability. The best design sees a bal-

[85] Güller M., & Henke, M. (2018), *Resilience Assessment in Complex Supply Networks, Revisiting Supply Chain Risk*, 10.1007/978-3-030-03813-7_5, (73–98).

ance between strengths and normal efficiency measures. For example, a single path through the activities in a process can create a vulnerability—if something happens at one point of the path, the whole process is at risk. The way to avoid these risks is, for instance, by designing a process with parallel paths. In this way, the flows may be moved from a disrupted path to one that is operating normally. It is also necessary to carry out continuous monitoring of outsourced services to assure their resilience.

- Capacity: Very often organizations have an urge to be lean and thereby reduce waste, such as in over-capacity or amount resources. This is fine, but the organization cannot overdo it. It should keep in mind the need to ensure an ability to recover and not be too lean. The organization must have some more additional capacity available in case of emergency.
- Collaboration: One of the most important ways to ensure resiliency is through the integration process, with several members who work together to solve common problems, although they may belong to different organizations. Without a basic level of cooperation, it is almost impossible to make any progress toward a truly integrated process. Collaboration can take many forms. It could range from informal discussions up to strategic alliances. The most common forms of sharing information are to increase perspicacity—with more formal arrangements for collaboration, planning, forecasting, resourcing, and synchronizing actions. There are several reasons why cooperation is difficult to achieve, but there are mechanisms available to achieve it and those responsible must be ready to use them. Sharing of information throughout the entire process is the basis of such visibility. This means that some part of the working activity of the process must be able to see what is happening at all points of the flow. Relevant information typically includes demand, seasonality, promotions, introduction of new products, industry and market conditions, operations and purchase schedules, benefits, risks, contingencies, lost sales, and any other relevant information. Many aspects of cooperation in the process can be summarized in terms of partner relationship management. This is a generic term for procedures that enable an organization to cultivate new partners in the processes, maintain existing partners,

reduce disruption by spreading activities among partners and the areas of service delivery, and to manage risks with unique sources. The sharing of ideas, methods, and information is an important part of outsourcing. This is the only way in which in the process states how it is possible to identify common risks of an initiative and to design effective ways to deal with them, achieving synergies from collaboration.

- Convergence in processes: Visibility is beneficial for risk management but can also bring other benefits, including the convergence of operations. In other words, operations tend to converge toward common standards and are then accepted as the normal mode of operation. Other initiatives have the same effect, in particular, quality assurance and risk management.
- Connecting: Resilience requires flexible connections, but being effective and able to act in support of unanticipated events. Connections or networks must act, in the informatics and telematics capacity, in such a way as to allow the provision of continuity using a back-up, if necessary. Connections also have commercial value, with the possibility of using the resources of other organizations to allow continuity in the provision of services in emergency conditions.
- Changing: Change management requires agility. It is based on creating the right mix of bureaucracy, agility, and speed that distinguish the most effective procurements.

Principles of Resilient Outsourcing Design

To analyze the principles of resilient outsourcing design, follow what is recommended for procurement management systems and make the appropriate changes.[86] The design of resilient outsourcing requires a fully integrated approach.[87] There are several basic principles inherent in an initiative of this type, such as the need for careful design, agile operations, visibility, relationships with customers and partners, culture, and so on.

[86] Waters, D. (2011). *Supply chain risk management: vulnerability and resilience in logistics.* Kogan Page Publishers.

[87] Kleindorfer, P.R, & Saad, G. H. (2005). Managing disruption risks in supply chains. *Production and Operations Management*, 14 (1), 53–68.

It is important first of all to have a strategic vision. In common with all major initiatives, resilience needs a strong commitment from an organization's leadership. Managers should be aware of the issues and should be able to allocate resources at short notice. Outsourcing is a strategic initiative that can have profound effects on an organization and the way it is handled. Put simply, with bad risk management there is less chance that an organization will survive in the long term. This need for high-level support becomes more apparent when the organization explicitly includes relationships with other organizations, as in procurement 4.0, as these inevitably need new strategies and policies.

The resilience of outsourcing requires that basic processes work properly. If an organization that intends to use outsourcing is not properly organized in the processes it intends to outsource, a partner should take responsibility to introduce them during transition to collaboration. This step must ensure a strong engagement direction, the presence of extensive policies for risk management, a well-defined team for risk management, the presence of necessary ICT systems, well-oiled processes, and related well-functioning information flows. A risk register must be well designed and up to date. The procedures must be tested and so forth. Only when everything works internally, can an organization's managers extend the processes outside.

An opposing view suggests that managers can learn valuable lessons in working with others on organizational issues, so they should not approach the organization partners with well-defined ideas and inflexibility. Rather, they should partner in a spirit of exploration. The best ideas emerge from a cooperative approach, combining thought and experiences so that everyone can learn new ideas and methods that the organization can then use within its domains.

Perhaps the best answer is intermediate between these two approaches, where managers make some progress in their risk management, and then try to improve and consolidate their methods by opening up to other organizations.

Before an organization can successfully plan its processes, the outsourcer and its customer must understand clearly what they are examining. They must properly grasp the concept of the risk—that is, the members, roles, communication, interactions, objectives, dynamic forces, power, and all other elements that make up the complex value network of an organization and its weak points. Then the organization can combine these two concepts in the integrated function of resilience management.

A process is only as strong as its weakest link. A disturbance at any point in a process causes problems for the whole stream. Customers and outsourcers must identify the risks throughout the process to find the weakest parts. There are always weaknesses in a value network. They could include individual routes, connections with long delivery times, members who face specific organizational risks, those who are not willing to share information, members who do not properly handle risks, and so on. Sometimes, parallel paths can be created around risky areas. This can be difficult—for example when there is only one data center. Managers need to pay special attention to risks in the weakest areas, in particular if these areas are outside of their control. They should take steps to reduce the consequences of risk or try to influence the managers who are responsible for their inclusion in the outsourced risk management process. Or they can redesign the procurement processes to bypass these areas of weakness.[88]

Management of an Emergency

Resilience also requires effective, efficient, and economic emergency management. When a risky event occurs, if the organization has created resilient, and hence flexible, operations it can avoid the worst effects and continue to function almost normally. Sometimes, though, the effects are too severe to be solved even by the most flexible operation. For example, if a material delivery is delayed, flexible operations allow a near-normal work, but do not eradicate entirely the effects of the delays. If the supply or stocks of materials are lost, even the most flexible operations cannot find a solution. The alternative is to build contingency plans for emergencies. These are used as a last resort when all other aspects of risk management have failed. They work on the basis that, if the organization does not know what will happen, the best plan is to be ready for everything.

Procurement should require that the service partner can act at all points throughout the cycle. A partner should be able to improve the characteristics of the processes by managing risks and disasters thanks to accumula-

[88] Mazlan, RMR, & Ali, KN (2005). Relationship between supply chain management and outsourcing. *Doctoral dissertation, Heriot-Watt University.*Kunreuther, H. & Heal, G. (2004), Interdependent security: the case of identical agents, *Journal of Risk and Uncertainty*, 23 (2): 103–120.

tion over time of its knowledge base on how to address any dysfunctions of processes and sub-processes in outsourcing.[89]

The first thing to do in an emergency is to restore service. Most often, this requires an organization to find a temporary solution (workaround) instead of solving all problems with one move. Once the workaround or solution has been applied, it is necessary to verify whether it works well. If the test is positive, the organization can start to regain a normal or a reduced rate of service.

The following operation is particularly important. The organization needs to find the causes of what has happened. A root cause is a factor (or factors) that caused non-compliance and should be permanently eliminated through process improvement.[90] The analysis of root causes (Root Cause Analysis—RCA) comprises a wide range of solutions, tools, and techniques used to identify the causes of a problem.[91] Once the organization has found the root cause, it is necessary to permanently solve the problem. Normally, it is not possible immediately to fully restore a reliable process. Before the organization applies the fix, it needs to be tested.

It is important to create and regularly update a knowledge base of all known incidents and information on finding solutions to fix incidents. This is vital to improve resilience of the system in terms of rapid recovery in case of known errors. There are many different ways to organize such a knowledge base. A simple but effective approach is to set up a wiki—an intranet or extranet site, which allows collaborative editing of content in the form of a storehouse of pertinent information.[92]

Resilience Metrics

The metrics of the KPIs of resilience must be the measure of customer satisfaction. Customers must be able to appreciate both a reduction in the severity of the occurrence of a risk and its minimum possible impact and duration.

[89] Kim, B. S., Kim, Y. D., Hwang, C. K., & Yoo, J. H. (2007, October). A mechanism of KEDB-centric fault management to optimize the Realization of ITIL based ITSM. In *Asia-Pacific Network Operations and Management Symposium* 72–81. Springer, Berlin, Heidelberg, Germany.

[90] Andersen, B., and Fagerhaug, T. (2006). *Root Cause Analysis: Simplified Tools and Techniques*. ASQ Quality Press, Milwaukee, WI.

[91] Rooney, J. J., & Heuvel, L. N. V. (2004). Root cause analysis for beginners. *Quality progress*, *37*(7), 45–56.

[92] - (2007), 1 *Encyclopædia Britannica*, Encyclopædia Britannica, Inc., London, UK, Accessed January 1, 2019.

To graphically show what happens in the occurrence of a risk, one can refer to a chart that illustrates how the risks could affect the performance of an organization in terms of sales, production levels, margins, and/or quality of customer service. It is possible to generalize what it has been introduced as the resilience triangle and to use a generalized model in the case of the outsourcing.[93] The KPIs, which measure resilience, are present in what can be termed the 'graph of resilience' (Fig. 3.7).[94] This graph shows the several stages of performance of the system response: after a process has been degraded by the occurrence of a risk and actions have been taken to restore the service as soon as possible (workaround), next the organization needs to identify the root causes and restore the performance as prescribed in its contracts. The graph of resilience visualizes these phases by tracing the organization's response over time. The graph displays in scale the impact and duration of negative performance of outsourced process or sub-processes. The Y-axis represents the severity of the interruption, that is, its duration and the impact of the damage associated with the disaster. The X-axis represents the recovery time of the service and the determination and remediation of the root cause.

This graph of resilience is important for procurement. Its objective is to negotiate with partners the reduction of the central area in Fig. 3.7. For this purpose, the contract should define the maximum permissible values for the parameters shown in Fig. 3.7.

Conclusions

In a situation where organizations increasingly depend on outsourcing to service partners, procurement 4.0 must take essential precautions to ensure reduction as far as possible of operational risks, which impact on the organization's operations. In the case in which part of activities are outsourced, it is important to ensure the resilience of these activities. This requires careful examination of activities outsourced by the organization and the characteristics, skills, and capabilities of the outsourcers. They must be resilient—in other words, they must be able to consider the potential risks and disasters and be prepared to reduce their impacts and respond effectively.

[93] Carvalho, H., Barroso, A. P., Machado, V. H., Azevedo, S., & Cruz-Machado, V. (2012), Supply chain redesign for resilience using simulation. *Computers & Industrial Engineering*, 62 (1), 329–341.

[94] Nicoletti, B. (2016). Resilience and outsourcing. *PMWORLD*, *2*, 16.

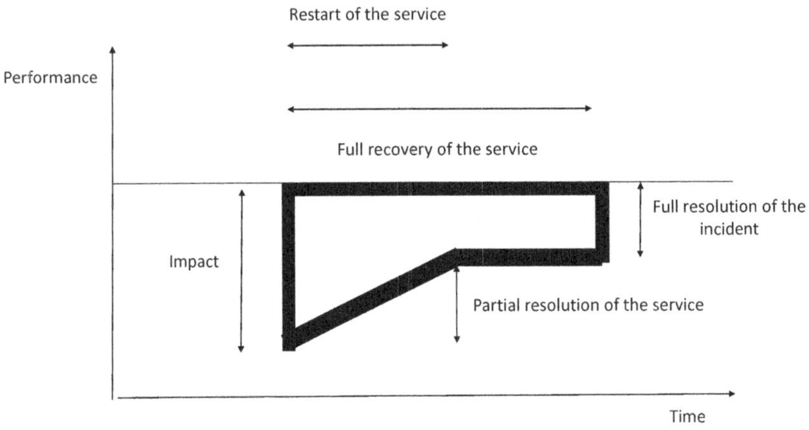

Fig. 3.7 Graph of resilience

To cope with the risks of outsourcing, it is essential to adopt a well-defined strategy for resilience. This implies:

- understanding the critical risks associated with outsourcing, and how they can be either a technical or an organizational issue that could have an impact on the continuity of the outsourced customer's business, and to create considerable damage in terms of reputation and financial position;
- considering drastic changes that guarantee improvements in the creation of a more resilient outsourcing environment;
- analyzing how the nine Cs, outlined in this chapter, can improve resilience;
- finding out at all levels how active engagement of the customer and outsourcer organizations and their management can progress toward better resilience.

3.6 Controllership: Procurement Finance 4.0

The World Bank forecasts an acceleration in international trade.[95] This is good news, although it will be coupled with the continuing difficulties in raising credit for international transactions, especially for small and medium-sized organizations.

[95] http://www.worldbank.org/en/publication/global-economic-prospects. Accessed March 10, 2019.

Fig. 3.8 Procurement finance

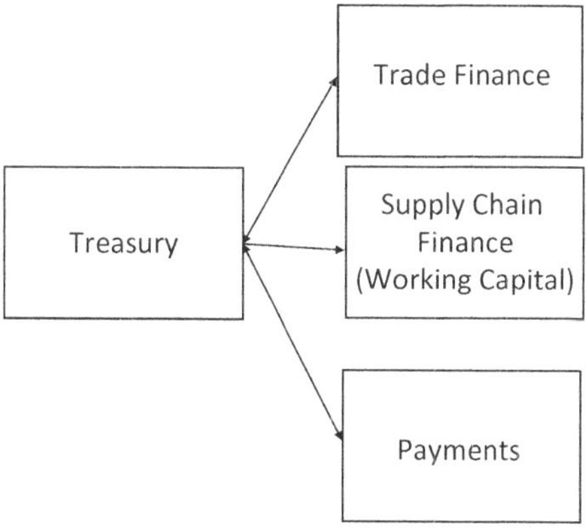

It seems pertinent to investigate the issue of granting credit related to procurement 4.0. It is important to have an integrated vision of the problem. The following functions need to be considered in an integrated manner (Fig. 3.8)[96]:

- Trade finance—a financial instrument related to trade financing, especially internationally. It also includes the identification and prevention of risks in the sales of goods and/or services. Other forms of commercial financing can be export credit insurance, factoring, forfeiting, and other similar instruments.
- Supply chain finance—this term covers all financial instruments for financing working capital. This financing requires organizations to rely not only on economic, financial, or business aspects but also on the role that the organization intends to play within the value network in which it operates.
- Payments, especially cross-border—these are complex due to the need often to take into account different currencies and their fluctuations.
- Treasury—these are tasks involved in the management of cash (receipts and payments) of an organization, whether public or private.

[96] Nicoletti, B. (2018), *Procurement Finance*, Springer International Publishing, London, UK.

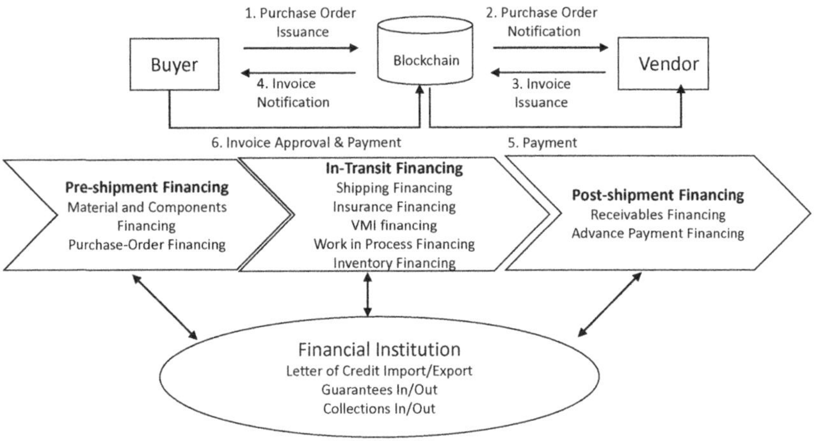

Fig. 3.9 Procurement finance 4.0 process

This function of the organization is also responsible for management of risks related to liquidity, credit, interest rates, and exchange rates.

All these financial instruments are described in this book as 'procurement finance.' This book encourages organizations to use this integrated approach and at the same time to pursue its automation, especially in the case of procurement 4.0 (Fig. 3.9).

The digital transformation, in the sense of using advanced ICT solutions, has found a fertile field in some organizations. Much less has happened in other organizations. This situation should change for several reasons, which can be named as other four Cs:

- Customers, especially foreign ones, are demanding new solutions in procurement financing. There are important financial instruments that can reduce costs and improve process efficiency.
- Computerization, or ICT, provides solutions that reduce costs, increase efficiency, and improve scalability, up or down. These applications are important to ensure flexibility concerning financial products.
- Competition is becoming increasingly active. It is represented not only by the traditional players but also by new players entering the

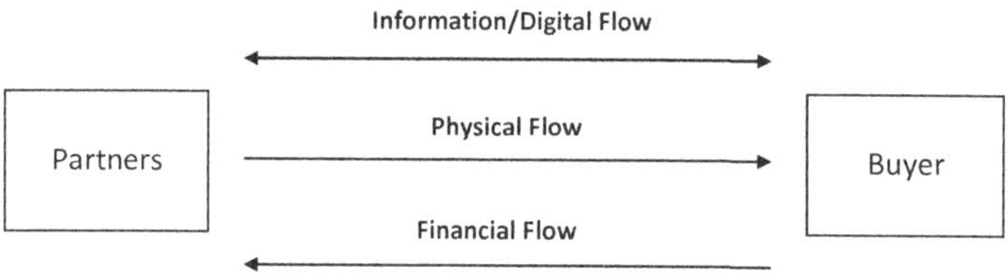

Fig. 3.10 Procurement flows

market. This is the case of the so-called fintech organizations.[97] Many of these new operators provide customized solutions. It is necessary to take into account new players not only as bank competitors but also as potential partners. The synergies obtainable are remarkable due, on the one hand, to the financial capacity of traditional banks, and on the other hand, through the innovations introduced by these new players.

- Finally, it is necessary to consider the requirements of Compliance, which are increasingly stringent. The digital transformation should also apply in this direction because compliance costs can be up to 80% of operating costs.[98]

In dealing with market changes, it is important not only to pursue improvements in procurement's physical processes (industry 4.0 and the like), but also in cash flow and digital/information (Fig. 3.10). There are five areas on which to focus:

- financial product innovation—documentary credits are an ideal field for the introduction of innovative solutions[99];
- Integration—made possible by new digital solutions and communication;

[97] Nicoletti, B. (2017), *The Future of Fintech*, Springer International Publishing, London, UK. ISBN 978-3-319-51414-7.

[98] Quayle, M. (2003). A study of supply chain management practice in UK industrial SMEs. *Supply Chain Management: An International Journal*, 8(1), 79–86.

[99] Documentary credits are payment techniques used in international trade. For more details consult: Nicoletti, B. (2018), *Procurement Finance*, Springer International Publishing, London, UK.

- back-office operations—these need to be digitized to the maximum possible extent, pushing so-called straight through processing and the dematerialization of copious documents associated with trade, especially if international[100];
- exploitation of data—organizations and banks have a treasure trove of information and data which is largely untapped. Its use allows to improve the effectiveness, efficiency, economy, and ethics (compliance)[101];
- risk management—an important aspect, especially when an organization considers international trade. Risks can be of different types: in connection with the market, customers, currencies, transport, and so forth. These risks should be managed and mitigated to the maximum extent possible, including the use of resilient solutions.

3.6.1 Fintech Finance and Procurement 4.0

One of the most interesting developments in the financial sector is so-called fintech organizations.[102] Their name is a portmanteau of financial and technology services and, in most cases, they are startups, using more or less advanced technology to offer innovative financial instruments and services.

Fintech organizations were born mainly in British and American English-speaking parts of the world. They are also very much alive in the Eastern countries, where the traditional financial world is still less innovative than in the West, with the possible exception of China. Fintech organizations are undoubtedly a characteristic of what can be described as business 4.0, namely extension of the Fourth Industrial Revolution into the world of services and, in particular, to financial services.

Procurement 4.0 is interested in fintech organizations since they can influence its development and revolutionize important sectors such as procurement finance. As mentioned in the previous section, procurement finance is the synthesis of closely related aspects of procurement, namely trade finance (trade credit), supply chain finance (financing the production world), and the world of payments (Fig. 3.8). Trade finance

[100] Stonebraker, M., Çetintemel, U., & Zdonik, S. (2005). The 8 requirements of real-time stream processing. *ACM Sigmod Record*, *34*(4), 42–47.

[101] Woerner, S. L., & Wixom, B. H. (2015). Big data: extending the business strategy toolbox. *Journal of Information Technology*, 30(1), 60–62.

[102] Nicoletti, B. (2017), *The Future of Fintech*, Springer International Publishing, London, UK. ISBN 978-3-319-51414-7.

was characterized by traditional financial instruments such as letters of credit, guarantees, factoring, and payment advances. The importance of these tools has increased in recent times, for several reasons. The main one is the increasing internationalization of trade. There is also the difficulty, especially for SMEs in accessing banks. Finally, the development of e-commerce for businesses is revolutionizing sourcing. Despite all these challenges, organizations increasingly need the support of the financial world. Commercial banks have been slow to respond. In some cases, commercial banks have even made it more difficult to access credit, for instance by increasing their costs, which were already high.

Before examining some of these initiatives, it is important to consider the business model of these winning organizations. The model is that of platforms—organizations that present themselves as intermediaries and facilitate meetings between sellers and customers. A platform is characterized by four players, which this book refers to as the four Ps:

- Proprietors or 'owners' are the controllers of the intellectual property platform. They decide who can participate and how. They act on the innovation of the platform by changing the business model or aggregating other business models.
- Providers or service partners make the platform available, from the infrastructure point of view.
- Producers offer their products or services (in the case of procurement finance, financial instruments).
- Purchasers are the buyers or customers of the products and services.

The examples of successful platforms in other sectors are relevant. Think of the cell phone. In the case of the iPhone, the roles are as follows:

- the owner is Apple who introduced the iOS platform;
- the providers are the vendors of the telecommunication infrastructure and devices;
- the producers of the Apps are the various suppliers;
- the purchasers are those who use the apps to buy or use a service.

There are also pertinent examples of platforms in the case of procurement finance.

Fabrick[103]

Fabrick is an independent ecosystem. It is based on the experience of a large Italian bank: Banca Sella. It exists on open banking platform.[104] Participants in this platform using the terminology are:

- Banca Sella is the proprietor. Based on its experience, the Banca launched this new business model and ecosystem.
- The producers are several organizations, such as HyperServe, Vipera, and Kubique.[105] These organizations offer omnichannel financial services and digital customer engagement. For example, Kubique is a fintech organization that creates platforms and software solutions for the financial management of the value network.
- The providers are Banca Sella and other financial institutions offering quality services with compliance that is simple and convenient.
- The purchasers are organizations and end-users who have access to efficient and tailor-made solutions created for their needs by the providers. They can cut operational costs through this platform solution. They can improve and optimize their business thanks to improvement of the customer journey.

Fabrick ensures full compliance with the European Directive Regulation PSD2.[106] It offers a sophisticated digital payment processing system, in store and online, to support electronic invoicing, value network financing, and equity crowdfunding.

The spread of platforms will take time. Fintech organizations in this sector are eager to occupy the market. Fabrick is also interesting in that it is a collaboration between a traditional financial institution and fintech organizations, with a very effective flexibility and agility.

[103] https://www.economyup.it/fintech/open-banking/banca-sella-lancia-fabrick-un-laboratorio-per-lopen-banking-ecco-chi-ce-dentro/. Accessed March 10, 2019.

[104] Zachariadis, M., & Ozcan, P. (2017). The API economy and digital transformation in financial services: The case of open banking. *Swift Institute Working Paper No. 2016-001*

[105] www.vipera.com. Accessed July 20, 2019. http://kubique.com/?lang=en. Accessed July 21, 2019.

[106] Cortet, M., Rijks, T., & Nijland, S. (2016). PSD2: The digital transformation accelerator for banks. *Journal of Payments Strategy & Systems*, 10 (1), 13–27.

3.6.2 *Innovation and Technology in Procurement of Financial Services*

As part of research conducted by the Master's in Procurement Management course at the University of Tor Vergata in Rome, Italy, the procurement function has been studied in several financial services institutions. This analysis shows that in the face of a changing financial services industry and, in many cases, even in an economic crisis, the procurement function is gaining increasing importance. The commoner aspects that characterize responses to such a crisis consist of innovation, often based on technology, but not only this. The procurement function of innovation invests in:

- services provided
- processes used
- resources used
- business models (in some cases).

On the other hand, in many cases indirect purchases can represent up to 80% of an organization's costs, even if direct purchases are growing. The general trend is to push toward agile procurement 4.0, thereby pushing toward flexibility of services provided and toward lean processes.

Some of the innovative aspects are:

- In terms of services, procurement in several organizations has introduced as internal marketplace. In this manner, pushing onboard contracts and self-service part of its services, it is possible for an organization to significantly increase the productivity of procurement services.
- In terms of processes, the trend is to streamline relationships with partners in a push toward the qualification of partner, consolidating them so that the organization can shorten acquisition times and improve services.
- In terms of resources, the trend is a push for internal resources to become as professional as possible, trying to reduce manual operations as far as they can be. Procurement 4.0 tends to improve the management of relationships with customers and automate exchange and documentation management.
- Finally, in terms of business models, the trend is heading in two directions:

- increasing outsourcing, both in the information systems sector and in the field of BPO and optimization.
- there is a push on collaboration between organizations, to simplify the purchase of 'commodity' services and products.[107]

This latter aspect is particularly intriguing and could be an example for other functions.

ABC: Procurement & Cost Management[108]
ABC Procurement & Cost Management is a consortium of Italian banks. It was founded in 2005 and operates in support of the departments of the banks in the consortium that deal with procurement and cost management.

The consortium's activities are developed along three interconnected dimensions:

- The collaborative dimension is an integral part of the consortium. It is the distinctive nature of the activities carried out by the consortium with the partner community.
- The existing synergistic dimensions between services have an operational nature (ICT solutions) and those related to the development and sharing of knowledge (skills, data, and information) to support of the different stages of procurement processes.
- The nonprofit dimension is also a constitutive nature of the consortium. It allows the delivery of services at the cost of production. Thanks to partner involvement, the majority share of consortium revenues is based on sources external to the consortium system.

(*continued*)

[107] A commodity is a generic product that, by its nature, is not different from those of competitors in terms of potential customers. It is, in other words, easily interchangeable with other products in the same product category that have similar functional characteristics and the same price range. The term 'commodity' is often used to denote the primary products or raw materials used in the production cycle of other products: for example, steel products, basic chemicals, and foodstuffs.

[108] https://www.consorzio-abc.it/. Accessed July 20, 2019.

(continued)

One of the major areas is the development and sharing of knowledge. The ABC consortium organizes training and analysis of expenditure data and individual product categories. ICT developments allow the planning of a series of services aimed at preventing risks of supply. Hence, the organization can guarantee the consortium's institutions. The consortium provides:

- information on partners (consortium info providing service);
- markets (market analysis by product category);
- information on regulatory and contractual aspects (supply and sale of goods/services);
- organizational aspects and sourcing processes (organizational assessment of procurement).

The consortium also provides operational services. A growing number of customers and partners use the consortium platform which has several computer modules to support the entire procurement process. These modules are fully manned by the consortium in terms of responsibilities and ownership of software. They are designed according to the real requirements of member organizations and best practices. These services are structured, in terms of continuity, according to the most significant solutions on the market.

Further, the consortium provides support in the areas of:

- partner pre-qualification/qualification (partner repository)
- categories of goods and services
- observatory cost management
- user groups
- training
- a LinkedIn group—of a buyer network.

3.7 Conclusions

This chapter has reviewed the transformation of processes that support procurement 4.0. It does not cover all procurement processes but those critical in supporting procurement 4.0.

Innovation in procurement can take many forms. Often, but not always, technology helps. It is particularly important to improve processes in this area. The crucial thing is to select the solutions which suit the needs of the organization. It is also vital not to forget that 'the organization that hesitates has lost.' This statement is true for organizations as well as in personal life.

CHAPTER 4

Platforms for Procurement 4.0

4.1 Introduction

Platforms in support of procurement have developed over time (Fig. 4.1).

This chapter considers the primary requirements for procurement 4.0 platforms, especially for industrial plants, in the industry 4.0 perspective. They are[1]:

- operations monitoring using computer numerical control (CNC) and programmable logic controller (PLC);
- user-friendly human–machine interface;
- information systems linked between the factory level and the machines for remote operations;
- automated integration with logistics and value network or with other machines on the shop floor;
- compliance with excellent worker safety parameters;
- tele-maintenance, remote systems diagnosis;
- continuous tracking of working conditions and process parameters with proper sensors and adaptive processes;
- Integration features among the physical machines, models, and simulation of processes.

[1] Tiboni, M., Aggogeri, F., Pellegrini, N., & Perani, C. A. (2019). Smart Modular Architecture for Supervision and Monitoring of a 4.0 Production Plant. *International Journal of Automation Technology*, *13*(2), 310–318.

B. Nicoletti, *Procurement 4.0 and the Fourth Industrial Revolution*,
https://doi.org/10.1007/978-3-030-35979-9_4

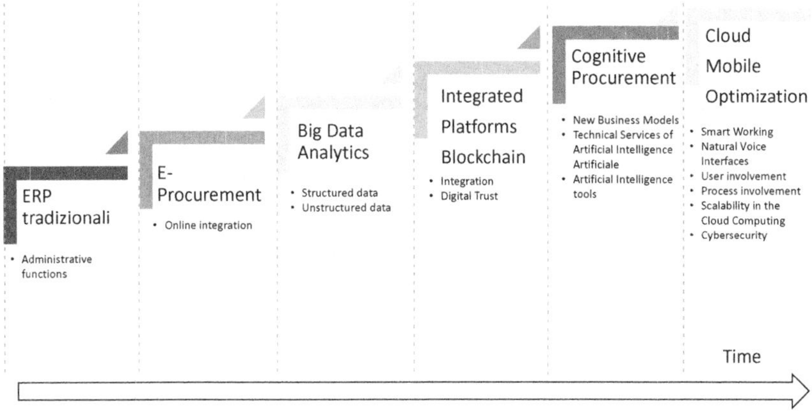

Fig. 4.1 Procurement systems transformation

Procurement 4.0 is characterized by the integration of traditional computing platforms with advanced automation platforms. For a comprehensive list, one may refer to the enabling technologies for industry 4.0 indicated by the Boston Consulting Group (BCG)[2]:

- Inputs
  - Internet of Things
  - mobility
- Process automation
  - blockchain
  - big data analytics and business intelligence (analysis, management, evaluation, and extrapolation of data of interest for the organization)
  - intelligent automation
  - cognitive procurement
  - process automation
  - advanced manufacturing solutions (advanced production systems including cobot[3])

[2] Lu, Y. (2017). Industry 4.0: A survey on technologies, applications and open research issues. *Journal of Industrial Information Integration*, 6, 1–10.

[3] Cobots are tools that interact with co-workers within an organization. They are also called co-processors, or more simply, collaborative robots.

- Output
  - robot(ic) process automation
- Support
  - cloud computing
  - cybersecurity and data privacy

Hardware architecture should include the following major features: modularity, easy implementation, and the use of broad technologies and devices. The idea is to create an industrial IoT network that connects all the machines to the PLC (or CNC) and every sensor distributed on them.

This chapter examines the major technology platforms and how they can be used in procurement 4.0. The order that this is set out corresponds substantially with that suggested by BCG.[4] These platforms are classified by taking into account the model of the eight Cs presented in Chap. 2 (Fig. 4.2), starting with architectural consideration related to e-Procurement, which can be considered the foundation for procurement 4.0.

The opportunities for CPOs in using better platforms is significant.[5] When employed properly, these solutions can provide important data and insights to support strategic decision-making. They can help with the accurate tracking and reporting of benefits. Furthermore, some transactional tasks can be automated. In this way, the procurement function of a business can focus on strategic responsibilities and thereby better contribute to the performance of their organization.

Research shows that digitalization of procurement processes has a multitude of benefits. Apart from the overall improvement of organizational performance, it supports daily administrative tasks and complex decision-making processes. These benefits will steer new focus on procurement as a strategic interface and increase the strategic importance of procurement to an organization. Organizational effectiveness and profitability will be heightened, alongside the potential for establishing new business models, services, and products. However, digitalizing procurement processes

[4] Lu, Y. (2017). Industry 4.0: A survey on technologies, applications and open research issues. *Journal of Industrial Information Integration*, 6, 1–10.

[5] https://assets.kpmg/content/dam/kpmg/pdf/2012/07/the-power-of-procurement-a-global-survey-of-procurement-functions.pdf. Accessed 13 May 2019.

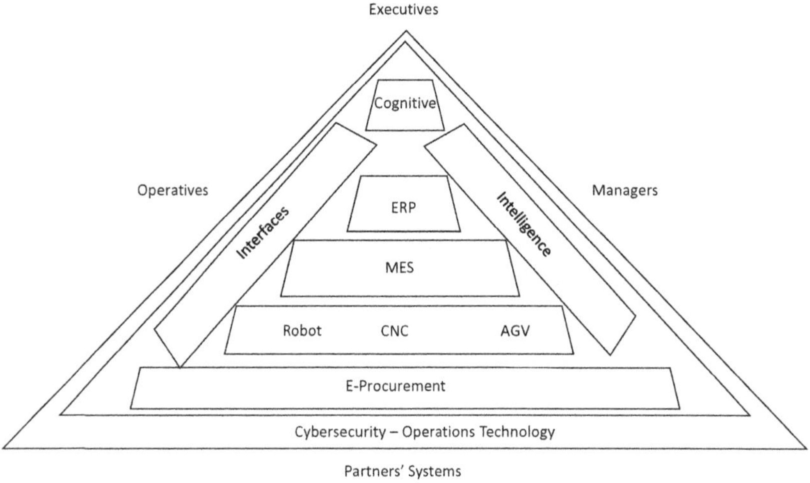

Fig. 4.2 Industry 4.0 architecture

comes with hurdles related to the existing procedures and processes that the systems of any company entail; these must be overcome to fully make use of industry 4.0 as an asset.[6]

4.2 Classification of the Platforms

The classification of platforms can be done by taking into account three different axes—related to the level of the physical automation, the type of connections, and decisional processes.[7] Referring to the first axis, platforms may be classified as manual, partially automated, or completely automated. The second axis concerns the capability of an object or machine to collect and transmit data. According to this axis, there might be non-connected objects that collect data manually or read barcodes. The second type of platform includes smart objects which sense and store data through sensors and RFIDs. The final type of platform covers

[6] Bienhaus, F., & Haddud, A. (2018). Procurement 4.0: factors influencing the digitisation of procurement and supply chains. *Business Process Management Journal, 24*(4), 965–984.

[7] Tappia, E. & Moretti, E. (2019). La Ricerca dell'Osservatorio Contract Logistics "Gino Marchet". *Euromerci*, no 4–5, 34–37.

storage and movements systems, which may also send and transmit structured information among resources. The third axis allows differentiation of platforms based on the relevant decisional process. Traditionally, decisions were taken in a centralized way, sometimes with the support of ICT applications. In the case of procurement 4.0, decision-making processes can be partially decentralized, with machines self-configuring, especially in standard situations, without the intervention of external agents, or being completely automated. In the latter case, platforms have wide decisional autonomy. They can interpret the context and take appropriate decisions.

4.3 Architecture for the Platforms

It is interesting to analyze the developments in the platforms relevant to procurement 4.0. This chapter refers to them as the seven Cs[8]:

- cloud computing;
- communication becoming increasingly mobile;
- cognition, meaning how to improve the knowledge of organizations through the tools referred to as big data and analytics;
- cybersecurity to assure protection from unauthorized accesses and protection of data privacy;
- collaboration, also through social networks;
- use of external contractors;
- costs being increasingly reduced, despite declining numbers of partners.

Each of these trends is a strong agent of change in procurement processes:

- Cloud computing is the use of computing resources, accessed through networks and payments for services provided and paid based on use. The impacts on procurement are significant, since they open new horizons for sourcing and accessing computing resources.
- Communication pushes toward working anywhere, anytime, on any device.
- Cognition within an organization, through tools such as big data and analytics, supports the analysis of the procurement processes not

[8] This classification is related but not the same as the model of the eight Cs in Chap. 2.

possible in the past, thanks to the increasing availability of large amounts of data, information, and documentation.

- New collaboration tools make it possible to develop integration along with the value stream.
- The need to be lean pushes the use of external resources, such as contractors or outsourcers, for specific needs. In this case, the difficulty is to evaluate partners. The acquisition of valuable resources and the introduction of mechanisms of productivity is not easily definable in contracts.
- Reduction of costs is particularly pressing in these times of deep and long financial crisis. In this situation, the pressure on the procurement function to achieve reductions in the prices of products/services procured tends to be great. This goes against the trend to create partnerships with the vendors rather than confrontation. The management of the energy costs (or the use of natural resources) is particularly important.
- Cybersecurity is the practice of defending computers, servers, applications, mobile devices, electronic systems, networks, and data from malicious attacks or unauthorized access.[9] It is also known as ICT security or operational technology security.[10] These terms apply in a variety of contexts, from the organization to wider ecosystem computing.

An interesting concept at the basis of industry 4.0 is that of the 'digital twin'.[11] The vision of the digital twin refers to a comprehensive physical and functional description of a component, product, or system.[12] A digital twin includes more or less all information that could be useful in all current and subsequent lifecycle phases. From a product lifecycle management point of view, there is a strong need to integrate all lifecycle data

[9] https://www.kaspersky.com/resource-center/definitions/what-is-cyber-security. Accessed 31 May 2019.

[10] Windelberg, M. (2016). Objectives for managing cyber supply chain risk. *International Journal of Critical Infrastructure Protection*, *12*, 4–11.

[11] Schleich, B., Anwer, N., Mathieu, L., & Wartzack, S. (2017). Shaping the digital twin for design and production engineering. *CIRP Annals*, *66*(1), 141–144.

[12] Boschert S, Rosen R (2016) Digital Twin –The Simulation Aspect. In Hehenberger, P. & Bradley D (eds.): *Mechatronic Futures: Challenges and Solutions for Mechatronic Systems and their Designers*, Springer International Publishing, 2016, 59–74.

artifacts into a comprehensive management system.[13] This system can be used by various actors for querying data, such as through-life performance information and making predictions about physical products or services from the digital twin for design optimization and manufacturing system improvement. A digital twin could also help procurement 4.0 organization to procure better products, services, or components, for instance with predictive maintenance.[14]

This chapter examines the most relevant of these platform developments one at a time, to analyze their possible uses in support of procurement 4.0.

4.3.1 General Architecture for the Procurement 4.0 Platforms

Before going into detail about the platforms, it is important to underline the connection of these platforms to the processes examined in Chap. 3 and the groundwork for the development of procurement 4.0 represented by e-procurement.

Lean and Digitize

The correct implementation of procurement 4.0 is done by combining process optimization and automation using the method known as 'Lean and Digitize,' as shown in Fig. 4.3.[15]

This approach is useful, as demonstrated in many organizations. In attempts to apply the digital transformation, organizations often fail to ascribe proper importance to the improvement of processes—especially to persons affected by the transformation and the partners, which are an important counterpart. The introduction of procurement 4.0 thus requires a cultural change. It is necessary to make the procurement processes integrated, simpler, and more immediate to manage. It is also essential to motivate the internal staff on the procurement processes to work with the new procurement 4.0 approach, so that its success is guaranteed.

[13] Rosen. R, von Wichert, G, Lo, G., & Bettenhausen, K. D. (2015). About the Importance of Autonomy and Digital Twins for the Future of Manufacturing, *IFAC-Papers OnLine*, 48(3), 567–572.

[14] Mobley, R. K. (2002). *An introduction to predictive maintenance*. Elsevier, Amsterdam, Netherlands.

[15] Nicoletti, B., (2012), *Lean and Digitize: An Integrated Approach to Process Improvement*. Gower Publishing, Farnham, UK. ISBN-10: 1409441946.

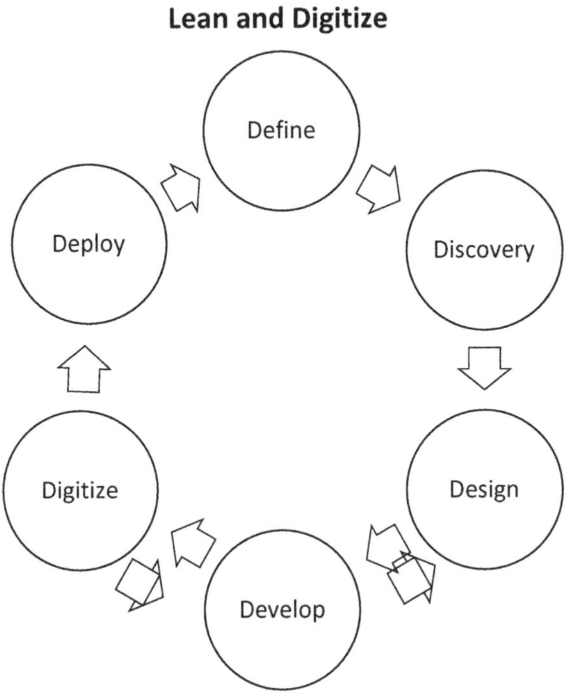

Fig. 4.3 Lean and digitize methodology

This section presents a cloud computing architecture for procurement 4.0. It expands on earlier developments, combining different technologies to create interoperable communities of e-platforms.

The development of e-procurement is also expanding in public and private organizations, part of the basis of procurement 4.0. It is important to have a clear vision of the final target architecture and to implement it through several generations. The proposed cloud computing procurement brings a series of benefits. The results of the analysis show that the implementation of a 'Software as a Service' (SaaS) scheme in cloud computing in e-procurement systems brings significant flexibility and cost reduction.[16] The main reason for such a use has been economics. In fact,

[16] Nicoletti, B., (2013), *Cloud Computing and Financial Services*, Palgrave Macmillan, London, UK (also translated in Chinese).

e-procurement in combination with cloud computing is much more than just a new solution or a cost-saving model: It can change the culture of an organization, its products, processes, organizations, and business models.[17]

The development of web-based e-procurement alters the way organizations work. There are still challenges connected with the reliability of connections, security, and the interoperability. It is important to implement a proper architecture, as described in the following section.

A Generalized Architecture for e-Procurement

To reap the benefits of e-procurement, it is necessary to adopt an advanced architecture (Fig. 4.4). This is based on cloud computing and, in particular, on the SaaS model. This solution assures proper connection with the organization, its customers, and partners, anytime, anywhere, and from any device.

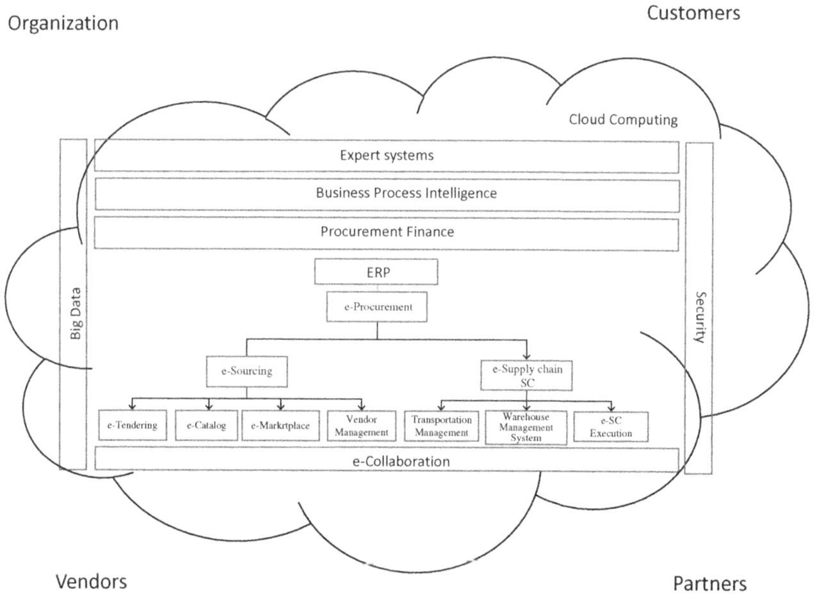

Fig. 4.4 Architecture for e-procurement

[17] Nicoletti, B., (2012), *Lean and Digitize: An Integrated Approach to Process Improvement*. Gower Publishing, Farnham, UK. ISBN-10: 1409441946.

The architecture is based on the following modules, also made accessible in cloud computing from an organization app store.

- The ERP manages the basic processes of the organization and specifically with regard to procurement. The e-procurement components integrate the ERP with a series of advanced and specific modules.
- The e-procurement system can be divided into two main areas:
  - E-sourcing defines the technical and economic requirements of the product until the time of placing an order. There are several sub-processes: from the solicitation of an offer to be sent to a partner, the collection of published offers, and the selection of the partner. The chosen partner must engage in contractual terms with the organization. The e-sourcing should provide support to the whole process P2P of (Procure to Pay) thus:
- streamline and automate the entire process from the acquisition request up to the payment of the invoice to the partner;
- develop the documentation (such as functional and technical specifications, orders, invoices, manuals, and so on) in electronic formats to avoid duplication and ensure continuous updating of the contents;
- Facilitate the partners to generate electronic invoices and manage catalogs online.
  - E-supply chain management needs to support supply operations and provide continuous assessment.

Each of these macro areas can be broken down into several specific areas. Thus, e-sourcing can be split into:

- Processes pertaining to the purchase of products or services in limited quantities and specifications (e-tendering). They include all activities from the search for new partners, their qualifications and certification, and the relevant negotiations. The process can be based on tools such as the request for information/proposal/quotation and the online auctions;
- Repetitive sourcing processes (e-catalog), web-based catalogs, products or services already defined, specified, and contractualized—normally standard and indirect products;
- Sourcing processes on the market (e-marketplace);
- Management of partners and contracts (vendor or partner management).

The e-supply chain management can be broken down into the following areas:

- Transportation management systems which support logistics operations after issuance of the order. This includes transportation management up to the storing of the goods or the delivery of services;
- The warehouse management system that supports activities related to the storing of goods;
- The e-supply chain execution supports the operational and administrative processes with the goal of making automated and integrated interfaces between operators and the phases of operations.

At the base of all these components is a model of e-collaboration that supports the relationships within the organization and with third parties (be they partners, distributors, or customers).

The ERP manages the stream of the physical supplies (be they goods or services). In its connection, there should be a module to take into account procurement finance and the material tracking and management.

All processes should be managed by a module of business process intelligence which helps extract, summarize, and visualize the data and supports the workflows to manage the processes.

All the modules should be connected with a big database, which will manage all the contents, whether structured or unstructured (such as documents, emails, and so on). The data will be in the cloud or on the premises, depending on security, compliance, and performance.

Finally, a module for access and security manages the access and the protection of the system, transmission, and interfaces from external or not properly authorized intrusions.

Benefits of e-Procurement

E-procurement, public or private, has spurred the interest of researchers from very different fields: computer and management science, the theory of organizations, law, and economics. It would thus be difficult to provide a comprehensive picture of the main research papers written since the turn of the millennium.

E-procurement is electronic tendering and procurement of goods and services.[18] Most organizations or public authorities implement some form

[18] Timmers, P. (1998), Business Models for Electronic Markets, *CommerceNet Research Report*, 9 September.

of e-procurement using the internet. They seek benefits, such as a wider choice of partners. This is expected to lead to lower costs, better quality products and services, improved delivery, shorter cycle times, and reduced total cost of ownership (for instance, tender specifications can be downloaded by bidders rather than mailed via post). Electronic negotiation and contracting, and possibly collaborative work in preparing the specifications, can further enhance time- and cost-savings and convenience. For the partners, the benefits are in the possibility to access more tendering opportunities, on a global scale and lower costs in participating in a tender. Another benefit is the possibility of tendering in ways better suited to smaller enterprises, or collaborative tendering (if the e-procurement site supports some form of collaboration). For the organizations using e-procurement, the main sources of increase in margins up to this point came from the reduction of costs (automated tender processing, more cost-effective offers, and similar).[19]

The emergence of internet platforms, such as eBay and Amazon, has gradually provided more and more data for economists and ICT experts to conceptualize and analyze aspects such as the structure of the information needed in e-marketplace, the nature of forces affecting price formation, the main performance dimensions, namely the degree of participation from both sides of the market (buyers and sellers), and level of competition.[20]

The benefits of e-procurement are substantial, and there is still room for e-procurement to expand. An example is in the realm of public procurement, which accounts for roughly 16% of GDP in the European Union (EU). The public procurement departments has not yet made full use of innovative models and tools to streamline value networks, to increase transparency and speed, as well as to reduce administrative cost and contract prices. E-procurement can also bring significant savings when used in public procurement. Such a change in process requires a new management culture and new tools. Several authors have analyzed the key lines of change to be pursued. They have shown that e-procurement and, particularly, e-tendering are the appropriate tools to implement such changes

[19] Timmers, P. (1998), Business Models for Electronic Markets, *CommerceNet Research Report*, 9 September.

[20] Oppong, S. A., Yen, D. C., & Merhout, J. W. (2005). A new strategy for harnessing knowledge management in e-commerce. *Technology in society*, 27(3), 413–435.

because, in connection with business process intelligence, they can support significant improvements to help cope with the strategic and tactical challenges of public procurement.[21]

Portugal is a relevant case study. It is the first EU member state to have mandatory public e-procurement including e-public tendering for any open, restricted, or negotiated procedures, since November 2009.[22] The different types of savings in Portugal were estimated using public procurement data for 2010, which shows that they brought overall savings between 6% and 12% for total public expenditure, thanks mainly to e-tendering.

Deutsche Bank's research department has underlined the importance of managing public procurement worth €2 trillion.[23] The School of Management at the Politecnico di Milano presented six main areas of intervention. They highlighted the benefits that could be achieved in Italy in the medium term (three years) from e-procurement, under certain assumptions.[24]

- E-procurement in the area of public administration: savings of around €7 billion per year.
- Electronic invoicing: savings of around €5 billion per year, €1 billion for the public administration and the rest for private organizations.
- Electronic payments to the public administration: saving around €0.6 billion per year.
- Electronic payments to partners: increased tax revenues of around €5 billion per year.
- Dematerialization and digital innovation in the processes of public administration: saving around €15 billion per year.

In the case of a given organization, a research framework suggests that alignment among business strategy, e-procurement strategy, e-procurement tools, strategic ICT capabilities, and strategic approaches have a positive influence on an organization's strategic performance.[25]

[21] Castellanos, M., De Medeiros, A. A., Mendling, J., Weber, B., & Weijters, A. J. M. M. (2009). Business process intelligence. In *Handbook of research on business process modeling*. IGI Global, Hershey, PA, 456–480,

[22] Tavares, L.V. (2011), A strategy to reduce public expenditure based on e-tendering and procurement Business Intelligence: The case of Portugal, *Eva paper*. 3 May.

[23] Meyer, T, (2011): E-Procurement, *Deutsche Bank Research Paper*, http://wwwdbresearchde/PROD/DBR_INTERNET_DE-PROD/PROD0000000000269867PDF, Accessed 8 February 2019.

[24] Scuola di Management del Politecnico di Milano (2012), *Osservatorio Agenda Digitale, Smau*, Milan, Italy

[25] Phillips, P., & Piotrowicz, W. (2006), e-Procurement: How does it enhance Strategic Performance?, *Working Paper No. 113, Kent Business School*, April.

Cloud procurement tools bring—directly or indirectly—significant tangible and intangible benefits:

- guarantee of transparency in relation to supply undertakings;
- an easier search for new sources;
- greater efficiency by aggregating the needs of most organizations with similar requirements, and the modernization and reorganization of the extended value network beyond internal processes;
- opportunity to optimize effectiveness of e-procurement processes through the use of several tools best suited to specific cases;
- attention to environmental sustainability and green public procurement.

Challenges of e-Procurement
The challenges connected with the proposed architecture are the need to assure:

- cultural change
- availability of the applications, platforms, network, and infrastructure
- security, privacy, and trust issues
- reliability
- controllability
- training
- user-friendliness.

4.4 Connection: IoT and Blockchain

Connection is one of the most important aspects of procurement 4.0. Several solutions can support it, but two are particularly relevant: the Internet of Things (IoT) and blockchain.

4.4.1 IoT

This defines the network of equipment and devices, connected to the internet, equipped with software capable of exchanging data with other related objects.[26] The objectives of these devices are collection of data and information, issue of commands, and the monitoring of activities.

[26] Atzori, L., Iera, A., & Morabito, G. (2017). Understanding the Internet of Things: definition, potentials, and societal role of a fast evolving paradigm. *Ad Hoc Networks*, 56, 122–140.

The two main features of a 'connected object' are to have:

- an IP address that allows unique identification on the network;
- the ability to exchange data over the same network without the need for human intervention.

According to Gartner, there are already about 8 billion connected objects and this figure is around 25 billion in 2020.[27] Other sources estimate that connected devices number between 8 and 10 billion.[28]

IoT Architectures

IoT devices, also known as microcontrollers, which are increasingly connected but with limited resources, must continually communicate with each other in a synchronized manner, according to precise protocols. They collect data using the sensors, store them in data structures, generally in the cloud or on edge computers,[29] where they are analyzed. In this manner, an organization gets information that is fed back into the real world to use for planned objectives. This leads to push messages on mobile apps, browser charts, QR codes, and so forth. The entire ecosystem of hardware/software objects that is part of an IoT project is based on an architecture composed of such connected elements.

There is not just a single architecture in the IoT. At a high level, it is necessary to take into account:

- hardware items
- communication protocols
- cloud computing services
- data storage
- software applications.

[27] https://www.gartner.com/en/newsroom/press-releases/2017-02-07-gartner-says-8-billion-connected-things-will-be-in-use-in-2017-up- 31-percent-from-2016. Accessed March 10, 2019.

[28] https://www.forbes.com/sites/forbestechcouncil/2018/03/16/developing-the-connected-world-of-2018-and-beyond/. Accessed April 25, 2019.

[29] Salman, O., Elhajj, I., Kayssi, A., & Chehab, A. (2015, December). Edge computing enabling the Internet of Things. In *2015 IEEE 2nd World Forum on Internet of Things (WF-IoT)*, 603–608. IEEE.

Hardware items can be:

- Short range—they communicate on the network through Bluetooth or cable or Wi-Fi and therefore require gateways/hubs for the connection into the network (usually the internet);
- Long range—they connect the network to the wide-area network thanks to their SIM.[30]

Through its typical features, such as elasticity, scalability, power, and its relative low costs, cloud computing is enabling the IoT. One of the reasons for the close connection between cloud computing and the IoT depends on the fact that the technology of intelligent devices is still in the process of expanding and being developed by innovative organizations. The main aspect that makes it so interesting is the blend of cloud computing and the IoT, and the amount of data that the IoT can generate. This data can be analyzed to draw relevant conclusions about users, market trends, and so forth.

Among the physical objects and end-users, the IoT is a platform that has the role of communicating with relevant objects and the information organization software, managing how data are transmitted and stored, and using algorithms to extract knowledge from data.

Application Areas

IoT applications can be divided into three degrees of maturity:

- consolidated applications
- experimental applications
- embryonic applications.

Consolidated applications are the simplest. Applications currently under development are those that are closest to the paradigm of the IoT. Plans for the future are the embryonic applications.[31]

[30] The name comes from the acronym SIM card, or subscriber identity module. This is a smart card inserted into a mobile phone or tablet and allows the device to securely store the IMSI, a unique number associated with all users of mobile GMS or UMTS networks. It thus becomes the subscriber's identity.

[31] Ma, T., & Zhang, C. (2011, December). On the disruptive potentials in internet of things. In *2011 IEEE 17th International Conference on Parallel and Distributed Systems*: 857–859.

The IoT brings intelligence in information processing systems. Through the IoT, objects can be controlled remotely, and are capable of transmitting data from which an organization can extract useful information on the functioning of such objects and about the interactions between these objects and those who use them (for example, the end-user). Hence the criticism[32] regarding security and data privacy in connection with the IoT, and the need for transparency in the processing of personal data.

The applications of the IoT can be:

- facility automation or technology applied to the facilities, to manage for example refrigerators, washing machines, phones, and so forth;
- robotics or engineering and technology that allow the robots to 'come to life,' or for robots to execute tasks that in the past were performed by persons.
- avionics, that is, the technology applied to the aircraft and the pilot, such as communication systems onboard aircraft, drones, autopilots, and so forth;
- the automotive industry for new applications for vehicles, such as intelligent wipers activated when it starts to rain. In time, smart cars with autonomous or assisted driving will be rolled out;
- industry biomedical with IoT applied to medicine, such as remote management of patients. Over time, it will be possible to have remote surgeries;
- telemetry to support data transmission and information.

At the organizational level, the most interesting applications are:

- Smart manufacturing or industry 4.0: Smart manufacturing was certainly one of the precursors of the IoT.[33] IoT applications have been active for many years, long before people started talking about them as part of the IoT as such. Today, this area is one of the most mature, combining issues related to automation with issues related to the world of robotics. Smart manufacturing overlaps with the industry

[32] Kraijak, S., & Tuwanut, P. (2015, October). A survey on internet of things architecture, protocols, possible applications, security, privacy, real-world implementation and future trends. *2015 IEEE 16th International Conference on Communication Technology (ICCT)*. IEEE. 26–31.

[33] Kang, H. S., Lee, J. Y., Choi, S., Kim, H., Park, J. H., Son, J. Y., & Do Noh, S. (2016). Smart manufacturing: Past research, present findings, and future directions. *International Journal of Precision Engineering and Manufacturing-Green Technology*, 3(1), 111–128.

4.0 world, namely with a true development policy to extend the introduction of digital industry in the organizational realm.

The use of IoT in the industry is a reality in many countries, as evidenced by the data collected by the smart manufacturing research group at the School of Management of the Politecnico di Milano. This survey shows that the IoT market is growing at a rate of 20% and represents a concrete thrust in support of the 'Made in Italy' brand.[34]

- Smart logistics: These include solutions for value network traceability, brand protection and monitoring of the cold chain, for safety in complex logistic poles and the management of fleets of vehicles (vehicle tracking and condition monitoring).[35]
- Smart asset management: remote management of value infrastructure (for instance, electro-biomedical devices, vending machines, and similar) for the purpose of detecting damage and tampering, localization, tracking, and inventory management.[36]
- Smart factory: implementation of new solutions in production management through the use of machines sensitive to the context in which they operate, which can detect real-time information, communicate, and take decisions.[37]

Among the factors that enable innovation at the procurement level, there are platforms to support collaboration between all stakeholders (internal and external). This implies the digitization of the value network processes, of sourcing, and logistics. These platforms enable IoT devices or other devices to collect and retrieve data. It is possible to 'see' the data to define what they are 'doing,' and finally to envision the future of procurement.

These platforms are also referred to as procurement collaboration.[38] They allow an organization to synchronize, integrate, and make digitally available real-time information to all concerned.

[34] https://www.internet4things.it/iot-library/internet-of-things-gli-ambiti-applicativi-in-italia/. Accessed April 25, 2019.

[35] Ferreira, P., Martinho, R., & Domingos, D. (2010). IoT-aware business processes for logistics: limitations of current approaches. In *Inforum*, 3(2010): 612–613).

[36] Nel, C. B. H., & Jooste, J. L. (2016). A technologically-driven asset management approach to managing physical assets-a literature review and research agenda for 'smart' asset management. *South African Journal of Industrial Engineering*, 27(4), 50–65.

[37] Wang, S., Wan, J., Li, D., & Zhang, C. (2016). Implementing smart factory of industrie 4.0: an outlook. *International Journal of Distributed Sensor Networks*, 12(1), 3,159,805.

[38] Yan, MR, Chien, KM, & Yang, TN (2016). Green component procurement collaboration for improving supply chain management in the high technology industries: A case study from the systems perspective. *Sustainability*, 8 (2), 105.

IoT can support platforms that allow organizations to incorporate the majority of their partners, even the smallest, with optimized order management and reduction of the associated costs. The logic of these platforms assumes that the search for the end-to-end value stream within an organization requires the creation of platforms to develop forms of data sharing between all actors. To achieve the maximum involvement of all partners, organizations require multi-platform solutions that integrate the sourcing and logistics processes in a connected manner among customers, partners, logistics providers, and public organizations.

Efficiency Improvement Through the IoT

IoT strategy must be based on four points: business process collaboration, retail efficiency improvement, cloud collaboration, and ecosystem resource and process management. Founded on this logic of partnership, these collaborative platforms can be used to manage procurement transactional processes: procurement marketing, sourcing, logistics, and execution. The main features of these processes are traced to independent modules (such as partner management or bid management, order management, advance ship notice, and receiving). The collaboration domain includes solutions for extended collaborative logistics, such as[39]:

- transport management systems
- governance
- risk management and compliance
- electronic data interchange
- e-invoicing.

These solutions are characterized by recognizing and managing the peculiarities of the different sectors and individual organizations. They can interact with all partners using all the tools available, overcoming the limitations of using only one channel, whether it is a structured flow as in the electronic data interchange or emails, both online and offline, through

[39] Adetiloye, TO (2012). Collaboration stakeholders for sustainable planning of city logistics operations. *Doctoral dissertation, Concordia University*, Montréal, Canada.

multiple channels. The latter frees organizations from the constraints and allows them to internally develop a unique process for a more efficient, effective, and economical management of the procurement 4.0 in full control of the organization's performance. This allows all stakeholders in an organization's value network to share structured information, business plans, forecasts, and all the documentation of the procurement cycle. In this way, the organization can enable dynamic relationships marked by real collaborative integration models.

Partnerships Through the IoT
Procurement collaboration solutions provide the visibility and tools to improve data and information sharing. They enable high levels of partnership, allowing the exploiting of data from business applications that integrate unstructured information usually found in emails and/or office documents. Thus, an organization can manage discrepancies, such as those between actual and forecasted orders and reprogramming, as the number required or delayed in the delivery of products, disseminating information among its different departments.

The implementation logic also recommended in the case of the IoT is a gradual introduction. It begins with a focus on the most important processes for each sector. The next move is giving support to customers, after obtaining the results and seeing the robustness of the solution. Later, the organization can extend its service to other areas. When an organization starts to develop collaboration processes, it must have a strategy that can support all of them, even if the organization initially focuses on only one service, knowing that the development of the other services may be gradual and evolutionary.

4.4.2 Wireless Sensor Networks

Wireless Sensor Networks (WSN) are systems that consist of sensors and wireless communication networks. WSN enable the collection and transfer of data between sensor nodes, access devices, and network users.[40] Sensors are used to identify objects and their physical characteristics—the characteristics of goods, transport and transshipment means, containers, loca-

[40] Radivojević, G., & Milosavljević, L. (2019). The Concept of Logistics 4.0. *4th Logistics International Conference,* 23–25 May. Belgrade, Serbia.

tions in warehouses and sales facilities, equipment and traffic infrastructure, and so on.[41] Some examples of the use of WSN in logistics are measuring vehicle load based on WSN and 3D cameras, and quality control of goods based on analysis of data obtained from sensors.[42] Sensors are installed in transport and transshipment equipment, infrastructure and facilities in logistics; work clothes with built-in sensors improve safety and health conditions of workers, and so forth.

4.4.3 Blockchain

The models of industry 4.0 and of procurement 4.0 are based on six Cs: cybernetics, communication, control, collaboration, connection, and cognition. Two other Cs are aspects relevant to procurement processes: co-division or sharing, and getting confidence (or trust). Deriving from the new interconnected and automated procurement 4.0 ecosystems, the matter of trust plays a vital and important role in the entire ecosystem. Within traditional buyer–partner relationships, trust is a powerful factor based on the interactions between both parties as well as external influence factors.[43] Considering value network ecosystems, trust must be maintained mutually between more than two parties. This challenges organizations in their traditional behavior and requires a change in organizational culture and solutions used.[44] An emerging solution can provide support to both: the blockchain.

The blockchain is a computerized open ledger in which it is possible to record every transaction in the network for a specific application.[45] The

[41] Radivojević, G., Bjelić, N., & Popović, D. (2017). Internet of Thing in Logistics, *Proceedings of the 3rd Logistics International Conference - LOGIC 2017*, 185–190, Belgrade, Serbia.

[42] Kückelhaus, M., Chung, G. (2018). Logistics Trend Radar, DHL *Customer Solutions & Innovation*, Germany. www.dhl.com, Accessed 14 July 2019.

[43] Keith, B., Vitasek, K., Manrodt, K. & Kling, J. (2016), *Strategic Sourcing in the New Economy: Harnessing the Potential of Sourcing Business Models for Modern Procurement*, Palgrave Macmillan, New York, NY.

[44] Harshak, A., Schmaus, B. & Dimitrova, D. (2013), Building a digital culture: how to meet the challenge of multichannel digitization", www.strategyand.pwc.com/media/file/Strategyand_Building-a-Digital-Culture.pdf. Accessed January 27, 2019.

[45] Zheng, Z., Xie, S., Dai, HN, Chen, X., & Wang, H. (2018). Blockchain challenges and opportunities: a survey. *International Journal of Web and Grid Services*, 14 (4), 352–375.

blockchain is available for all participants; they may see and check it whenever they wish. If registered, a participant may also enter new data into the blockchain. There is a log that allows shared visibility of operations and services. This vision in common eliminates the need for data transfer between organizations. One can also imagine blockchain as a network of "digital trust".[46] This expression indicates that the blockchain is a set of data that can be considered reliable because their 'authenticity' is based on the consensus of a large number of actors. Not coincidentally, the blockchain was created to support Bitcoin, a virtual currency, since the use of a currency requires confidence in the possibility of using it.[47]

From a technical point of view, a blockchain is a secure database. It is managed through a global network of independent servers. They provide a shared vision. The blockchain eliminates the need to transfer information between the organizations through files, messages, or similar media. As a result, it erases any difference of data between partners and customers. Everything is held in the cloud and so is easy to access from any location.

The blockchain helps to eliminate all differences in data between partners and customers. For example, blockchain solutions could be used to manage products and partner quality certificates, proof of ownership, references of a specific partner, contracts, and purchase orders. They could help organizations quickly resolve delivery discrepancies in the recovery of data end-to-end throughout the process from order to payment. They may also provide tests according to which the materials originate from areas certified to be environmentally and socially responsible.

The blockchain can be classified as a development over time of data management (DM 4.0), in terms of this sequence:

- DM 1.0—dataset in an application
- DM 2.0—database architecture
- DM 3.0—relational database
- DM 4.0—blockchain in the cloud.

[46] Nofer, M., Gomber, P., Hinz, O., & Schiereck, D. (2017). Blockchain. *Business & Information Systems Engineering*, *59*(3), 183–187.

[47] Wolf, R. A. (2016). Virtual Currencies, M-Payments and VAT: Ready for the Future?. In *Bitcoin and Mobile Payments,* 231–249. Palgrave Macmillan, London, UK.

The blockchain is a type of master electronic ledger created to ensure that once a partner transfers digital activity, the same party may not assign (or even sell) to anyone else. Unlike other ledgers, each participant controls the blockchain; decisions about which records it contains are subject to the consent of all participants.

The multiplication of tenures guarantees the accuracy of a registration. Each participant controls an entire copy of the ledger. Discrepancies resolution mechanisms ensure that all copies reflect an identical story. Although permits can be managed with a good degree of control, by default, each authorized participant can view all transactions. Transparency is thus a basic feature of the blockchain.

The characteristics of a blockchain solution can be summarized like so[48]:

- Distributed database: Each party on a blockchain has access to the entire database and its complete history. No single party controls the data or information. Every party can verify the records of its transaction partners directly, without an intermediary.
- Peer-to-peer transmission: Communication occurs directly between peers instead of through a central node. Each node stores and forwards information to all other nodes.
- Transparency with pseudonymity: Every transaction and its associated value are visible to anyone with access to the system. Each node, or user, on a blockchain, has a unique 30-plus-character alphanumeric address that identifies it. Users can choose to remain anonymous or provide proof of their identity to others. Transactions take place between blockchain addresses.
- Irreversibility of records: Once a transaction is entered in the database and the accounts are updated, the records cannot be modified since they are linked to every transaction record that came before them. Several computational algorithms and solutions are deployed to ensure that the recording on the database is permanent, chronologically ordered, and available to all other participants on the network.
- Computational logic: The digital nature of the ledger implies that blockchain transactions can be tied to computational logic and in essence programmed. Users can set up algorithms and rules that automatically trigger transactions between nodes.

[48] Iansiti, M., & Lakhani, K. R. (2017). The truth about blockchain. *Harvard Business Review*, *95*(1), 118–127.

The Blockchain in Procurement

Blockchain solutions can support procurement 4.0.[49] The blockchain can be a shared database that supports the several stakeholders associated with the ecosystem of the procurement: organizations, customers, partners, distributors, and, if necessary, regulators or public administration entities. It can manage a portfolio of partners, their administration, sourcing, and management of any complaints. The blockchain can provide excellent visibility for all such data. It can provide a messaging service that is seamless and reliable, and uninterrupted ecosystem-wide shared information on the procurement of an organization. It is an effective method to facilitate the availability and exchange of data among several parties involved in procurement processes. It allows organizations to increase the effectiveness, efficiency, and economy of a procurement ecosystem.

Blockchain applications can range across all areas of procurement 4.0. Figure 4.5 shows the typical processes of procurement at a high level. The blockchain can be useful throughout the entire procurement cycle (Fig. 4.6).

- The blockchain can be used at the time of the partners participating in a tender, or in their qualifications, to verify the identity of the partner or to limit the risks associated with sourcing from that partner.
- The blockchain can help in the exchange of order documents, warranties, invoices, and other documents, as certified and accessed by all parties involved. An example of the use of the blockchain is provided by SafeShare, a British organization.[50] It employs the blockchain to confirm the bonds between two parties, such as in insurance. This solution facilitates the agile delivery of a product that meets the needs of customers. Other examples include the management of different types of contracts (for example, procurement contracts), certificates, and similar documents.
- A blockchain solution can support the management of shipments of finished goods' inventory. The finished goods warehouse receives products from the factory. It identifies and stores them. It is important to ensure inventory accuracy and product availability. Subsequently, the blockchain can include information on the carrier shipment, transport,

[49] Akaba, T. I. (2019). A Framework or the Adoption of a Blockchain-Based E-Procurement System: A Case Study of Nigeria. *Thesis for: Msc. E-Governance Technologies and Services*. Tallinn University of Technology, Tallinn, Estonia.

[50] http://www.safeshareinsurance.com/. Accessed March 29, 2019.

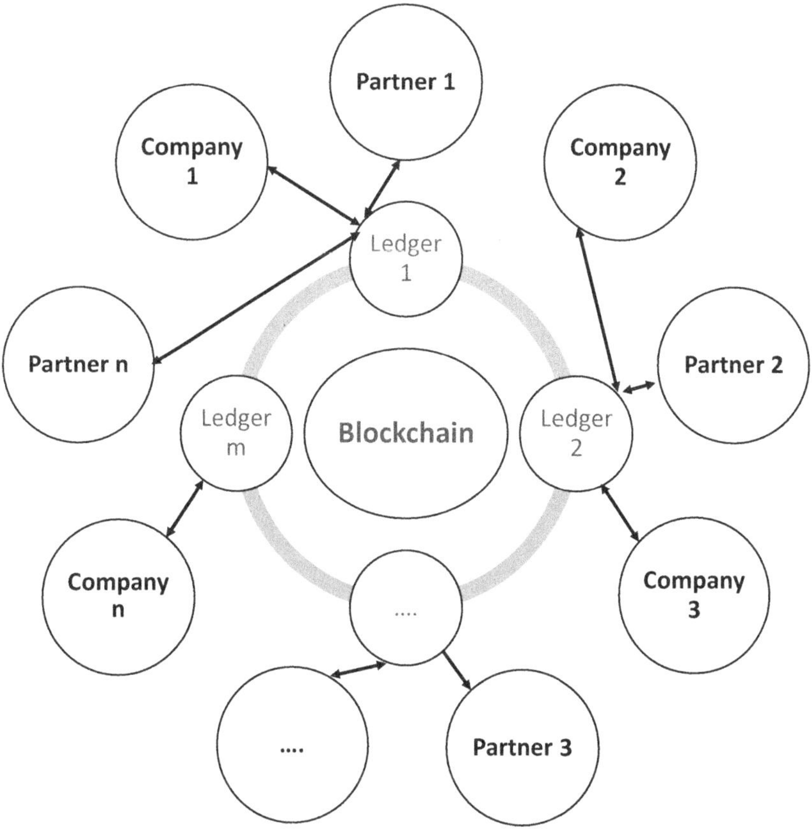

Fig. 4.5 Blockchain and procurement processes

and delivery of the product to the customer. At the same time, it supports the processing and verification of the transport documents, customs clearance, cargo insurance, and invoices for services provided. In this series of transactions, there are many agencies and organizations involved. With the blockchain, all parties may refer to the same ledger.

- The blockchain can also help to manage cash flows associated with purchases, so-called trade finance. The blockchain can record the different movements between the parties. It allows authorized customers to track and improve transactions securely and fast in a paperless mode. All parties are able to immediately examine the status of the reconciliation documents. The blockchain allows a transparent link between the parties involved in a given transaction, simplifying management, moni-

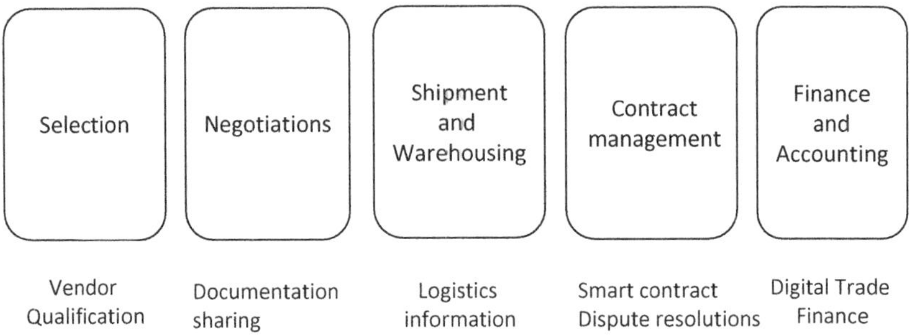

Fig. 4.6 Blockchain framework for procurement

toring, and settlement of domestic and international transactions not only for large organizations but also for small and medium-sized enterprises. Accounting of transactions would be recorded on the blockchain, speeding up all the processes with full transparency and security.

Digital Trade Chain[51]

Seven European banks (Deutsche Bank, Natixis, Société Générale, Rabobank, HSBC, KBC, and the Italian UniCredit) and IBM have signed an agreement for the development of payment services.[52] This is based on a shared platform and built on a blockchain solution aimed at simplifying business transactions of small and medium-sized enterprises with the financial institutions. The banks have collaborated in the development and commercialization of a new product, called the Digital Trade Chain (DTC). DTC allows authorized customers to track and refine paperless transactions securely and fast. The platform was tested by all the banks involved in the agreement in their respective home countries (Italy, Germany, France, Holland, United Kingdom, Belgium, and Luxembourg).

Thanks to DTC, KBC won the Efma Accenture Innovation Award for Best New Product or Service 2016.[53]

[51] https://www.bankingtech.com/tag/digital-trade-chain/. Accessed July 20, 2019.

[52] Lipton, A., Hardjono, T., & Pentland, A. (2018). Digital trade coin: Towards a more stable digital currency. *Royal Society Science Open*, 5 (7), 180, 155.

[53] https://distributionmarketingblog.accenture.com/kbc-uses-blockchain-to-transform-international-trades. Accessed July 20, 2019.

Besides reducing bureaucracy, this blockchain solution provides end-to-end transparency of the entire process, dropping the barriers of fear and distrust that often hinder things, especially for small organizations when they operate in new markets, for example foreign ones.

Tradle[54]

Tradle is a startup. It can store information with high resilience to potential hackers and cyberattacks.[55] It has created a platform to compensate for the limitations of normal blockchain solutions, such as low throughput of transactions, data storage limits, absence of transactional semantics, and the high cost of the calculations.

Trust in Motion (TIM) is an application of Tradle on this platform.[56] It allows users to initiate a secure line of communication and go on-the-record for the exchange of confidential documents, checks, assignments, and agreements. The resulting records are stored securely and irrevocably, with high resilience to hackers, unauthorized access, and a remarkable ability to respond to many needs.

This allows, for instance, financial institution partners to share data with their customers. The organization's financial institution partners can offer a very quick process and simplified ordering of a product without requesting data which are already in the possession of the financial institution.

Fluent Network[57]

Fluent Network is a blockchain-based software platform for cross-border B2B trade aimed at the businesses and financial institutions that play key roles in a value network.

The Fluent Network is a financial operational network utilizing blockchain solutions which greatly facilitate financing value net-

(*continued*)

[54] https://tradle.io/ Accessed March 28, 2019.

[55] Grisoni, A. (2016), If insurers look to blockchain, Bank Organization Also, Mar: 66:67.

[56] https://www.trust-in-motion.com/, Accessed September 11, 2018.

[57] https://www.pymnts.com/news/b2b-payments/2016/blockchain-supply-chain-network-makes-its-debut/. Accessed July 20, 2019.

(continued)

works. Blockchain is a potential means to overhaul an array of aspects in B2B payments, including cross-border and smart documentation. Fluent Network uses the technology for supply chain management, including payments and invoicing.

The network allows businesses and banks to manage and trade invoices and payments in real time at lower costs. Such a network allows the whole to be exponentially greater than the sum of its parts and eliminates the inefficiencies that exist in disconnected systems. Global supply chains have dealt with siloed systems for far too long.

Carrefour Italy[58]

The Carrefour Group, the leading distributor in Europe and second in the world, operates in Italy with more than a thousand outlets.

The evolution of consumer demand and the renewed attention to the origin of the retailers' products impose on the industry a growing commitment to transparency of information. Carrefour Italy has adopted a blockchain solution to track food digitally, with information accessible to its consumers. The first product to be covered was chicken reared in the open air and without antibiotics, for which the entire supply chain will be drawn in, that is, 29 farms, two feed mills, and a slaughterhouse. The second industry supported by blockchain was citrus fruits under the Carrefour brand.

The blockchain solution is a covenant of trust between Carrefour Italy and its end customers. It takes place directly and with real-time information related to the product value network, from origin to the arrival to the point of sale. Consumers can access information through a QR Code present on product packaging through an interface realized by Carrefour Italy. Through this they will know how animals are reared and fed, and how the fruits have been grown.

The blockchain solution ensures the immutability of the recorded data. For Carrefour Italy, the traceability of the value network chain is a further assumption of responsibility toward its customers and an additional step toward complete transparency.

The trial of blockchain in Carrefour has already provided positive results in France, where it was first launched, starting with the d'Auvergne chicken chain and widened to cover the Marmande tomato.

[58] https://www.carrefour.it/Organizzazione/UfficioStampa/blockchain. Accessed March 10, 2019.

TradeLens[59]
Shipping processes are largely manual. They can greatly benefit from digitization and the blockchain can help to solve the problem as these technologies can easily follow the flow of shipments along with the chain and ensure that the immutable record has not been altered at any point.

Mærsk A/S, also known as simply Maersk, is a Danish business conglomerate in the transport, logistics and energy sectors. Maersk has been the largest container ship and supply vessel operator in the world since 1996.

IBM and Maersk announced a blockchain-based shipping tool, TradeLens, in 2019. The organizations have worked to get other major shippers onboard. CMA, CGM, and MSC Mediterranean Shipping Company have joined TradeLens. The platform now encompasses nearly half of the world's cargo container shipments, according to Tech Crunch.

TradeLens, with its commitment to open standards and open governance, is a key platform to help usher in this digital transformation.

4.4.4 *Digitization of the Contracts Lifecycle*

An element of the procurement process that is often neglected is contract lifecycle management (CLM). This is the proactive management and methodology of a contract from its creation, up to its renewal or termination. Implementation of CLM can lead to significant improvements in terms of savings and efficiency. Understanding and automating CLM can also limit the exposure to litigation and improve compliance with legal requirements.

The CLM process can be managed using the support of commercial software, which more and more widely available and powerful. Contract management software is a program or set of programs related to the storage and management of legal agreements with partners such as contracts, leases, and license agreements. An important objective of contract management software is to simplify contract administration and reduce the workload by providing a single, unified view of processes and documentation associated with each contract.

[59] https://techcrunch.com/2019/05/28/ibm-maersk-blockchain-shipping-consortium-expands-to-include-other-major-shipping-companies/?guccounter=1&guce_referrer_us=aHR0cHM6Ly93d3cuZ29vZ2xlLmI0Lw&guce_referrer_cs=6qvJbu5ZEydjveq8TWkvhg. Accessed May 20, 2019.

Smart Contracts

One of the most interesting implementations of blockchain solutions is the so-called intelligent contract (smart contract). This model is still being fully defined from a technical and legal standpoint. This solution aims to make contracts 'live,' with the self-application of some specific contractual provisions for their self-execution in a blockchain solution. In the context of value network management, these programs can be self-executing intelligent contracts that manage the flows of funds based on the application of the automatic contract terms. In this way, it is possible to apply effectively, efficiently, economically, and ethically (that is, correctly) contractual arrangements through a digital application. Potentially, there would be no need for human involvement for the execution of an agreement. Contracts can be created algorithmically to clarify and enforce independently the rules of the transaction. All interactions, related for example to the delivery of products or services, can be automated according to fixed rules and agreements.

The potential savings here could be significant. A smart contract allows a reduction of administration costs, the reconciliation, and the elimination, or at least reduction, of potential errors. It would be possible to reduce the risks and disputes related to contractual relationships. Smart contracts, with the support of a blockchain solution, could provide retrieval modes of information and agreements to handle any claims in a transparent manner, one that is responsive and irrefutable. Contracts and complaints may be registered on a blockchain solution and validated by the network, ensuring that only valid claims are paid (Fig. 4.7).[60]

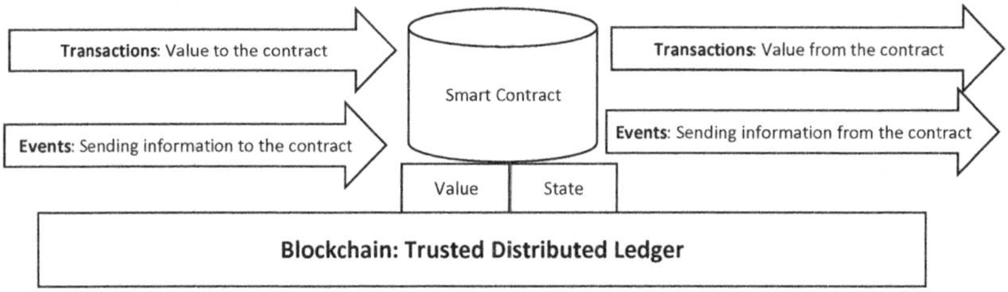

Fig. 4.7 Smart contract. (Adapted by the author from *Blockchain solution and its potential in taxes*, Deloitte, 2017.)

[60] Deloitte (2016), Blockchain: democratized confidence in *Tech Trends 2016*: Innovating in the digital age.

An example supporting these uses is provided by a document describing a clever application of smart contracts within the Department of Defense of the United States of America.[61] A smart contract ceases to be a static document filed on a server computer—the contract 'manages' itself. The contract could become empowered to execute contractual agreements throughout its life.

In computer jargon, 'object' refers to a component with properties and methods. Properties are what an object knows about itself. And methods are what an object knows it can do. A smart contract, as an object, will therefore know things about itself.[62] It will know its economic value. It will have all the essential information, such as who signed the contract, the persons who administer the contract, the payment schedule, the events that trigger these payments, and when it is assumed that the contract is terminated. With further developments in smart contracts, the contract would be able to interact with other objects. This would allow all stakeholders to learn from the same source movements of funds between customers, partners, and financial institutions, and when funds need to be released. If a problem occurs, such as unspent funds with the contractor which is no longer in business, the contract would know how to handle the situation.[63]

Cognitiv+[64]

Cognitiv+ is a legal and compliance analytics and technology startup. Its solutions can emulate structured processes and predefined tasks that normally are done manually. Its solutions collect information from thousands of documents and structure them in a way that brings anomalies to light faster. Traditionally, audits are based on taking samples of populations. With the power of big data analytics, the auditor can choose to analyze all items in certain populations.

(*continued*)

[61] Chesebro, R. (2015). *A contract Which managed itself.* Working Paper. Univ Ft Belvoir, VA.

[62] Morabito, V. (2017). *Business Innovation Through Blockchain: The B3 Perspective.* Springer. Cham, Switzerland: 101-124.

[63] https://www.kinno.fi/en/smartlog, Accessed September 15, 2018.

[64] http://www.cognitivplus.com/company/. Accessed June 20, 2019.

(continued)

AI can read thousands of contracts and extract what the auditors are after, without the need to read them in person. Systems can also analyze entire sets of expenses sheets, read the entire text, categorize expenses, and potentially expose non-authorized claims. Systems can identify indications of fraud, just by reviewing changes in patterns of invoices over time or spotting unusual invoiced items, and quantities based on the previous history. Auditors have some leads to identify mismanagement and save their organizations huge sums.

AI introduces the idea of continuous auditing and proactive analysis. Investigations can be programmed regularly. Auditors will have the opportunity to focus on more advanced analysis. AI can apply risk indicators to large datasets to detect risks that would otherwise remain hidden.

Basic Functions of Smart Contracts

The main functions of CLM in terms of automating contract management in specialized software are (Fig. 4.8):

1. Capture: The first step in CLM consists of centralizing all existing paper contracts into a single central point accessible to all authorized persons. If the organization does not have a clear idea of which contracts it holds, then the organization has no idea of what the organization's potential exposure to risk might be.
2. Tracking: The next step is to acquire the data from the contracts once the organization can account for all of its contracts. The objective is to keep track of all the important data so as not to miss any important data or dates. This applies to both old as well as new contracts.
3. Preparation of new contracts with monitors in place. The focus here is on accelerating the process of creating a new contract. The 'authoring' process involves the creation of contract templates and libraries to allow internal users to connect to them; the objective is for users to create new contracts quickly but in a controlled manner.
4. Drafting: The draft of a contract can emerge in two ways. First, it is appropriate to empower users in the organization by creating self-service draft contracts, based on intelligent templates preap-

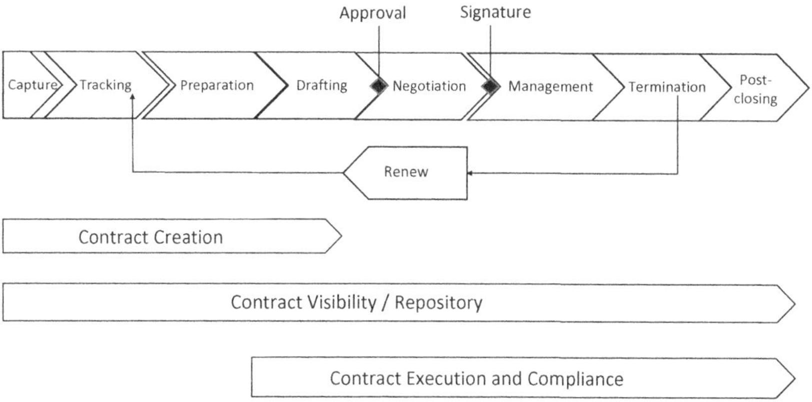

Fig. 4.8 Contract lifecycle management

proved by the legal department. Second, the organization can simplify the work of the legal department when they prepare complex offers, or review and modify trade contracts.

5. Approval: Organizations need an approval workflow to ensure that risky contracts are reviewed and approved by the correct parties. Some risks need to be approved by the legal department, some by the management, others by a certain organization's specific entities such as credit managers, and so forth. Ideally, simple contracts should be preapproved once the clearance on the budget is obtained.
6. Negotiation: The typical role of negotiator needs to include a list of potential problems of control for each type of business; a way to track the differences compared to the original or last draft; and a way to capture and report these differences.
7. Signature: When the contract is final and agreed upon, it must be signed (physically and, increasingly, in digital form) from all subjects and the signed copies must be filed. Someone has to ensure that the final signed version has not been modified in any way after sending copies around for their execution.
8. Analysis: Organizations with many contracts need to analyze these for potential risks, rights, and obligations. Executives, lawyers, and professionals working in risk management need scanned reports and alerts to manage the most common risks. Ad hoc reports should have contingency scenarios. Fast access to the terms and contractual information allow personnel to react quickly to new scenarios and address the risks related, for instance, to the time factor.

9. Management: Capabilities such as monitoring of complex contracts with more applications, additions, amendments, and specifications for the management of changes or evolutions of the initial contracts are very important and help prevent errors, criminal payments, or similar actions. Management also includes alerts about important dates.
10. Termination or automatic renewals: Reminders of upcoming deadlines and closing tasks of contracts or basis for their renewal or extensions are very important to avoid penalties.
11. Post-closing: Support for any disputes, providing the history of the contract and all its variations and respect over time.

An interesting use of blockchain in procurement 4.0 is in connection with the vendor-managed inventory (VMI). The VMI is a widely used collaborative inventory management policy in which partners manage the inventory of manufacturers or retailers.[65] They take responsibility for making decisions related to the timing and extent of inventory replenishment. There are several critical success factors for a successful VMI strategy implementation, such as information sharing, trust, systems integration, and long-term collaboration. However, in current value networks, complex processes, high number of participants, and complex procurement 4.0 channels make successful adoption of VMI strategies difficult. It is interesting to consider a new interaction framework based on smart contracts and blockchain for governing the relationship between the partners. Tests performed using a local private blockchain show the applicability of this architecture along with the significant benefits for each participant.[66]

CLM Software Applications

Today, many software partners offer CLM systems as presented in this section. Typical functions are:

[65] Ryu, C. S. (2016). Review of vendor managed inventory: Investigation on how it improves supply chain performance, *Journal of Distribution Science*, 14(9), 47–64.

[66] Dasaklis, T., & Casino, F. (2019). Improving Vendor-managed Inventory Strategy Based on Internet of Things (IoT) Applications and Blockchain Technology. In *2019 IEEE International Conference on Blockchain and Cryptocurrency* (ICBC), 50–55. IEEE.

- creation of the contract, based on existing contracts or third-party agreements
- support contracting
- contracts repository
- contract negotiation
- support of several types of contracts
- approval of contracts
- complete contract monitoring
- optimization of contracts
- management of contractual processes
- alerts about relevant dates
- integration with other documents
- termination of contracts or their renewal and extension.

Benefits of CLM Solutions

Implementation of the CLM can lead to significant improvements in terms of savings and efficiency. The CLM software category is expected to grow on average between 15% and 20%.[67] The reasons for this are several. These solutions do more than simply creating a legal archive. They optimize and automate contracts, and they allow the organization to follow and support the management of all the stages of the life cycle of the contract.

Some specific benefits support a business case for their evaluation, in which companies should[68]:

- rationalize the authoring process, using libraries of legal clauses and improved collaboration;
- create time for contract production to be substantially reduced compared to the old ways of operation—there are substantial savings in time and costs in the adoption of the CLM;
- automate the tracking of compliance—integration with transactional systems ensures the issuance of orders with correct economic clauses, and it enables organizations to demand what was agreed as discounts or benefits associated with volume;
- reduce total administrative costs—this enables the resources of procurement and legal entities to focus on more important and complex tasks that add more value to the organization.

[67] http://www.digitaljournal.com/pr/3814597. Accessed March 30, 2019.

[68] https://www.bearingpoint.com/files/0553_WP_EN_Vertragsmgt_final_web.pdf. Accessed March 30, 2019.

In this perspective, there will be several self-adaptive contracts, for example in the logistics sector.[69] They will act without significant human intervention and allow an organization to implement more flexible and faster systems. They will require greater decentralization, an agile approach, and autonomous interaction.

4.4.5 3D Printing

The 3D printing process builds a three-dimensional object from a computer-aided design model, usually by successively adding material layer by layer, which is why it is also called additive manufacturing.[70] 3D printing or additive manufacturing is a powerful tool to reduce complexity in the value network, from the consolidation of components into a single product: by replacing previously assembled parts with a single component. Thus, the manufacturing process can be simplified significantly.[71] The 3D printing market is forecast to be worth $30.18 billion by 2022.[72]

Trends driving the impact of this solution are:

- Component consolidation lowers not only the number of components in the manufacturing flow,[73] it can also permanently reduce the number of stock-keeping units (SKUs) in the system.
- 3D printing replaces many of the assembly steps required during the production phase in the supply chain with a single task.[74] Process complexity is reduced, making the flow of the material more transparent and easier to control.[75]

[69] Plattform Industries 4.0: Aspects of the Research Roadmap for Application Scenarios, https://www.plattform-i40.de/I40/Redaktion/EN/Downloads/Publikation/aspects-of-theresearch-roadmap.pdf?__blob=publicationFile&v=10. Accessed March 9, 2019.

[70] Dawes, J., Bowerman, R., & Trepleton, R. (2015). Introduction to the additive manufacturing powder metallurgy supply chain. *Johnson Matthey Technology Review*, 59(3), 243–256.

[71] Gao, W., Zhang, Y., Ramanujan, D., Ramani, K., Chen, Y., Williams, C. B., & Zavattieri, P. D. (2015). The status, challenges, and future of additive manufacturing in engineering. *Computer-Aided Design*, *69*, 65–89.

[72] www.marketsandmarkets.com. Accessed June 20, 2019.

[73] https://timreview.ca/sites/default/files/Issue_PDF/TIMReview_November2015.pdf#page=20. Accessed June 20, 2019.

[74] Janssen, G. R., Blankers, I. J., Moolenburgh, E. A., & Posthumus, A. L. (2014). *The Impact of 3-D Printing on Supply Chain Management*. The Hague, Netherlands.

[75] Janssen, R., Blankers, I., Moolenburgh, E., & Posthumus, B. (2014). TNO: The impact of 3-D printing on supply chain management. *The Hague, Netherlands: TNO*.

- Rationalization of inventory and logistics 3D printing allows for production to happen on demand and at the point of consumption. The need to transport physical goods can be replaced by placing manufacturing close to the customer. This leads to the rationalization of warehousing and logistics.[76] Furthermore, the movement of physical goods across long distances can be substituted by sending electronic files to printers.[77] Digital inventory in the form of 3D model files for the entire product portfolio could replace physical inventory for technically complex products, further reducing the number of SKUs and the total number of stored parts.
- The combined effects of 3D printing on several sections of the value network could potentially bring a decrease in demand for the global transportation of physical goods and inventory activities.
- 3D printing has an impact on the volume of the inventory and on the inventory mix. This includes a shift to inventory in the form of raw materials (for instance, powders or filament coils) rather than semi-finished parts and components. The handling of these raw materials is cheaper, safer, and requires fewer skilled workers than the handling of semi-finished goods and final product modules to handle the materials. Distribution logistics will become more reliable.

3D printing is a powerful tool also to reduce complexity in the value network, from the consolidation of components into a single product: by replacing previously assembled parts with a single component, the manufacturing process can be simplified significantly.[78] Consequently, there is great potential for savings on internal cost and time through reduced value network complexity.

[76] Manners-Bell, J., & Lyon, K. (2012). The implications of 3D printing for the global logistics industry. *Transport Intelligence*, 1–5.

[77] Nyman, H. J., & Sarlin, P. (2014). From bits to atoms: 3D printing in the context of supply chain strategies. In *2014 47th Hawaii International Conference on System Sciences*. IEEE, 4190–4199.

[78] Gao, W., Zhang, Y., Ramanujan, D., Ramani, K., Chen, Y., Williams, C. B., Wang, C. C. L., Shin, Y. C., Zhang, S., & Zavattieri, P. D. (2015). The Status, Challenges, and Future of Additive Manufacturing in Engineering. *Computer-Aided Design*, 69: 65–89.

Additive Manufacturing
A very interesting platform under development is that 3D printing can give rise to a completely different type of operation, known as additive manufacturing or discrete manufacturing systems, when applied to manufacture, adjustable manufacturing systems, and flexible manufacturing systems.

The additive manufacturing (or 3D printing) is a production method that, using 3D printing and other solutions, allows the creation of objects (components parts, semi-finished or finished products) by generating and adding successive layers of material. This mode is very different from traditional processing techniques which proceed by subtraction from a raw component (turning, milling, and so forth).

Benefits of 3D Printing
3D printing allows for on-demand production and potentially at the point of consumption; therefore, the need to transport physical goods can be replaced by placing manufacturing closer to the customer. This leads to rationalization of warehousing and logistics.[79] The movement of physical goods across the globe can be substituted by sending electronic files to printers.[80] Digital inventory in the form of 3D model files for the entire product portfolio could replace physical inventory for technically complex products, further reducing the number of SKUs and the total number of stored parts.[81]

3D printing has the power to impact well beyond basic ICT technologies, allowing for custom manufacturing. This technology can reduce the use of materials in the production and change the paradigm of production, resulting in a highly distributed production model. Such technology also has benefits for the environment in terms of reduced use of materials, energy, and transport costs. It also enables more effective recycling of materials for regeneration.

[79] Manners-Bell, J., & Lyon, K. (2012). The Implications of 3D Printing for the Global Logistics Industry. *Transport Intelligence*. Bath, UK.

[80] Nyman, H. J., & Sarlin, P. (2014). From Bits to Atoms: 3D Printing in the Context of Supply Chain Strategies. In *47th Hawaii International Conference on System Sciences*, Waikoloa, HI, January 6–9, 4190–4199.

[81] https://timreview.ca/sites/default/files/Issue_PDF/TIMReview_November2015.pdf#page=20. Accessed June 20, 2019.

DHL[82]

DHL is a logistics company that offers international transport of goods and logistics contracts. DHL has identified 3D printing as a major disruptive trend for its impact on the logistics industry in the medium term.[83] DHL identifies the very positive potential of 3D printing capabilities for simplifying the production of products and spare parts of complex customizable products.[84] Through these means, DHL intends to obtain benefits such as greater customization, less waste, and more localized production and deliveries. It involves using supporting technology and advanced distribution models.

DHL describes four possible implementations of 3D printing in the field of logistics:

- The first use is based on a 'virtual warehouse.' Spare parts are not physically stored here, but rather their digital model, which can then be produced at the customer's request. The result is a low inventory cost and no loss of obsolete or expired stock.
- A second option is to use distribution centers and stores as small factories for the production of tailor-made products.
- Logistics organizations can collaborate with manufacturers to offer the 'postponed services.' Here the final assembly of the product is performed in the distribution centers close to the customer.
- The last option of using 3D printing by DHL is the so-called runway end services where the 3D printing warehouses could locate itself at major airports. In this manner, it can provide quick response times and speed to market for timely shipment.[85]

[82] Horenberg, D. (2017). Applications Within Logistics 4.0: A research conducted on the visions of 3PL service providers, Bachelor's thesis, University of Twente, Enschede, Netherlands.

[83] Chung, G., Niezgoda, D., & Beissmann, R. (2016). 3D Printing and the Future of Supply Chains. DHL Trend Research: 1–17.

Mohr, S., and O. Khan. (2015). 3D Printing and Supply Chains of the Future. *HICL*, 147.

[84] Chung, G., Niezgoda, D., & Beissmann, R. (2016). 3D Printing and the Future of Supply Chains. DHL Trend Research: 1–17.

[85] Chung, G., Niezgoda, D., & Beissmann, R. (2016). 3D Printing and the Future of Supply Chains. *DHL Trend Research*: 1–17.

Panalpina[86]

The Panalpina Group is one of the world's leading providers of supply chain solutions. The company combines its core products to deliver globally integrated, tailor-made end-to-end solutions for 12 core industries.[87]

Panalpina places the possibilities of 3D printing in the last stages of the value network. It focuses on the construction of logistics hub manufacturing services (LMS).[88] It is a perfect complement to Panalpina logistics processes; 3D printing is a powerful solution that allows customization of products as late as possible in the procurement chain.[89] Panalpina emphasizes the benefits of 3D printing at local production sites capable of limiting the transport to the last mile.[90] Panalpina began research with Cardiff University to explore the possibilities of 3D printing in terms of logistics.[91] The research seeks to identify which products are most interesting to consider for 3D printing, which processes can be transformed, and what effects these may have on the transformation of procurement processes.[92]

(*continued*)

[86] Horenberg, D. (2017) Applications Within Logistics 4.0: A research conducted on the visions of 3PL service providers, *Bachelor's thesis*, University of Twente, Enschede, Netherlands.

[87] https://www.panalpina.com/www/global/en/home.html. Accessed August 5, 2019.

[88] Todd, S. (2017). Panalpina Sees Future of LMS as Contract Logistics – Lloyd's Loading List. http://www.lloydsloadinglist.com/freightdirectory/adviceandinsight/Panalpina-sees-LMS-asfuture-of-contractlogistics/69375.htm?mc_cid=a8d195357c&mc_eid=ce7b0e5092. Accessed March 10, 2019.

[89] Panalpina World Transport. (2017). 3D Printing (Additive Manufacturing). Panalpinaon 6 Continents. http://www.panalpina.com/www/global/en/home/pr oducts_solutions / logistics / 3d_printing.html. Panalpina World Transport (2017). 3D Printing. "http://www.panalpina.com/content/www/global/en/home/products_solutions/logistics/3d_printing/_jcr_content/contentParSys/download/downloadList/flyer.spooler.download/3D%20printing%20onepager.pdf. Accessed March 10, 2019.

[90] The Business Debate. (2017). Panalpina – Supply Chain of the Future. Youtube. https://www.youtube.com/watch?v=E71M9lga3Vg. Accessed March 10, 2019.

[91] Cinar, D., Gakis, K., & Pardalos, P. M. (Eds.). (2018). *Sustainable Logistics and Transportation: Optimization Models and Algorithms*, 129. Springer, Cham, Switzerland.

[92] DVV Media Group GmbH. (2017). "Panalpina Launches Research into 3D Printing and the Supply Chain." Air Cargo News. http://www.aircargonews.net/events/air-cargo-newsevents/cay-2014/news/panalpina-launches-researchinto-3d-printing-and-the-supply-chain.html. Accessed March 10, 2019.

(continued)
Panalpina's vision is to transform its warehouses into hubs where it customizes the client's products and ships them very quickly.[93] According to Panalpina, these services will lead to lower value network lead times and inventory levels, guaranteeing highly customized products at a comparatively favorable cost and improved service levels.

4.4.6 Automatic Guided Vehicles

Automatic guided vehicles (AGV) have been in use for several decades in different industries, production processes, and warehouse facilities.[94] AGVs are driverless vehicles based on sensors and video detection technologies, AI, and other automated solutions. AGVs may be used in logistic processes as: tractors for towing trailers, vehicles for unit loads, pallet trolleys, trolleys with additional forks, light load vehicles, assembly line vehicles, special vehicles, and so forth. These vehicles are used for traditionally demanding tasks. They can enable automatic handling of goods, materials, and equipment. The application of AGVs in logistic processes reduce costs and labor, increase reliability, productivity, safety, and quality of work, while reducing risks of damage due to human error and the like.[95]

4.4.7 Drones

Unmanned aerial vehicles, or drones, are not expected to replace the traditional modes of transport. They can be used for safe operation in remote and potentially dangerous locations.[96] Commercial use of drones has been tested in recent years in some large organizations (Amazon, Google, DHL).[97] One

[93] http://www.trasportoeuropa.it/index.php?searchword=panalpina&ordering=&searchphrase=all&Itemid=71&option=com_search. Accessed March 16, 2019.

[94] Radivojević, G., & Milosavljević, L. (2019). The Concept of Logistics 4.0. *4th Logistics International Conference*, May 23–25. Belgrade, Serbia

[95] Kückelhaus, M., & Chung, G. (2018). Logistics Trend Radar, DHL *Customer Solutions & Innovation*, Germany. www.dhl.com, Accessed July 14, 2019.

[96] Radivojević, G., & Milosavljević, L. (2019). The Concept of Logistics 4.0. *4th Logistics International Conference*, May 23–25. Belgrade, Serbia

[97] Bamburry, D. (2015). Drones: Designed for product delivery. *Design Management Review*, *26*(1), 40–48.

of the expected applications of drones is in intralogistics processes, monitoring of logistics activities, and delivery of goods to end-users. Drones simplify intralogistics operations in terms of transportation between production units, urgent delivery of spare parts, or for the transfer of goods from warehouses to retail sections. Drones can be used for monitoring facilities, infrastructures, and equipment, stock control, and checking incoming vehicles on receiving gates. Drones for delivery of goods to end-users may transform existing methods of delivery in large cities and especially in rural areas.[98]

4.5 Cognition: Cognitive Procurement

The lean approach originated in Japan around 1946. At that time, use of computers very limited. The expression 'lean' was introduced in the United States by groups associated with the organization and management of HR.[99] At the same time, the computer was born and developed independently. Only in the 1990s did the two solutions started to be analyzed concurrently.[100] Computer applications at the time were rather rigid and therefore not suited to supporting the concepts of slenderness and agility associated with lean approaches.

Over time, computer applications have become more flexible. In recent decades, the concept of computer applications, open and integrated with other solutions, have become popular. Solutions based on the blockchain are an example of how ICT has become a powerful tool of integration inter-organizationally.

The real development of agility can greatly benefit from AI and, in particular, from cognitive solutions.[101] Cognitive technologies are products that can capture data and continually learn in the same way that humans would but using data at a very large scale.[102] These technologies, with their

[98] Kückelhaus, M., Chung, G. (2018). Logistics Trend Radar, DHL *Customer Solutions & Innovation*, Germany. www.dhl.com, Accessed July 14, 2019.

[99] Nicoletti, B., (2013), *Lean Procurement*, FrancoAngeli, Milan, Italy.

[100] Nicoletti, B., (2012), *Lean and Digitize: An Integrated Approach to Process Improvement.* Gower Publishing, London, UK.

[101] Zheng, N. N., Liu, Z. Y., Ren, P. J., Ma, Y. Q., Chen, S. T., Yu, S. Y., & Wang, F. Y. (2017). Hybrid-augmented intelligence: collaboration and cognition. *Frontiers of Information Technology & Electronic Engineering*, 18(2), 153–179.

[102] Fekete, N. (2016). What Artificial Intelligence Can Do for You?. *Procurement Leaders*, June 20.

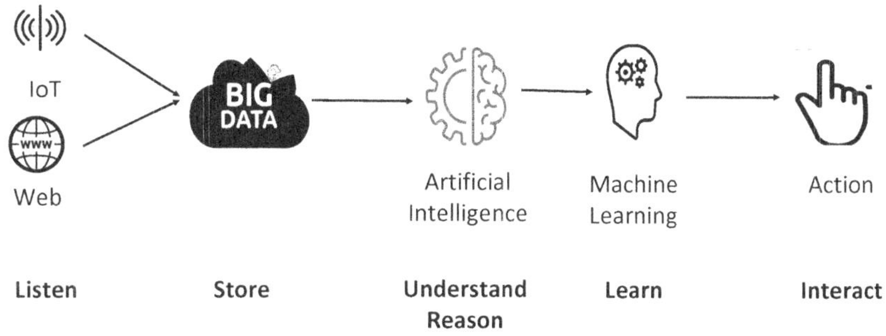

Fig. 4.9 Cognitive procurement

acquired data (including unstructured data), can understand meanings, reasons, context, and possible impacts. Cognitive technologies can generate hypotheses, arguments, and recommendations. Moreover, these technologies can perform tasks that only humans could before. In so doing, they allow persons to focus on the most innovative and critical activities. These solutions are particularly interesting in procurement 4.0, so-called cognitive procurement.[103] This is another step in the digital transformation of procurement (Fig. 4.9).

The platforms presented in this section represent the next generation of procurement applications. They provide intelligent automation, predictive analytics, and proactive interventions. The AI of advanced and machine learning is integrated into the different components of IoT architecture as part of the complex cognitive procurement platforms.[104] These components are composed of many solutions and techniques (for instance, deep learning, neural networks, and natural language processing. These tools move beyond traditional rule-based algorithms to create autonomous systems that understand, learn, predict, adapt and operate autonomously. They give rise to an intelligent implementation, including physical devices (for instance robots, autonomous vehicles, industrial electronics, and so on) as well as application and services (such as virtual personal assistants,

[103] Schoenherr, T. (2018). System Capability and Technology. *CPSM Study Guide*, 3rd.
[104] Vermesan, O., & Bacquet, J. (Eds.). (2017). *Cognitive Hyperconnected Digital Transformation: Internet of Things Intelligence Evolution*. River Publishers, Gistrup, Denmark.

smart advisors, and so on). In this context, the platforms deliver a new class of intelligent application and objects. They provide embedded intelligence for a wide range of processes, software platforms, and service solutions in support of procurement 4.0.

Some of the initial applications of cognitive procurement are:

- to replace humans in complex repetitive tasks of procurement;
- to provide integrated support in the acquisition of new partners;
- automatically provide prices, create new business models, and evaluate partners;
- manage emergencies, due to difficulties in procurement from a specific partner or territory;
- integrate with robots for the implementation of automated and integrated solutions to support the procurement processes in so-called robot process automation (RPA).[105]

The possibility to access cognitive procurement from mobile phones and tablets can further benefit its use, through[106]:

- allowing it to navigate multiple channels and procurement systems;
- recommending a corresponding product in the best possible way to the demands by adding transparency to the buyer work;
- recommending actions on sourcing from preferential partner catalogs based on requests from users;
- allowing interacting in natural language for improved user experience.

The benefits associated with cognitive procurement are several:

- increasing workforce productivity and reducing the need for education and training;
- logging on to a richer and larger set of data;
- allowing the organization to discover hidden information;

[105] Madakam, S., Holmukhe, R. M., & Jaiswal, D. K. (2019). The Future Digital Work Force: Robotic Process Automation (RPA). *JISTEM-Journal of Information Systems and Technology Management*, 16.

[106] Khuan, L. S., & Swee, M. F. S. H. (2018). Technologies for Procurement: Current Trends and Emerging Trends. *Emerging Technologies f or Supply Chain Management*, 45.

- automating repetitive tasks;
- improving approvals for purchase orders and enhancing their accuracy;
- increasing efficiency in providing customized information suited to particular circumstances.

IBM[107]

IBM has created a "map of the cognitive path" of procurement processes to analyze where AI solutions can help organizations. Procurement has access to huge amounts of data about partners and their products, such as purchase orders, bills, and login information on the internet. Some of the AI solutions used by IBM teams are:

- A system to provide information on the partners, called Supplier IQ. Through an app for smartphones, buyers can find specific information about partners, including IBM's spending with them, what they buy from IBM, how they compare with the competition and the market sentiment toward the organization based on social networks.
- A system to support management of contracts called Watson Contract Analyzer. Using a database of digital contracts and scanned images of contracts, Watson can read hundreds of millions of pages per second and find out if any of them contain specific clauses.
- An AI solution to assess contracts in terms of procurement risks based on specific metrics. These metrics can be computed by selecting appropriately the data. Data are then visually displayed on a dashboard which highlights the partners for which it is useful to improve and strengthen the contractual terms.
- A system to prepare General Data Protection Regulations (GDPR) in support of personal data privacy.[108] This tool is particularly important to manage the increasing number of regulations, controls, and requirements from regulators and governments.

[107] Schoenherr, T. (2019). Outlook to an Exciting Future. In *the Evolution of Electronic Procurement*, 117–125. Palgrave Pivot, Cham, Switzerland.

[108] Tankard, C. (2016). What the GDPR means for businesses. *Network Security*, 2016(6), 5–8. Calder, A. (2018). *EU GDPR: a pocket guide*. IT Governance Publishing Ltd., Ely, UK.

UCB[109]

Global biopharmaceutical company UCB has used AI and robotics to develop an assistant for cognitive procurement. The system employs natural language processing to answer questions about procurement processes. It provides automated responses in interacting with human professionals. As AI capabilities are currently limited, UCB intends to scale the system through an agile development process that allows the project team to quickly modify the prototype. Governance can be a big problem in developing a machine learning robot. There are limitations that need to be mediated during the prototyping phase to prevent the learning of negative behaviors. UCB has held workshops for members of the procurement team to define the graphical user interface appearance of a best-in-class system and determine the processes and contact points to be automated. UCB assembled a cross-functional team that included professionals from ICT, finance, and procurement to oversee the development of this solution. The prototype has been used to determine how the parties use the facility. The solution was built internally, with its main integration into the global system of the company's ERP.

4.5.1 Analytics and Big Data

Integrated analytics are related to the ability to analyze large amounts of data by applying multidimensional layers and statistical analysis criteria. These analyses allow an organization to move from elementary data to information, and from information to knowledge through aggregation processes, statistical inference,[110] and multivariate analysis.[111] The potential applications of integrated analytics support functionality of different types[112]:

[109] Busa-Fekete, R., & Kégl, B. (2009, June). Accelerating AdaBoost using UCB. In *Proceedings of the 2009 International Conference on KDD-Cup 2009-Volume 7*, 111–122. JMLR.org.

[110] Casella, G., & Berger, R. L. (2002). *Statistical inference* (Vol. 2). Duxbury, Pacific Grove, CA.

[111] Var, I. (1998). Multivariate data analysis. *Vectors*, 8(2), 125–136.

[112] https://www.digital4.biz/procurement/ufficio-acquisti-digitale-cose-quali-benefici-del-procurement-4-0/. Accessed March 9, 2019.

- descriptive analytics is used, for example, to contextualize the behavior of the partners, grouping them into homogeneous classes;
- predictive analytics is used to predict the future behavior of the partners based on their past behavior and the specific context as shown by the descriptive algorithms;
- prescriptive analytics, or decision-making, allow the relation of all elements of a decision to try to predict the outcome and thus support managers in decision-making.

Analytics are models for data analysis. They are especially valuable in areas rich in data. This situation is increasingly common due to the use of pervasive information systems also for procurement. This analysis can be the production of statistics, reports, or executive dashboards. These outputs allow organization to gain better management visibility. For example, in the case of sourcing, analytics tools allow analysis of costs in a very accurate manner (so-called spending review or spending Visibility).[113]

These analytics may require the processing of huge masses of data (big data).[114] These big data can serve as a basis for the development of strategy formulations and risk assessments of different partners for several categories.[115] The gathered, cleaned, and stored data is defined as master data.[116] Reliable master data is crucial for several applications such as the spending and category analysis or supplier management.[117] Spending visibility is the process of the accumulation, cleaning, and analysis of corporate spending to lower costs and increase operational performance.[118] An organization is

[113] Angeles, R., & Nath, R. (2007). Business-to-business e-procurement: success factors and challenges to implementation. *Supply Chain Management: An International Journal*, 12(2), 104–115.

[114] McAfee, A., Brynjolfsson, E., Davenport, T. H., Patil, D. J., & Barton, D. (2012). Big data: the management revolution. *Harvard business review*, 90(10), 60–68.

[115] Capgemini. (2018). Digital Procurement Research 2018: Uncovering the solutions that bring you forward. https://www.capgemini.com/nl-nl/wp-content/uploads/sites/7/2018/10/CapgeminiDigital-Procurement-Research-2018_web-version1.pdf. Accessed July 24, 2019.

[116] Berson, A., & Dubov, L. (2007). Master data management and customer data integration for a global enterprise: McGraw-Hill, Inc. Accessed July 24, 2019.

[117] Capgemini. (2018). Digital Procurement Research 2018: Uncovering the solutions that bring you forward. https://www.capgemini.com/nl-nl/wp-content/uploads/sites/7/2018/10/CapgeminiDigital-Procurement-Research-2018_web-version1.pdf. Accessed July 24, 2019.

[118] Trkman, P., & McCormack, K. (2010). Estimating the benefits and risks of implementing e-procurement. *IEEE Transactions on Engineering Management*, 57(2), 338–349

not able to maximize its buying leverage, arrive at intelligent sourcing decisions, ensure compliance with partner contracts, raise partner performance, optimize budgeting and planning, and anticipate the impact of changes in cost, inflation, and other factors without appropriate spending visibility.[119] Low spending visibility is accountable for a significant percentage of maverick buying.[120] Appropriate spending visibility is mandatory to achieve best-in-class sourcing decisions and total value management.[121] Several vendors such as Ivalua or Coupa provide algorithm-based solutions that support the automated classification of business spending.[122]

Another important function provided by big players, such as SAP Ariba or Smart by GEP, is category analysis. This refers to the in-depth examination of attributes and drivers of specified categories.[123] The goal is to enhance stakeholders' understanding of supply market characteristics, demand profiles, and key category drivers.[124]

In this area, an Italian survey highlights a situation in progress.[125] In terms of spending visibility, over 85% of merchandise categories are covered by analytics in large organizations. This percentage drops to 15% for micro, small, and medium-sized organizations.

[119] Angeles, R., & Nath, R. (2007). Business-to-business e-procurement: success factors and challenges to implementation. *Supply Chain Management: An International Journal*, 12(2), 104–115.

[120] Capgemini. (2018). Digital Procurement Research 2018: Uncovering the solutions that bring you forward. https://www.capgemini.com/nl-nl/wp-content/uploads/sites/7/2018/10/CapgeminiDigital-Procurement-Research-2018_web-version1.pdf. Accessed July 24, 2019.

[121] Lamoureux, M. G. (2018). The Strategic Sourcing Lifecycle: A Brief Introduction. https://www.coupa.com/products/strategicsourcing/sourcing-optimization/. Accessed July 24, 2019.

[122] Coupa. (2019). Coupa Spend Analysis. https://www.coupa.com/products/spend-analysis/. Accessed July 24, 2019.

Ivalua. (2019). Strategy & Analytics. https://www.ivalua.com/solutions/process/strategic-sourcing/strategy-analytics/. Accessed July 24, 2019.

[123] SAP Ariba. (2018). SAP Ariba Spend Analysis- Data Sheet. https://www.ariba.com/-/media/aribacom/assets/pdf-assets/sap-ariba-spend analysis-datasheet.pdf?la=en-us&hash=143116B9886776FA3E62B02E251963B 1D92D295F. Accessed July 24, 2019.

Smart by GEP. (2019). Spend Management Software https://www.smartbygep.com/procurement-software/spend-management. Accessed July 24, 2019.

[124] Zycus. (2019). Category Management. https://www.zycus.com/blog/glossary/category-management/. Accessed July 24, 2019.

[125] https://www.logisticaefficiente.it/procout/supplychain/approvvigionamenti/maturita-procurement-italia-europa-risultati-parte-1.html. Accessed March 10, 2019.

4.5.2 Artificial Intelligence

Also known as augmented intelligence, AI is the ability of computers to solve complex problems and react like human beings and show intelligent behaviors.[126] AI can also be defined as: scientific study of the computational principles behind thought and intelligent behavior.[127] With AI, computers can learn, plan, recognize, and solve problems by themselves. AI solutions have three characteristics[128]:

- It operates intentionality. AI algorithms can use real-time data to support sophisticated analysis and decision-making, using sensors and digital data to combine information from a variety of different sources and analyze them instantly.
- AI is undertaken in conjunction with machine learning and data analytics. It thus has actual 'intelligence.' Machine learning collects data and looks for underlying trends. When it spots something relevant for a practical problem, software designers can take that knowledge and use it to automatically analyze specific issues.
- AI can operate in an adaptable way, adapting as it makes new decisions. The AI system can collect a large amount of data and use their advanced algorithms to learn and achieve 'experience' from other similar machines, then predict the upcoming situations.

The strengths of AI are especially connected with machine learning. Machine learning is concerned with enabling computer programs automatically to improve their performance at some tasks through experience.[129] The field is closely related to pattern recognition and statistical

[126] Burgess, A. (2017). *The Executive Guide to Artificial Intelligence: How to identify and implement applications for AI in your organization.* Springer, Cham, Switzerland.

[127] Skilton, M., & Hovsepian, F. (2017). *The 4th Industrial Revolution: Responding to the Impact of Artificial Intelligence on Business.* Springer, Cham, Switzerland.

[128] West, J. R. A. D. M., & Allen, J. (2018). How artificial intelligence is transforming the world. https://www.brookings.edu/research/how-artificial-intelligence-is-transforming-the-world/. Accessed June 2, 2019.

[129] Pham, D. T., & Afify, A. A. (2005). Machine-learning techniques and their applications in manufacturing. Proceedings of the Institution of Mechanical Engineers, Part B: *Journal of Engineering Manufacture*, 219(5), 395–412.

inference. Several pieces of research in machine learning have focused on classification—the task of developing a model, from a set of previously classified examples, that can correctly categorize new examples from the same population. This classification has a wide range of applications, including manufacturing, telecommunications, marketing, and scientific analysis. Many procurement problems fall under the category of classification, where procurement professionals need to assign a class label to an object or a situation based on the specific values of a set of parameters.

Machine-learning solutions include inductive learning algorithms such as decision-tree induction and rule induction, instance-based learning, neural networks, genetic algorithms, and Bayesian-learning algorithms. Among the several machine learning solutions developed for classification, inductive learning from instances is the most commonly used in real-world application domains. Inductive learning techniques are fast in comparison to other techniques. Another benefit is that inductive learning techniques are simple. They allow the generation of models that are easy to understand. Finally, inductive learning classifiers obtain similar and sometimes better accuracies compared with other classification techniques.

The market for AI is huge. The market size for machine learning in 2016 was $61.34 million. It is expected to grow to $3.75 billion by 2020 with a CAGR of 43.7% from 2016's $702,021.[130]

Technologies such as AI, AR, and VR are opening up new scenarios. They will change the way the world works. It is possible to envision the emergence of mixed work teams, composed of humans and smart technologies. This is the opinion of 43% of Italian manufacturing SMEs, which have already adopted or intend to introduce innovative technologies/processes including ICT security, cloud computing, collaborative robotics, and the IoT.[131]

[130] www.marketsandmarkets.com. Accessed June 10, 2019.

[131] https://www.mecspe.com/en/comunicati-stampa-en/osservatorio-mecspe-focus-nazionale/. Accessed August 5, 2019.

Staples[132]

Staples, the American retailer specialized in office products, has developed a range of different modes for customers to buy its products as easily as possible. On its website, there is a button that can allow the site understanding voice commands. The mobile app is also able to identify products from pictures. These simplifications of the buying process have direct and positive impacts for the retailer. They can also be useful in the procurement office to delegate internal users to buy directly from the organization's portal and in this way avoid maverick sourcing.

4.5.3 *Robotic Process Automation*

RPA is the use of robots (based on software or physical) for the automation of simple and repetitive tasks.[133] Organizations can thus free up the time of the expert procurement professionals.

The use of software robots is particularly innovative.[134] They are based on agents or programs with an appropriate level of AI and are capable of replicating some human actions. As an example, software robots can carry out data entry tasks, interacting with the interface of a management system as a human operator would. It is possible to train an RPA in the process, through the realization of process flow charts using graphical user interfaces. Over time, the software robot should be able to learn and improve its performance through machine learning techniques.[135]

[132] Burgess, A. (2017). The Executive *Guide to Artificial Intelligence: How to identify and implement applications for AI in your organization*. Springer, Cham, Switzerland.

[133] Anagnoste, S. (2017, July). Robotic Automation Process-The next major revolution in terms of back office operations improvement. *Proceedings of the International Conference on Business Excellence*. 11(1), 676–686. De Gruyter Open, Berlin, Germany

[134] Perona, M. (2019). Procurement 4.0, the check list for Purchasing Digital, https://www.digital4.biz/procurement/ufficio-acquisti-digitale-cose-quali-benefici-del-procurement-4-0/. Accessed March 9, 2019.

[135] Mohri, M., Rostamizadeh, A., & Talwalkar, A. (2018). *Foundations of machine learning*. MIT Press, Cambridge, MA.

Alpha

Alfa is a multinational food business operating in the global market, with annual sales of €2 billion.[136] In moving to procurement 4.0, it used the following solutions:

- RPA is the automation of simple and repetitive tasks, which need no longer be carried out by the procurement team. This solution can verify if the order has been approved by the managers and all administrative steps required have been completed.
- Integrated analytics are used to switch from the provision of elementary information and from information based on the knowledge of analysis of aggregated processes to statistical inference and multivariate analysis
- Cognitive procurement processes suggest the best course of action in response to the context. Cognitive computing, for example, allows the interpretation and response to requests of the partners made via email, chat, or voice.

These technologies can bring benefits, such as the possibility of reducing the number of employees of the procurement office of 41 FTEs out of 112, corresponding to 37% of the total.

The benefits can be analyzed based on the organization's point of view and that of the processes. Organizational analysis can be divided into back-office, middle-office, and front-office benefits:

- Savings in the back office are up to 89%. This area is mainly formed by repetitive and standardized activities. They can be done using RPA.
- The front office needs more creativity and interpersonal skills. It has savings equal to 7% of the FTEs.
- The middle office can achieve savings of 75%.

(*continued*)

[136] Perona, M. (2019). Procurement 4.0, the check list for Purchasing Digital, https://www.digital4.biz/procurement/ufficio-acquisti-digitale-cose-quali-benefici-del-procurement-4-0/. Accessed March 9, 2019. The name is fictitious due to a non-disclosure request.

(continued)

Improvement in the processes can be divided into strategic, tactical, and transactional results.

- At the transactional level, the application is so significant as to generate savings of 12.2 FTE, equal to 90% of the current job content. This level includes all routine and repetitive activities. They are well suited to the adoption of analytics tools.
- At a tactical level, the savings are 15.7 FTE. They correspond to 36% of the total employment at this level.
- At a strategic level, there are savings of 13.1 FTE, equal to 24% of the total workforce at this level.

4.6 Communication

4.6.1 Cloud Computing

Cloud computing is a set of technologies that allow the processing and/or storage of data through the use of distributed hardware/software virtualized in the network (normally the internet). Customers pay for the services on a pay-per-use basis, as with the provision of other utilities, such as electricity or gas. The service is fully managed by the provider (be it private, community, public, or hybrid) and the customer only requires an access device and an internet connection. Users can access the cloud anyplace, anytime, and on any device.

The NIST, the American standardization body, defines cloud computing as a model to enable, via the network, widespread easy access, upon request, to a shared set of configurable computing resources (for instance networks, servers, memory, applications, services, and cybersecurity) that can be acquired and promptly released with minimal management effort or interaction with the service partners. The NIST cloud computing model is composed of five essential characteristics, three service modes, and four deployment models.[137]

[137] Nicoletti, B., (2013), *Cloud Computing and Financial Services*, Palgrave Macmillan, London, UK (also translated in Chinese).

There are many types of cloud computing services. The most popular are:

- The Software as a Service (SaaS) model, where the full software suite (including the applications and their updates) is provided by a service provider. The customer cannot change or modify the software but only configure it in a self-service mode. For this service, the user pays a fee based on usage or a monthly charge (which can move upwards or downwards based on usage).
- Platform as a Service (PaaS) offers an entire platform (operating system, servers, relational database but not applications) to customers for several purposes. As with SaaS, the platform is managed and kept stable and current by the service provider. The platform can be accessed by both in-house and remote staff. This enables all persons in the organization to view, edit, and share data no matter their location. Each user has the option to utilize only the services they need. These services tend to be very customizable.
- Infrastructure as a Service (laaS) is an infrastructure on-demand service in which customers outsource servers, storage, network components, and so on. The service provider owns the equipment and is responsible for its deployment, operations, upgrade, and maintenance.

Cloud computing is expanding fast. Use in European organizations was estimated at 26% in 2018. Large organizations use cloud computing more (56% of organizations with 250 or more people) than smaller companies (23% of organizations with employees numbering between 10 and 49).[138] There is a lot of scope to research this area.[139] A major interest in cloud computing is in developing countries, where the current infrastructure is still weak. Cloud computing can provide almost instantaneous working environments. It requires only a good telecommunication infrastructure (fixed or mobile). For example, cloud computing has been proposed in e-governance models in India, as a new and ideal solution for future gov-

[138] Eurostat (2018), *the EU Statistical Office*, December.

[139] Nicoletti, B., (2013), *Cloud Computing and Financial Services*, Palgrave Macmillan, London, UK (also translated in Chinese).

ernment projects, including e-procurement.[140] Cloud computing was also examined in its application in the context of e-governance. E-governance projects in India face many challenges, from the development phase to implementation. Similarly, cloud computing has been proposed as part of the architecture for e-procurement systems in Indonesia (Jawa Barat) to reduce the ICT costs for implementing e-procurement systems.[141] The results of this analysis show that significant cost reduction can be achieved by implementing the IaaS scheme of cloud computing in an e-procurement system at Jawa Barat.

Cloud computing can be useful in very varied economic sectors. For instance, cloud computing can be an enabler of a full dematerialization of the whole building lifecycle.[142] The use of e-procurement in this sector improves efficiency and increases market competitiveness thanks to cloud computing support. Particularly important in this sector is the application of these solutions in the procurement and construction phases of building development projects.

Cloud Procurement

The support of procurement by cloud computing is referred to as cloud procurement.[143] Cloud procurement concerns the use of well-established systems in the cloud, such as ERP, for administration and management activities. Thanks to cloud technology, information can be viewed, updated, and applied at any time or place, with the only requirement being a device connected to the internet. Cloud procurement follows the

[140] Tewari, N., Sharma, M.K. (2011), Towards e-Governance Framework in India using Cloud Computing Research Note #98–21, *Proceedings of the 5th National Conference, INDIACom-2011, Computing for Nation Development*, New Delhi, India, March 10–11.

[141] Galih, S. (2011), Cloud Computing Approach for IT Cost Reducing in Indonesia Government's e-

Procurement System: Case Study Jawa Barat e-Procurement System Unit (LPSE Jabar Indonesia), *ICID 2011 Conference*, 26 November, Yogyakarta, Indonesia.

[142] Grilo, A., Jardim-Goncalves, R. (2010), Changing e-procurement in the AEC sector with BIM, *Proceedings of the CIB W78 2010: 27th International Conference* – Cairo, Egypt, November 16–18.

Grilo, A., Jardim-Goncalves, R. (2010), Electronic public procurement of construction and public works: towards a new reality, *Journal of Public Procurement*, 10(3).

[143] Kroes, N. (2012, January). Setting up the European cloud partnership. In Speech at the World Economic Forum, Davos.

entire procurement process, from the design phase to product delivery and the payment of invoices to partners.

Cloud procurement is becoming more and more popular as an element in procurement 4.0.[144] The reason is simple: its features, such as its ease of use and guaranteed ICT assistance, meet all the different needs of an organization. Thus, the organization can spend less time on technicalities and more on its core activities: buying well, buying better, satisfying internal and external customers, and increasing organization revenues and margins.

Cloud procurement helps organizations manage new challenges faster. Some fear that if all members of the organization can access the data from anywhere, even unwanted persons might have access to sensitive information. Experts believe that the cloud is as secure as an on-premises system, even under increasingly stringent regulations. Administrators have complete access control, so they can decide who is authorized to see which data are in the system. As for the possibility of being hacked, many cloud service providers include 24/7 security support to avoid data breaches.

Cloud procurement is a solution that helps organizations in many ways. One of the benefits is that the ICT team in the buying organization does not have to take care of software maintenance, including technical support, hardware maintenance, upgrade, and hardware/software security. Cloud procurement is an excellent choice since it is the same provider of cloud computing that manages all the incidents and service requests related to its infrastructure.

Cloud procurement allows the reduction of capital expenditure. For example, a cloud ERP eliminates some of the higher long-term costs that occur in legacy ERPs. Here, there is a reduction in ICT expenses that are not required for ERP software in the cloud as opposed to on premises. There is also greater security and reliability with regard to uptime and disaster recovery, and there is no initial investment (usually very high) for software licenses and upgrade fees since it is sufficient to pay a monthly fee (usually low).

[144] Boss, G., Malladi, P., Quan, D., Legregni, L., & Hall, H. (2007). Cloud computing. *IBM white paper*, 321, 224–231.

Mladenović, T. (2018). Cloud Computing in logistics, *Master Thesis, Faculty of Transport and Traffic Engineering*, University of Belgrade.

Cloud procurement enables savings to be made thanks to the possibility of implementing the new system, processing data, and processing orders more quickly. Cloud procurement can accelerate all processes, automating the communication between operations and accounting. Even if the distribution of components in the warehouse has not been recorded, it is in any case automatically inserted by the system as part of the work in process, so it is shown that these materials/products are no longer available. Hence, procurement can improve the accuracy, maintenance, and management of the inventory.

Some research describes how Building information modeling (BIM), service-oriented applications, and cloud computing can change traditional e-procurement functions, namely the processing of tendering documents, as the technical data can be automatically coupled with transactional information orders, as in RFX, or invoices, and published in e-procurement platforms. Despite the potential to move to cloud computing practices in some parts of the world (such as the ASEAN Economic Community), there are some hurdles to overcome before it reaches a tipping point.[145]

B2B Cloud

A further interesting use of cloud procurement is the so-called B2B cloud.[146] This solution helps to address an important aspect of procurement 4.0: collaboration and integration among partners and customer organizations when:

- there is a need for frequent exchanges of information between different organizations;
- organizations that want to cooperate are geographically distant;
- there are standard formats for the connection of different ICT solutions.

A situation of this type allows the implementation of partnerships in B2B outsourcing and management of a community of trading. This is a

[145] Galih, S. (2011), Cloud Computing Approach for IT Cost Reducing in Indonesia Government's e-Procurement System: Case Study Jawa Barat e-Procurement System Unit (LPSE Jabar Indonesia) *ICID 2011 Conference*, 26 November, Yogyakarta, Indonesia.

[146] Kim, J., & Shunk, D. (2004), Matching indirect procurement process with different B2B e-procurement systems, *Computers in Industry*, 53

typical situation in procurement. It could greatly alleviate the procurement processes thanks to the possibility of collaboration via computers and networks.

The best solution might be, at least initially, a hybrid B2B. This would allow an organization to connect directly with its most important partners. At the same time, the organization may use a B2B cloud to connect with the remaining partners. The cloud also makes it easier to build a procurement social network to improve collaboration between partners. Cloud procurement promotes shared collaboration and a greener environment, while reducing the need for expensive equipment. It also provides other benefits in connection with the proposed architecture:

- flexibility
- security and data privacy
- capital investment and (potentially) cost savings
- ease of access, implementation, and usage
- resources elasticity and expandability (such as manpower and energy savings)
- increased efficiency.

With cloud computing, organizations could open up new possibilities for further improving the efficiency and flexibility of procurement 4.0. The combination of data from all locations provides new prospects for process optimization. This includes more efficient control of material flows, early detection and elimination of supply bottlenecks and process disruptions, and the optimized operation of machinery and equipment in all plants and locations of the ecosystem.

The cloud-based platform, with its simplified data exchange, is an essential prerequisite for organizations to provide new solutions and innovations rapidly at several locations. These include RPA and data analytics functions to analyze and check procurement processes within the ecosystem. With the cloud-based platform, new applications, for example in ICT security for shop floor systems, can be scaled up directly to all locations throughout the world. Organizations can leverage cloud procurement innovation best practices to become more agile and react faster to industry trends.

Cloud procurement, by definition, is an open platform. The objective is to integrate organizations from the entire value network and to build up an ecosystem of partners with a database and information pooling that bring benefits to all concerned. The value network in procurement 4.0

needs to integrate with the partner organizations in its ecosystem. The cloud platform will generally be accessible to other organizations. In the case of manufacturing organizations, this can create a steadily growing global industrial ecosystem.

Volkswagen[147]

Volkswagen and Amazon Web Services developed the Volkswagen Industrial Cloud as part of a multi-year, global agreement. The Volkswagen Industrial Cloud combines the data of all machines, plants, and systems from the 122 facilities of the Volkswagen Group. The Volkswagen Industrial Cloud creates the essential prerequisites for achieving substantial productivity goals in production. In the long term, the global supply chain of the Volkswagen group—with more than 30,000 locations and over 1500 partner organizations—could be integrated into this initiative. By leveraging Amazon Web Services technology and services, Volkswagen is creating its Industrial Cloud as an open industry platform which other partners from the industry, logistics, and sales may use in future.

Expert teams from Volkswagen and Amazon Web Services work together on the Volkswagen Industrial Cloud. In the medium term, about 220 specialists will work on the project. They are based at several Volkswagen ICT competence centers, as well as a joint Industrial Cloud Innovation Center in Berlin. Experts in Dresden, Munich, and Wolfsburg are in support. The teams started with 140 projects for integration. These projects include a system for tracing the transfer of goods inside and outside the factory, by trucks (by using vehicle locating service) and services for the cross-plant analysis of the system efficiency (overall equipment effectiveness).

Edge Computing

With new and advanced tools such as IoT, the amount of data that can be created is enormous. In this situation, centralized computing in the cloud would increase network costs. For this reason, whenever possible, it is

[147] https://www.volkswagenag.com/en/news/2019/03/volkswagen-and-amazon-web-services-to-develop-industrial-cloud.html. Accessed May 5, 2019.

good to have some processing and storage done locally. This is called edge computing.[148] The use of intelligent edge devices can reduce the data sent to the cloud through quality filtering and aggregation. Edge computing allows integration of more functions into intelligent devices and gateways closer to the edge. This reduces latency and improves response times. By moving some of the intelligence to the edge, local devices can generate value when there are challenges related to transferring data to the cloud. Think, for example, of vessels or of remote locations, such as in the desert, where it is necessary to use satellite communication, which is still rather expensive. This allows for protocol consolidation by controlling the various modes. Devices can communicate with each other. There are different edge computing paradigms, such as transparent computing and fog computing, fully described in the literature.[149]

4.6.2 *Mobility*

Cloud computing supports the trends in technology and social networks in mobility communication. Mobile computing is the interaction of an operator with information systems anyplace, anytime, and on any device using a network (such as the internet or Wi-Fi). The possible uses of mobility in the context of procurement 4.0 are several, while devices and applications in this domain are multiplying and spreading. Procurement has been involved in a limited way so far, but this situation is changing. Examples of possible uses are:

- Mobility for sourcing: Mobile devices can be used to detect requirements directly on the shelf, to send orders, and get their acceptance directly in store or in the warehouse. Spend visibility would be available on the move.
- Mobility for logistics: Mobile devices are also very important for logistics. In the case of transportation, mobility can help in detecting the location of carriers or be used for long-distance communication, written or verbal.

[148] Vermesan, O., & Bacquet, J. (Eds.). (2017). *Cognitive Hyperconnected Digital Transformation: Internet of Things Intelligence Evolution*. River Publishers, Gistrup, Denmark.

[149] Zhang, Y., Ren, J., Liu, J., Xu, C., Guo, H., & Liu, Y. (2017). A survey on emerging computing paradigms for big data. *Chinese Journal of Electronics*, 26(1), 1–12.

- In the case of warehouses, mobile devices can be used for picking activities, deciding the arrangement of the items on the shelves, receiving, or shipping.
- Mobile devices can be used very efficiently for inspections, as they allow operators to work in the proximity of the materials or components to inspect or verify the quantity and/or quality on site.
- Mobile devices can also assist in making administrative processes leaner. The most important application is the inventorying, wherein the detection of stocks is not done manually and reported by hand on the workstations. Rather, it is carried out directly in the warehouse or in places of transit, thus accruing several benefits.

It is worthwhile to examine mobility in connection with procurement 4.0. The connection between the two words can be interpreted in different ways and all of them are pertinent.

In the case of procurement 4.0, mobility can be seen from various points of view. The first is the mobility of the organization's products. In this case, mobility and procurement are closely connected with logistics and of course with value network management. In the case of logistics, there are different forms of services, often referred to as 1LP, 2LP, 3LP, and so forth (with LP standing for logistics provider). The industry is rapidly changing and procurement needs to seize the opportunities presented these new environments as they can greatly help to make an organization more agile.

Another point of view is associated with the mobility of personnel within an organization. Procurement acquires and manages personal mobility services. There can be different meanings of this application in the sense of temporary mobility or medium- or long-term mobility, meaning the movement of persons to work in different locations for extended periods. With globalization, both meanings have an increasing economic value on which the procurement can and should act to develop and add value to customers and the organization.

Mobility can also be connected with the acquisition of devices or mobility services. This form of mobility is greatly expanding, in fields such as those associated with the shared economy, as in the cases of Uber, Enjoy, or similar.[150]

[150] Zhang, H., & Xu, J. (2018, April). Research on design strategy of marketing experience in shared economy. In 2018 IEEE International Conference on Applied Invention System (ICASI). IEEE: 888–891.

The most interesting meaning of mobility in connection with the procurement is linking the word mobility to mobile, as in mobile phones or tablets. Procurement is connected with mobility in different ways, depending on whether one considers mobile devices as a support to the procurement function or relative to the product category of mobile telephony. In the first meaning, there are several examples of the use of mobile in procurement. The use of mobility in this meaning is increasing due to the growing importance of mobile devices in all sectors and thus also in procurement.

The procurement of mobility, understood as a mobile device, is a field of increasing importance because, despite the relative reduction in terms of numbers of vendors in the industry in recent years, competition among operators continues to be lively, due to these products having substantial value as commodity types and thanks to their growing volumes and the possible effects of scale.

One area that has still received little attention is the management of mobile devices, especially in organizations. New services and products are spreading, such as the following[151]:

- Managed Mobility Services (MMS) facilitate ICT organizations in addressing the complexity of managing multiple platforms for mobile devices. MMS enable communication with employees who work out of the office. It enables them to interact with the resources that are traditionally accessible only to users of workstations within the organization, such as databases, email, and other content and organization applications. To do this, a multimedia provider makes available the content of these applications in a mode suitable for access by mobile devices that have been specifically authorized.
- Mobile Workforce Management (MWM), or management of a workforce is similar to MMS and the two expressions are sometimes used interchangeably. However, MMS is focused on mobile connection to the applications of an organization by staff when out of office, allowing them to interact with applications, servers, and databases, but also with other associates and partners. The MWM generally

[151] Pierer, M. (2016). *Mobile device management: Mobility evaluation in small and medium-sized enterprises*. Springer, Cham, Switzerland.

provides devices, software, and services. The focus is more on field workers, especially in the utility sector (gas, water, electricity, telephones, and the like). Some applications in this area are particularly important, for example those supporting workers carrying out maintenance for utility organizations. In this case, mobile devices can help in identifying the location in which to perform the services, and the network that provides these services. It is possible through appropriate AR viewers to allow employees to have simultaneous access to the maintenance or installations manuals, helping them carry out often quite complex tasks.

- Finally, there are solutions contained in Mobile Device Management (MDM), another term similar to the previous terms and sometimes confused with them. MDM is support given to the administration and management of mobile devices. It provides an aid to distribution, assures security, control, integration, and management of mobile devices such as smartphones, tablet computers, and laptops, in any place where an organization works. MDM is an aspect of MMS.

It is crucial not to forget insurance policies connected with mobility. They can be of different types, depending on whether they refer to damage or economic life. Cybersecurity insurance is gaining importance. The latter requires specific insurance besides adopting emergency systems to support business continuity and disaster recovery.

Figure 4.10 shows classification, in broad terms, of the most important aspects highlighted in this section, although it is restricted to high levels and does not go into details. In short, mobility is an interesting procurement category that lends itself to allowing the organization to add value to its internal and external users of procurement 4.0.

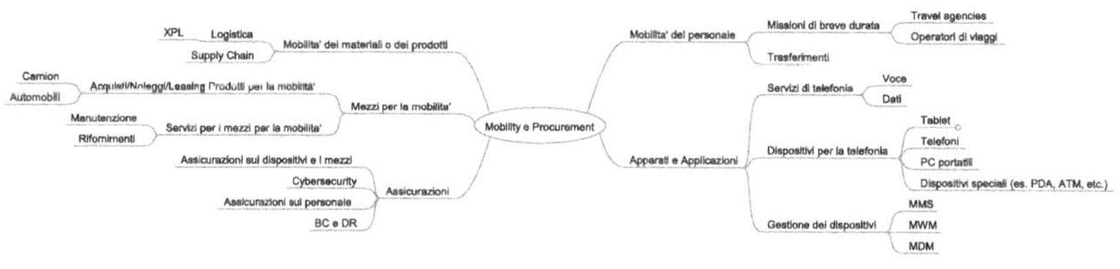

Fig. 4.10 Mobility for procurement 4.0

4.6.3 *Augmented Reality*

An AR (augmented reality) system can be defined by the following characteristics[152]:

- combines real and virtual objects in a real environment;
- registers (aligns) real and virtual objects with each other;
- runs interactively, in three dimensions, and in real time.

AR can support improvements in packaging, handling, storage and transportation phases where manpower and personnel play an important role. To decrease the error rate of object selection and decision-making time, it is necessary to simplify logistics operations execution. It is also necessary to make it more user-friendly when human resources are involved. Modern technologies can improve those processes through the use of AR. It offers key technologies to solve stressful situations and warehouse worker routines by allowing them to make decisions based on computer-generated visualizations and 3D model presentations. The successful use of AR technologies in several industries and some experimental applications in warehouse environments confirms its potential.[153]

Some AR solutions in procurement 4.0 are, for instance, the application of smart goggles in warehouses for collecting, sorting, and packing operations; smart handling of forklifts and vehicles; smart delivery of goods to the end-user, and so on.[154] The use of instructions in three-dimensional space instead of text and image-based guides is one of the improvements possible with AR. R&D of AR devices aims at recognizing images and connecting devices with software applications; this creates the conditions for the application of AR in all logistics processes.[155]

[152] Azuma, R. T., Baillot, Y., Behringer, R., Feiner, S. K., Julier, S. Andmacintyre, B. (2001). Recent Advances in *Augmented Reality. Computergraphics and Applications* 21, 6, 34–47.

[153] Cirulis, A., & Ginters, E. (2013). Augmented reality in logistics. *Procedia Computer Science*, *26*, 14–20.

[154] Radivojević, G., & Milosavljević, L. (2019). The Concept of Logistics 4.0. *4th Logistics International Conference*, May 23–25. Belgrade, Serbia.

[155] Kiickelhaus, M., Chung, G. (2018). Logistics Trend Radar, DHL *Customer Solutions & Innovation*, Germany. www.dhl.com. Accessed July 14, 2019.

4.7 Cybersecurity and Data Privacy

Cybersecurity is a characteristic of the vulnerabilities that computer systems present. In industry 4.0 there is a strong connection between several systems, which makes the system more fragile. This fact reveals the impossibility of data protection, either internal to the various processes that the organization holds or externally.

Many organizations still rely on management and production systems that are unconnected or closed.[156] With the increased connectivity and use of standard communication protocols that come with industry 4.0, the need to protect critical organizations' systems and manufacturing lines from cybersecurity threats increases dramatically. As a result, secure reliable communications as well as sophisticated identity and access management of machines and users are essential.[157]

Research demonstrates the growing importance of security in the field of procurement, especially with regard to a number of virtual information flows and automated transactions.[158] There is a concern for cybersecurity in procurement 4.0 overall and the possible risks for organizations in cases of malevolent attack.[159] It is essential to extend the developments of security and related security systems within procurement 4.0 based on a common approach by including all procurement stakeholders and to create common solutions and systems to secure the future common value network ecosystems against external violence or even internal attacks.[160]

[156] Lezzi, M., Lazoi, M., & Corallo, A. (2018). Cybersecurity for Industry 4.0 in the current literature: *A reference framework. Computers in Industry*, 103, 97–110.

Rübmann, M., Lorenz, M., Gerbert, P., Waldner, M., Justus, J., Engel, P., & Harnisch, M. (2015). Industry 4.0: the future of productivity and growth in manufacturing industry. *Boston Consulting Group (BCG) Raporu.*

[157] Rodrigues, M., Sousa, B., & da Costa, J. B. (2019). The Improvement of the Supply Chain Channel Based on Digital Transformation: An Exploratory Study in the Sustainable Industry 4.0 *4th Regional Helix- Book of Abstracts* Parallel Session 4, Porto, Portugal.

[158] Stephens, J. and Valverde, R. (2013), Security of e-procurement transactions in supply chain reengineering, *Computer and Information Science,* 6(3), 1–20.

[159] Barron, S., Cho, Y.M., Hua, A., Norcross, W., Voigt, J. & Haimes, Y. (2016), Systems-based cyber security in the supply chain, *IEEE Systems and Information Engineering Design Symposium (SIEDS)*, June 10, 20–25.

[160] Johnson, T.A. (2013), *Cybersecurity: Protecting Critical Infrastructures from Cyber Attack and Cyber Warfare*, CRC Press, Boca Raton, FL.

The type, number, and specificity of data collected from billions of devices through the IoT and big data create concern among users vis-à-vis their privacy, and between organizations regarding the confidentiality and integrity of their data.[161] The partner support of these solutions needs to offer valuable products and services, to provide transparency on what data is used and how, and to ensure they are adequately protected. Some organizations sign contracts with partners that offer products (such as IoT), without realizing that the organizations are authorizing the use of their data for commercial purposes by third parties.

The legislative scenario for data privacy is still not fully clarified. In Europe, the regulations to monitor are the GDPR, the ePrivacy Regulation, and the European Data Protection Regulation.[162]

Security is a big problem with the IoT. Organizations that collect data from billions of devices must be able to protect such data from unauthorized access. They also face new categories of risks that the IoT can introduce. These extensions of the ICT world create greater dangers of cyberattacks that must be managed.

The first malevolent campaign, based on IoT as its driver, saw more than 750,000 phishing and spam emails launched from 100,000 apparent everyday objects. The cyberattack, detected by Proofpoint, a provider that operates in the field of security as a service, occurred between December 23, 2013 and January 6, 2014. There were several waves of malicious emails intended for businesses and individuals around the world.[163] The news of this attack, which quickly went global, has cast a shadow on the use of intelligent tools. If organizations consider that IoT devices are set to grow more than four times the number of connected computers, it is clear that their weak points in terms of security can have a major impact on business and on the goals of organizations.

[161] Kozlov, D., Veijalainen, J., & Ali, Y. (2012, February). Security and privacy threats in IoT architectures. In *Proceedings of the 7th International Conference on Body Area Networks, 256–262. ICST (Institute for Computer Sciences, Social-Informatics and Telecommunications Engineering).*

[162] Carey, P. (2018). *Data protection: a practical guide to UK and EU law*. Oxford University Press, Inc., Oxford, UK.

[163] https://www.proofpoint.com/us/proofpoint-uncovers-internet-things-iot-cyberattack. Accessed March 30, 2019.

For criminals, new platforms, and especially the IoT, represent a healthy environment rich in poorly protected devices that they can freely move through via identity theft and infiltration in the ICT systems of organizations. It is important to protect access to such devices, yet at present organizations have limited experience and tools to detect or fix these types of infection.[164]

When these advanced solutions are used to control any sort of physical activity, whether it be of factories or vehicles, the consequences related to a security breach extends beyond even the unauthorized release of information. It may even cause a catastrophe.

4.8 A Roadmap for Digital Transformation

It is interesting to analyze the way that innovative platforms can become part of business as usual in an organization. One study suggests how foundational technologies and their business use cases evolve over time.[165] The first factor to consider is novelty, the degree to which an application is new. The more dramatic the innovation, the more effort will be required to ensure that users understand what problems it can help to solve. The second dimension is complexity. This is represented by the level of the ecosystem coordination involved. It can be measured by the number and diversity of parties that need to work together to produce value through the new solutions.

The same study developed a framework that maps innovations against these two contextual dimensions, dividing them into quadrants. Each quadrant represents a stage of technology development. Identifying which one an innovation falls into can help managers understand its challenges, the level of collaboration and consensus it needs, and the legislative and regulatory compliance it will require. The map also suggests which kinds of processes and infrastructure must be established to facilitate the adoption of innovation. Managers and professionals can use this model to assess the state, for example, of blockchain applied to procurement 4.0 development in an organization, as well as to evaluate strategic investments in their innovation solution capabilities.

[164] Atzei, N., Bartoletti, M., & Cimoli, T. (2017, April). A survey of attacks on Ethereum smart contracts (sok). In *International Conference on Principles of Security and Trust*, 164–186. Springer, Berlin, Heidelberg, Germany.

[165] Iansiti, M., & Lakhani, K. R. (2017). The truth about blockchain. *Harvard Business Review*, *95*(1), 118–127.

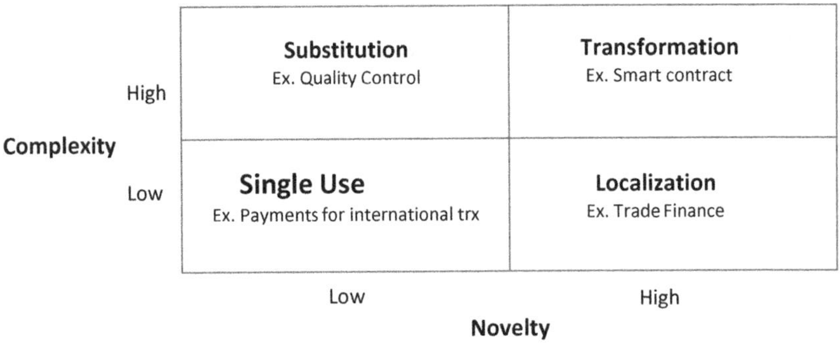

Fig. 4.11 Roadmap for a digital transformation

In this model, the stages in the innovative solution introduction are (Fig. 4.11)[166]:

- Single use—The first quadrant refers to low-novelty and low-coordination applications that create better, less costly, and highly focused solutions.
- Localization—The second quadrant comprises innovations that are high in novelty. They need only a limited number of users to generate immediate value. As a consequence, it is easy to promote their adoption.
- Substitution—The third quadrant contains applications that are low in novelty because they build on existing single-use and localized applications. They need high coordination because they involve broader and increasingly public uses. These innovations aim to replace entire ways of doing business. They face high barriers to adoption.
- Transformation—The last quadrant includes completely innovative applications that, if successful, could change the very nature of economic, social, and political systems. They involve coordinating the activities of many actors and gaining institutional agreement on standards and processes. Their adoption requires major social, legal, and political changes.

[166] Iansiti, M., & Lakhani, K. R. (2017). The truth about blockchain. *Harvard Business Review*, *95*(1), 118–127.

In the case of the blockchain applied to procurement 4.0, the potential applications at each one of these steps could be:

- Low novelty and low complexity—single use: payments for international transactions, where at least two financial institutions are involved.
- High novelty and low complexity—localization: management of trade finance within a limited ecosystem, composed by the financial institutions involved, the customers, and potentially the regulatory authorities.
- Low novelty and high complexity—substitution: quality control with procurement and delivery in several locations and potentially several countries to benefit the end customers and, as an intermediate stage, the retailers.
- High novelty and high complexity—transformation: use of smart contracts to support procurement relationships.

In a survey of the Italian market, participating organizations plan to concentrate investments in industrial IoT (48%), industrial analytics (39%), and advanced automation (33%). Considering a 3–5-year horizon, the priorities become advanced automation, the cloud, and additive manufacturing.[167] AI and the blockchain are not yet that relevant in the investment plans of the next few years, with some exceptions for large organizations.

4.9 Conclusions

This chapter has considered the main platforms that support procurement 4.0. The list is not exhaustive and it is dynamic. Over time, new solutions will be introduced. The greatest successes can be achieved by a combination of more than one technology. There are several good examples. Think of the cell phone or smartphone: it is a combination of a telephone with a computer. This rule applies also for procurement 4.0. Thanks to the combination of information technology with industrial automation technologies, procurement 4.0 can bring big benefits, but also challenges, such as cybersecurity.

[167] https://www.corrierecomunicazioni.it/industria-4-0/rallenta-la-corsa-di-industria-4-0-nel-2019-crescita-in-calo-del-10-15/. Accessed June 22, 2019.

IoT, cognitive computing, and big data analytics are key drivers for the transition of organizations to procurement 4.0. They are able to increase profitability and competitiveness on a new level. Within value network ecosystems, the flow of information and therefore deriving data is the critical factor for organizational success or failure.[168]

Deloitte in its CPO Survey 2017 found that 50% of 480 respondents do not see CPO automation and robotics (AI, machine learning, chatbots, and so forth) due to their concern on the benefits introduced by these new solutions. However, in 2025, that percentage is expected to have reduced to 7%.[169]

The Italian market for the industry 4.0 in 2018 stood at €3.2 billion, recording a 35% growth compared to 2017.[170] It was driven by the results of the investments made in 2017 (and invoiced in 2018). This increase benefitted of the National Industry 4.0 Plan. If one considers the previous four years, the number of organizations moving to industry 4.0 solution grew by 140%. €700 million should be added for 'traditional' digital innovation projects (about €300 million more than the previous year). Of these figures, 85% are made up of industrial IoT, industrial analytics, and cloud manufacturing. Eight hundred applications 4.0 were surveyed in Italy, on average four per organization. The consolidated projects have brought flexibility and lower costs. The most widespread 4.0 technologies are ICT, in particular industrial IoT (the components for connecting machinery to the network) which, with a value of €1.9 billion in 2018, represents 60% of the market and has recorded the biggest growth (+40%). They are followed by industrial analytics, with €530 million (17% of the market, +30%), and cloud manufacturing, with €270 million (8%, +35%). Among operational technologies, advanced automation wins the largest market share with €160 million and growth of 10%, followed by additive manufacturing with €70 million. The interface application between

[168] Bucy, M., Hall, S. & Yakola, D. (2016), "Transformation with a capital T", available at: www.mckinsey.com/business-functions/mckinsey-recovery-and-transformation-services/our-insights/transformation-with-a-capital-t. Accessed January 4, 2017; Zhong, R. Y., Neman, S. T., Huag, G. Q. & Lan, S. (2016), Big Data for supply chain management in the service and manufacturing sectors: challenges, opportunities, and future perspectives, *Computers & Industrial Engineering*, 101(2016), 572–591.

[169] https://www2.deloitte.com/bn/en/pages/operations/articles/cpo-survey-2017.html. Accessed April 28, 2019.

[170] https://www.corrierecomunicazioni.it/industria-4-0/rallenta-la-corsa-di-industria-4-0-nel-2019-crescita-in-calo-del-10-15/. Accessed June 22, 2019.

humans and machines marks the most robust growth (+50%, €45 million). The last part of the market consists of consultancy and training activities related to industry 4.0 projects, estimated at €220 million (+10%). This figure is lower than expected. It shows that there is still much to do in terms of skills improvements.

A quick overview shows that new platform solutions in procurement 4.0 achieve the maximum benefits from the combination of becoming lean and digitization.[171]

It is useful to report the results of some experiments of these new solutions in procurement 4.0. As for the monetized benefits, in some applications it is estimated that the possibility of reducing the number of employees in procurement is over 37%. The results were stratified in two different perspectives: organizational and processes.[172] The organizational analysis allows sharing of benefits between back office categories, middle office, and front office.[173] The analysis shows that the most significant impacts in terms of savings is 89% and this occurred in the back office. This sector is mainly characterized by repetitive and standardized activities that suit well procurement 4.0 solutions such as RPA. The activities in the front office need greater creativity and relational capabilities. They allow savings of just 7% of staff costs. Finally, the middle office could bring a saving of 75%.

The benefits in terms of processes can be divided into strategic, tactical, and transactional activities. In some cases, these results are in line with findings at the organizational level. A transactional level application is significant enough to generate savings of 90% of the current job content. This level includes all routine and repetitive activities based on the adoption of analytics solutions. At the tactical level, the analysis shows a reduction of 36% in the total employment. Finally, the strategic level could bring a saving of 24% of the total, thus showing a less effective response.

[171] Nicoletti, B., (2012), *Lean and Digitize: An Integrated Approach to Process Improvement*. Gower Publishing, Farnham, UK. ISBN-10: 1409441946.

[172] https://www.digital4.biz/procurement/strategie/procurement-4-0-la-check-list-luf-ficio-acquisti-digitale/. Accessed March 9, 2019.

[173] Perona, M. (2019). Procurement 4.0, the check list for Purchasing Digital, https://www.digital4.biz/procurement/ufficio-acquisti-digitale-cose-quali-benefici-del-procurement-4-0/. Accessed March 9, 2019.

Overall, procurement 4.0 projects bring tangible benefits, especially in terms of flexibility and cost reduction. The main benefits declared by the organizations with projects that have been active for over a year are improved production flexibility (47%), increase in plant efficiency (38%), reduction in design times (34%), and the opportunity to develop innovative products (33%).[174] The challenges most perceived by organizations in the development of procurement 4.0 applications are difficulties in the use of new technologies and the adoption of standards (59%), organizational issues and skills management (41%), change management difficulties (20%), and dissatisfaction with current solutions available in the market (17%).

These results refer to one implementation in a large organization. They demonstrate the benefits potentially associated with procurement 4.0. The greatest potential savings have been achieved with the RPA technology applied to the poorest activities for their intellectual content or relational possibilities. Benefits can be achieved in transactional and execution activities that typically belong to the back or middle office. Activities with the greatest intensity of relationship or that require greater intellectual contributions, typically of a strategic type and concentrated in the front office, are expected to see fewer benefits with the introduction of procurement 4.0 solutions. In this case, it is more difficult to replace human labor with the solutions presented in this chapter.

The non-monetary benefits here are made up of quality increases due to improved accuracy of processes and better results. With the platforms presented in this chapter, organizations can analyze a sample of data much larger than before and define a more accurate resulting confidence interval. The solutions presented in this chapter can improve the compliance and consistency of an organization's activities to the various relevant regulations, procedures, and codes of conduct. This is possible thanks to codified and standardized processes. It is potentially possible to minimize the likelihood of errors in the execution of activities and/or of non-compliance to internal procedures.

[174] https://www.digital4.biz/procurement/strategie/procurement-4-0-la-check-list-lufficio-acquisti-digitale/. Accessed March 9, 2019.

A challenge that comes with the introduction of procurement 4.0 is the use of advanced platforms.[175] A survey found that large organizations are on track in moving to procurement 4.0 in terms of the use of the platforms presented in this chapter (percentage of use in support of the procurement was between 45% and around 80% of Italian participants cited by the survey organization). For micro businesses and SMEs, the percentage is 56% of organizations that use advanced solutions on 45% of their assets. Results of this type are due to the backwardness in the technologies used in support of the procurement in many SMEs. The reason, in this case, is mainly due to the persistence of the traditional functional organization model prevalent in SMEs. Another reason for the fact that few SMEs have adopted procurement 4.0 platforms to manage their procurement is due to solutions in the market mainly being suited only to large organizations. In their context, these solutions are expensive, complex, and of no immediate use. Instead, SMEs need cheap and simple platforms (which would allow such organizations to manage the portfolios of their partners and the basic activities of the procurement cycle) but especially that are easy and immediately usable. From this point of view, cloud computing offers interesting prospects for more widespread use of these solutions. Cloud computing makes simple the acquisition and implementation, activation, and management of new advanced solutions.

In connection with advanced solutions, there are also problems of the safety of the workers affected, for example with AGVs. This subject is very extensive and the reader can refer to the several texts on the subject.[176]

[175] https://www.logisticaefficiente.it/procout/supplychain/approvvigionamenti/maturita-procurement-italia-europa-risultati-parte-1.html. Accessed March 10, 2019.

[176] Marvel, J., & Bostelman, R. (2013, October). Towards mobile manipulator safety standards. In *2013 IEEE International Symposium on Robotic and Sensors Environments* (ROSE), 31–36. IEEE.

CHAPTER 5

Persons in Procurement 4.0

5.1 Introduction

Persons are the most important factor in any organization and especially when introducing innovations. Procurement 4.0 is no exception. Dealing with persons presents a challenge but also many opportunities. The procurement function in any organization should prepare to build up required capacities and capabilities to support the organizational vision and mission from a more strategic and innovative position. The discipline of value network management is highly influenced by the new role of procurement 4.0 as a strategic network node within the operations ecosystems. This requires a rethinking of tasks, roles, and responsibilities of all procurement parties and the setting up of cross-functional interdisciplinary roles to speed up transactions and processes—all to stay at the cutting edge of new solutions and to drive future organizational success in the most efficient and effective way based on sustainable and diversified profitability.[1]

All personnel should be properly prepared, informed, and trained in procurement 4.0 solutions. This is a challenge, since most of the current employees in an organization will have started working when industry 4.0 did not even exist as a concept. On the other hand, it is an opportunity to revitalize interests of workers and provides opportunities for the most

[1] Bienhaus, F., & Haddud, A. (2018). Procurement 4.0: factors influencing the digitisation of procurement and supply chains. *Business Process Management Journal*, *24*(4), 965–984.

B. Nicoletti, *Procurement 4.0 and the Fourth Industrial Revolution*,
https://doi.org/10.1007/978-3-030-35979-9_5

intelligent. For this reason, this chapter focuses on training for procurement 4.0: education 4.0.

Organizations must digitally re-engineer all their procedures and activities in such a way that procurement 4.0 functions can support all of their procurement processes. Use of new solutions allows organizations to have an integrated view, which facilitates decisions that affect the entire value network. At the same time, the use of innovative solutions removes broken processes and more smoothly coordinates processes and activities in such a way to increase productivity and ease of use. In this phase of transformation, the determining factor is represented by human resources. To further extend and deepen innovation and adopt digital solutions, the role of personnel is decisive. In this line, e-competencies are essential.[2]

In a survey of the Italian market for industry 4.0,[3] it has been shown that organizations that have started using 4.0 solutions in their processes need to manage their impact on the organization. Most such organizations pay attention to changes in the process and flow (54.2% of the sample), in personnel activities and work methods (45.3%), and technical skills (42.7%). Less than 20% focused on the impact on roles, managerial, and relational skills and expected behaviors. When organizations focus on organizational aspects, they do so in 18.8% of cases at the start of the project, for the introduction of procurement 4.0, and 20.8% during its development.

Often, the promoter of 4.0 initiatives is a top manager (43.8% of the sample) or the production or plant manager (35.4%). The R&D function is involved above all in the development of the project. The HR function, on the other hand, participates in very few cases in the various phases of the digital transformation. Only in 6.8% of cases was it involved in all steps; in 27.1% it was only informed of the start of the project; in 23.4% it did not have a role in any aspect of the industry 4.0 initiative. The involvement of buyers and office operators was also limited: only 7.8% of organizations involved them in all phases of the industry 4.0 project, while 25% did not assign any role. In only 26.6% of cases were operators informed of the 4.0 strategy.

[2] Dobozy, E., & Ifenthaler, D. (2014). Initial teacher education by open and distance modes: A snapshot of e-competency experiences in Australia. *eLearning Papers: Digital Literacies & eCompetencies*, *38*(May), 57–67.

[3] https://www.corrierecomunicazioni.it/industria-4-0/rallenta-la-corsa-di-industria-4-0-nel-2019-crescita-in-calo-del-10-15/. Accessed June 22, 2019.

Of organizations surveyed, 57% have taken steps to identify 4.0 skills shortages and started actions necessary to fill them. About three out of ten consider their current level of skills adequate and as many are working to improve them. There is a strong participation of entrepreneurs, top managers, and project managers 4.0 in decisions to evaluate the competencies necessary. The HR managers tend to remain in the background and acquire importance only in the implementation phase.

According to Italian entrepreneurs, investments in training represent the best strategy to enhance human capital in an organization (49%).[4] They still have to struggle against certain stereotypes that are present mainly among young persons, who see work in the factory as tiring and manual (64%), repetitive, not very creative, leaving little room for personal fulfillment (48%), little recognized socially (41%), and even technologically backward (29%), making it difficult for organizations to find persons with highly specialized technical profiles. Industry 4.0 can resolve some of these difficulties.

5.2 Transformation Roadmap

It is important to consider the roadmap for how to migrate from being a traditional procurement organization toward application of the paradigm of procurement 4.0. There are three basic steps to guide this change, attributing the correct value to HR[5]:

1. Develop appropriate education and training processes. The design must be an integrated process that starts to create awareness and sensitivity from the top management downwards. It should disseminate the knowledge of procurement 4.0, going top down to the more operational layers of the organization. However, organizations often follow a completely opposite process, failing to act with a top-down logic and rather developing in a bottom-up direction, which starts with the training of operational personnel in the use of advanced solutions. This approach is doomed to fail. The most fre-

[4] https://www.mecspe.com/en/comunicati-stampa-en/osservatorio-mecspe-focus-nazionale/. Accessed August 5, 2019.

[5] This section follows the guidelines introduced and pioneered by Prof. Marco Perona and presented in https://www.digital4.biz/procurement/strategie/procurement-4-0-la-checklist-lufficio-acquisti-digitale/. Accessed March 9, 2019.

quent issue is not explaining to those who must use them how to handle these new solutions. It is important to teach and train all levels of an organization on what to do that is new and different to before. This must be consistent with the procurement strategy and in general with the strategy of the entire organization. Digital skills are essential at all levels.[6]

2. Redesign the way persons work and interact. Digitizing and automating a process involves not only adopting new and advanced tools to perform the same activities as before, with greater efficiency, effectiveness, and economy. The greatest effect is not in boosting but in transforming what was done before. It should begin with the spread of digital tools and enable and encourage their use through the top-down training processes described above. The organization needs to push on, accelerating organizational changes and its digital transformation. It should completely redesign the work experience of persons within the organization. It is necessary to work toward a professional experience of more focused activities with rich relational and intellectual points of view; and it is vital to eliminate or reduce repetitive and flat activities. In this way, the organization can increase employee satisfaction. This brings better products, which are at the basis of customer satisfaction. It is further necessary to increase the involvement of workers, stimulating a proactive and collaborative approach. This is a precondition for the success of procurement 4.0. Once this is achieved, the organization can enable a gradual phasing out of the traditional operating models, based on hierarchy and standard roles, in favor of more collaborative models with flatter organizations and less defined roles.
3. Attract new talent from the labor market. The transition from a traditional to a digital operating model, no matter how well prepared an organization may be, tends to result in a non-negligible percent-

[6] In 2006, the European Parliament proposed a first definition of 'Digital Competence' in the "Recommendation of the European Parliament and of the Council of December." This indicates eight key competences for lifelong learning. "Digital competence is to be able to use with confidence and critical information society technologies (IST) for work, leisure and communication. It is underpinned by basic skills in ICT (Information and Communication Technology): the use of computers to retrieve, assess, store, produce, present and exchange information, and to communicate and participate in collaborative networks via the Internet." This definition was later also adopted by the Agency for Digital Italy, the Agid. https://www.digital4.biz/hr/competenze-digitali-cosa-sono/. Accessed April 26, 2019.

age of failures. The innovative way of working (new roles, new skills, new relationships and partnerships, new tools, and so forth) can be difficult for some persons in an organization to accept and integrate within their jobs. The opening of new roles, professional groups, and related digital competencies requires the introduction of new competencies and therefore often of new persons. Working in this sort of digital and automated environment entails overcoming several constraints of time and space. It requires a thorough review of the relationship between the organization and its associates.

5.3 Persons' Contribution to Procurement 4.0

The personnel of an organization must contribute to procurement 4.0 on two levels. At the base level, employees are at the very core of organizational procedures and processes. Therefore, they are integral to the transformation to procurement 4.0. On the one hand, employees are affected by this transformation with regard to there being a change in working processes. On the other hand, employees have the chance to be part of a successful transformation by identifying areas for improvement. Employees should be open- minded about the Fourth Industrial Revolution and should support the opportunities it presents, instead of fearing the risks. Based on a survey of workers,[7] employees are somewhat undecided on these issues on the micro-level perspective, apropos which technologies will leverage digital transformation; however, on the macro-level perspective, employees understand the importance of digitization as a success factor in any organization's future.

At the management level, the shift to procurement 4.0 and increasing global connectivity with cross-functional teams, catalyzes management to create a working environment that frees the potential of creativity and innovation. On the one hand, managers have to guide employees through the process of transformation to procurement 4.0. On the other hand, it is important to make room for employees to accomplish this change process on their own terms and to ensure sustainable long-term success. Managers and leaders need to build trust and reliability in a first step to fostering a safe environment where employees can also speak about their

[7] Bienhaus, F., & Haddud, A. (2018). Procurement 4.0: factors influencing the digitisation of procurement and supply chains. *Business Process Management Journal*, *24*(4), 965–984.

fears and concerns. Regarding the change process, managers need to identify the bottlenecks and challenges on the macro-level and then define appropriate actions to resolve them as well as to ensure efficient, effective, and economical operations throughout the organization.

5.4 Training 4.0

Industry 4.0 concerns the digital transformation of organizations, especially in the manufacturing environment. It is associated with the convergence and integration between traditional ICT and systems/automated machinery. Some aspects that characterize industry 4.0, and hence procurement 4.0, are[8]:

- Cooperation–digitization enables the creation of virtual procurement associations (clusters) through which organizations can exchange data and information.
- Connectivity–digitization enables horizontal and vertical integration in the value network and visibility of information in all network links.
- Adaptiveness–the system of connected digital and automation resources must be flexible. It must be able to respond to different changes in the environment (requests, users, partners, and so on).
- Integration–in the digital world, the integration of the procurement systems is the process of connecting different computer systems, software applications, machinery automation, physically or functionally, to facilitate coordination of procurement flows.
- Autonomous–smart objects, which have the ability to communicate and undertake independent decision-making based on data processing of their own and wider environmental characteristics, are increasingly present in the procurement 4.0 solutions.
- Cognition–application of devices and systems for the automation of tasks requiring human skills, knowledge, perception, and cognitive skills (planning, reasoning, and learning).

Procurement 4.0 launched at the level of an organization requires a great effort and also the rethinking of education and training.

[8] Kayikci, Y. (2018). Sustainability impact of digitization in logistics, *Procedia Manufacturing*, 21, 782–789.

To analyze training 4.0, it is interesting to follow the sequence suggested by Rudyard Kipling to describe phenomena: It is necessary to examine the Why, What, Who, When, Where, and How.[9] And it is worth giving special attention to procurement issues, which are not always managed correctly within industry 4.0 initiatives.

5.4.1 *Why*

Underlying industry 4.0 are some key components of organizations, summarized as the four Ps: processes, platforms, persons, and partnerships. Persons are fundamental to design, develop, monitor, and control the new solutions. Hence the importance of educating and training in the new vision, involving the maximum possible number of persons and developing their digital competencies.

E-competencies are the ability to design and use, with confidence, critical advanced solutions and those for automating work, wherever the person is within the organization. Competencies involved in procurement 4.0 are useful skills for all persons and, in particular, to those who occupy managerial positions in procurement 4.0.

E-competencies are centered on basic skills in information, communication, and automation solutions: the use of computers to retrieve, assess, store, produce, present, exchange information, and communicate and participate in collaborative networks via the internet.[10]

5.4.2 *What*

Training 4.0 must relate persons to the other three Ps: processes, platforms, and partnerships. Some persons believe that procurement 4.0 is only about automation and digitization. Instead, it is important to review all relevant processes and re-engineer them in the direction of procurement 4.0 and organizational goals.

Attention should be paid primarily to providing training in small and medium-sized organizations through practical research and tailor-made knowledge transfer. The issues here are several, such as automation,

[9] Kipling R. (2013), *Just So Stories*, CreateSpace Independent Publishing Platform, Scott Valley, CA.

[10] https://www.aicanet.it/competenza-digitale. Accessed March 30, 2019.

mechatronics engineering, and process re-engineering, accompanied by business model engineering.

The training and the application of procurement 4.0 should be done in teams. It is important to promote training on how to improve teamwork and make it more effective and efficient.

5.4.3 *Who*

Training 4.0 must be directed at all levels and roles in an organization. It should not be limited to persons working on automation and ICT. On the contrary, it is necessary to develop e-competencies in all areas.

Procurement professionals must take into account the procurement 4.0 approach. Furthermore, the management, staff, procurement, maintenance, marketing, sales, and administration should be involved in the procurement 4.0 training too.

It is useful in the training 4.0 to include any partners, at least those critical to the organization. In a situation where the procurement of goods and services can reach 70% of overall costs (such as in BMW[11]) the organization cannot limit procurement 4.0 to within the walls of the organization.

It is useful to start with activities to 'train the trainers,' that is, training other trainers or at least the key users of these new processes and schemes throughout the organization. The number of persons involved in an organization can be very high. Training trainers in the organization can thus be extremely helpful to reduce costs and foster the creation of 4.0 'evangelists' who will spread good practice across the organization.

5.4.4 *When*

Ideally, training for industry 4.0 should start in schools and universities. It is also important to train persons already employed by an organization, in order that they may be converted to the initiative and become active supporters thereof. Procurement 4.0 calls for new competencies and capabilities. As a result, an organization's personnel should be involved well before the beginning of the digital transformation.

[11] https://businesslogisticsupf.wordpress.com/2016/11/25/bmw-outlines-new-plans-to-transform-logistics-efficiency/. Accessed July 19, 2019.

5.4.5 *Where*

The ideal is to do training 4.0 in or near an organization's premises. Training on the job, with frequent applications and interactions, is important. Training limited to the classroom will not fully achieve the purpose of the transformation. If the organization is unable to apply prototyping and proofs of concept for procurement 4.0, it may use training as the playground to try out the first successful implementations of procurement 4.0. In this way, it is possible to strengthen participants' awareness of the importance and especially the viability of this digital transformation.

5.4.6 *How*

Apart from training in the classroom and on the job, it is important to carry out visits to other organizations that have successfully implemented procurement 4.0. A visit to German organizations or research centers can be useful here. The non-profit German organization Fraunhofer-Gesellschaft is an excellent research center on industry 4.0, being the largest organization for applied research in Europe.[12] The institute collaborates with industry to promote research that generates benefits for the whole of society. The Fraunhofer-Gesellschaft was the first research institute in Germany to work on the concept of industry 4.0 and to successfully implement it.

A visit to such a research center would also be useful in terms of expanding the network of relationships and to be able to draw on funds allocated to research and competence centers for the development and testing of procurement 4.0 within an organization.

There are now several initiatives that work on training 4.0. The approach suggested in this chapter is the right one to follow, as it is holistic and integrated.

5.5 Conclusions

Education and training are important for procurement 4.0. They must be addressed in a holistic way that takes into account the system in its entirety and addresses these aspects as part of a consistent and integrated framework.

[12] www.fraunhofer.de. Accessed April 26, 2019.

To consolidate a culture that supports procurement 4.0, it is important to take into account five fundamental skills. They are vital to implementing a true digital transformation 4.0 in an organization:

- ability to manage innovation in the human–machine relationship;
- digital value network management;
- special focus on intelligent maintenance, particularly important for procurement would be the best practices in predictive maintenance;
- application of lean production 4.0[13];
- core competencies in safety management and cybersecurity both in the ICT domain as (and especially) in operations technology domains.[14]

The Osservatorio del Politecnico di Milano (Italy) conducted a survey that tracked the profile of some Italian organizations in their ratio of industry skills 4.0.[15] Half of the organizations knew about industry 4.0 or claimed to have assessed their skills for industry 4.0. This news is positive. It should be seen in a context where another 25% say they want to do this soon. The survey revealed that training was directed to personnel engaged in production, factory workers, employees, and figures that are directly involved in work on automation systems. Sensitivity to this new frontier in training courses does not stop at the factory floor. Rather, managers and entrepreneurs should be involved in the roadmap to skills 4.0.

The survey was useful to determine some important aspects of training 4.0. Training of internal staff (24%) or external acquisition (11%) of skills required are the two findings from organizations engaged in the 4.0 transformation. The survey does raise some concerns about the marginal role of HR in this training. Only 12% of the sample involved HR to guide and direct their training roadmap to digital transformation. For 70% of survey participants, HR either was not involved or only in a marginal way.

[13] Elg, M., Gremyr, I., Hellström, A., & Witell, L. (2011). The role of quality managers in contemporary organisations. *Total Quality Management & Business Excellence*, 22(8), 795–806.

[14] Hickson, D. J., Pugh, D. S., & Pheysey, D. C. (1969). Operations technology and organization structure: An empirical reappraisal. *Administrative science quarterly*, 378–397.

[15] https://www.industry4business.it/osservatori/osservatorio-industria-4-0-industrial-iot-analytics-e-cloud-manufacturing-spingono-il-mercato-a-24-mld-con-un-30/. Accessed May 25, 2019.

CHAPTER 6

Partnerships in Procurement 4.0

6.1 Introduction

This book does not use the term 'supplier,' preferring 'partner.' There are several reasons for the use of this terminology. The first is that partners can be of very different types: suppliers of products, services, and systems, partners external to or from the same group or even from the same organization, or academic research institutions, consultants, and so forth. The real reason for using 'partner' is that a provider really is a partner. A partner is a person, natural or legal, with which an organization works on activities in which their development requires the participation of more than one person and more than one skill. A partner is thus an ally. If delivery is unsuccessful, both the partner and the customer suffer from the standpoint of their reputation, if not directly in a monetary sense. In the case of procurement 4.0, partners play an essential role in the value network, because of their relevance to the advances being made and their close interconnection.

AI systems and, more generally, advanced ICT solutions will generate an increase in the market for digital products. Therefore, the increased role of partners in such components and a concomitant decline of the importance of partners in physical components can be expected.[1]

[1] Porter, M. E., & Heppelmann, J. E. (2014). How smart, connected products are transforming competition. *Harvard business review*, *92*(11), 64–88.

B. Nicoletti, *Procurement 4.0 and the Fourth Industrial Revolution*,
https://doi.org/10.1007/978-3-030-35979-9_6

Procurement 4.0 reflects an increasing emphasis on the importance of partners. Partner relations are changing to cooperate with selected suppliers. The activities that procurement 4.0 organization must implement are quite different from a few decades ago. Procurement 4.0 requires partner developments, partner design engagements, use of full-service providers, selection of total cost partners, long-term partner relationships, strategic cost management, enterprise resource planning, and integrated internet connections and shared databases as ways to create new value within the value network.[2]

The integration of operations with partners enables organizations to capture benefits from the exchange of information. ICT use is also an important foundation for the integration with partners in procurement 4.0 perspectives.[3]

6.2 Procurement in Teams

The right approach in procurement 4.0 is to consider the four Ps: processes, platforms; persons, and partnerships. There is much talk of teamwork in procurement due to the increasing importance and complexity of the value network. Procurement thus takes on a new role as team coordinator. It seems appropriate to analyze this view (Fig. 6.1). The existing procurement model will change within a future perspective with regard to functions, responsibilities, and stakeholders—also driven by the increase of digitization and the opportunities it presents within the next decades supported by the future trends outlined in this book.[4]

[2] Rodrigues, M., Sousa, B., & da Costa, J. B. (2019). The Improvement of the Supply Chain Channel Based on Digital Transformation: An Exploratory Study in the Sustainable Industry 4.0 *4th Regional Helix- Book of Abstracts* Parallel Session 4, Porto, Portugal.

[3] Vanpoucke, E., Vereecke, A., Muylle, S. (2017). Leveraging the impact of supply chain integration through information technology. *International Journal of Production Management*, 37 (4), 510–530

[4] Sengupta, S. (2013), 10 trends in supply chain management, *Supply Chain Management Review*, 17(4), 34–39.

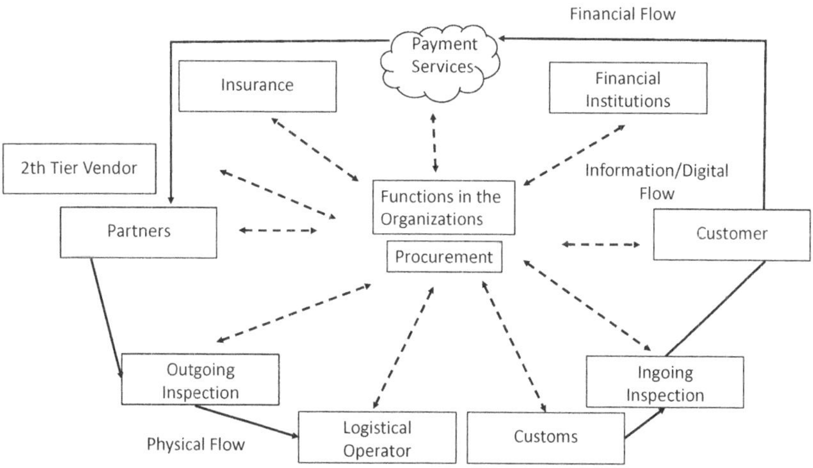

Fig. 6.1 New role of procurement as a team coordinator

6.2.1 *Persons and Organizations*

Procurement 4.0 is always about teamwork. Teamwork here may refer to that within the procurement sector; it can also mean teamwork within an organization. For example, in the case of a project, it is important to have someone in the project team dedicated to taking care of procurement. He/she would be a full or part-time member depending on the size of the project. For organizations that are part of a group, it is interesting to work within the group to achieve synergies in common purchases, such as those related to indirect purchases like equipment and office materials. In the case of public administration, both local and national, teamwork is important to providing procurement support for smaller departments. This is done, for example, in certain nations by a central procurement agency.[5] In the case of organizations not part of the same group, one organization can team up with other organizations in the same industry sector. This happens quite often in the retail sector. Another example is the setup of a purchasing center among different organizations. An example of this type is the ABC consortium in Italy, sponsored by the association of Italian banks (ABI) with the banks belonging to the association.[6]

[5] http://www.consip.it/. Accessed March 30, 2019.
[6] https://www.consorzio-abc.it/. Accessed March 30, 2019.

An example of an advanced procurement team is to use the internet for crowdsourcing. This can be defined as the use of ICT to outsource any organizational function to a strategically defined population of human and non-human actors in the form of an open call.[7]

6.2.2 *Processes*

In any procurement team, teamwork is particularly effective in supporting the marketing of procurement. In this case, participation of many persons with diverse experiences can be of great help. Similarly, evaluation of partners can be of great use for sharing experiences in groups with other buyers and therefore in selecting future partners.

6.2.3 *Platforms*

The support that ICT can provide for teamwork is growing and improving over time. For telematics platforms, it is useful if the platform includes three fundamental aspects of teamwork:

- Communication—the backbone of the teamwork. A procurement platform supporting teams uses a variety of media, chats, email, video and audio conference calls, and so forth, available at several levels of sophistication.
- Coordination—based on rules, explicit or implicit, to enable the various components of a team to operate in synergy. Typical tools in procurement 4.0 teams are group calendars and automatic software packages for planning and document sharing.
- Cooperation—this implies the sharing of a context that varies with the characteristics of the project, which is aimed at the working group.

In the past, platforms for teamwork were proprietary. Today, commercial solutions provide an important standardization when an interested procurement team works in more than one division of an organization., There are excellent telematics solutions for teamwork now available. Think of an organization-wide chat or the so-called groupware. The latter term is used to describe methodologies and tools that enable users with workstations connected via a network to:

[7] Kietzmann, J. H. (2017). Crowdsourcing: A revised definition and introduction to new research. *Business horizons*, 60(2), 151–153.

- communicate in several ways, from the exchange of messages (email, chats, and similar), voice calls, and videos on a computer screen;
- share multimedia documents (text, data, images, and sounds);
- use the same application programs, whether a simple Excel spreadsheet or complex applications, and to schedule jobs in which different actors may take part;
- agree on decisions at several stages of the process, using tools that facilitate discussion and idea generation, such as online brainstorming sessions.

Cloud computing solutions can be exploited intra-organization and inter-organization. Organizations that have an advanced approach to cloud computing tend to maximize their benefits through hybrid solutions. This enables them to effectively use these solutions as a means to integrate information across the organization. It also allows the organization to use cloud computing as a way to interact with its partners effectively, efficiently, economically, and in total transparency.

An pertinent variation of the distribution models of cloud computing is cloud B2B.[8] This solution helps to enhance cooperation and integration between buyer and seller organizations.

6.2.4 *Security*

Procurement has always been a matter of teamwork. This aspect is now increasingly appreciated and valued. Support tools in this area are the management of persons, processes, and platforms.

There are some particular things to consider for data security and confidentiality. The benefits of teamwork here can be significant, not only from the standpoint of efficiency and economy. The greatest benefits are to be found in increasing the effectiveness of procurement, both in terms of response times but also in the satisfaction of customers' internal and external procurement.

Moreover, with teamwork it is necessary also to consider security in the protection and tracking of information, and transparency of data for all partners and users. At the same time, it is essential to control access to the teamwork and its tools, and to control data sharing in order to avoid data breaches by competitors or hackers.

[8] Nicoletti, B., (2013), *Cloud Computing and Financial Services*, Palgrave Macmillan, London, UK (also translated in Chinese).

Ansaldo Energia[9]

Ansaldo Energia is an Italian power engineering company based in Genoa. Its R&D plan, lasting three years and starting in July 2018 was based on the industry 4.0 model, with partners such as Politecnico di Milano, University of Genoa, and other technology partners. Ansaldo Energia will invest a total of €14 million in this initiative. The business case provided a four-year payback that has been reduced to three years thanks to financing and incentives.

The project includes initiatives such as:

- Implementation of manufacturing execution systems and manufacturing operations management solutions that allow real-time tracking of work on the shop floor;
- Floor workshop operations, which are essential to support a highly variable market trend. Ansaldo Energia expects an average of around 35 releases per year of the production plan, with substantial changes in the mix;
- Smart tracking, necessary to guarantee synchronization with partners thanks to digital solutions in a situation that uses a large number of components, materials, and equipment;
- Asset optimization carried out in collaboration with the Politecnico di Milano, which plans to make a series of 'intelligent' machine tools to generate information. This will make it possible to move from a planned maintenance model to a predictive maintenance model.
- The use of big data and business analytics both in production and quality management. The organization is particularly keen on quality here. The objective is to reduce assessment costs by automating the collection process, by analyzing information, and intensifying prevention activities. In this way, it will be possible to evaluate the components with greatest risk of error, and so to better direct correction activities.

(*continued*)

[9] Bevilacqua, E. (2018). Ansaldo Energia, un percorso di digitalizzazione 4.0. https://www.zerounoweb.it/casi-utente/ansaldo-energia-un-percorso-di-digitalizzazione-4-0/. Accessed May 5, 2019.

(continued)

- Particular attention is paid to cybersecurity. Ansaldo Energia is developing a solution for the SCADAs (factory control and data acquisition control systems) with the possibility of replicating it and making it portable in power plants and critical customer infrastructures.

A fundamental element of the transformation in Ansaldo Energia is the concept of the digital twin, that is, the use of digital technology to replicate real industrial processes in a virtual model. The project involves strong involvement of value network partners, both machine tool and equipment partners, and SMEs. Attention to the value network also goes to startups, 160 of which responded to the call for innovation (Digital X Factory, October 31–December 1, 2017), contributing 90 proposals. Eleven selected startups and SMEs will work on implementation of the project.

The prospect is to create a technology platform to develop a digital twin with customers and experiment with the possibility of digitally managing the plant. There is a need to no longer manage physical assets, but to coordinate, thanks to integrated platforms, the energy supply and demand sector of, which is changing dramatically—this is a difficult step for a company whose current job is above all to produce turbines in the best way possible.

In perspective, the first objective is to increase digital capabilities of the persons within the organization, with the ability to create new roles for them, to learn to work more easily with customers, partners, SMEs, and innovative startups in a healthy procurement 4.0 ecosystem.

6.3 Partner Evaluation in Procurement 4.0

Assessment of partners (partner rating) is important and especially relevant to the processes of procurement 4.0, as it allows:

- better selection of partners;
- correction during work of any defects or inadequate performance;
- involvement of the entire ecosystem in procurement processes.

Assessment of partners should be done at different times:

- before the organization places an order, at the time of the selection of the partners;
- during the provision of services or supply of goods purchased;
- at the end of the service or supply of goods.

In the real life, rarely will the process be followed throughout the life of a supply. For example, in the evaluation at the end of a supply process, it is very difficult to get a proper written evaluation from users. The problem is that persons are often over-committed and do not have time or do not give priority to the assessment of partners.

One may wonder whether the digital transformation can also aid in the assessment of partners. This is important, as in many cases the percentage of the total purchases over the total operating costs is increasing over time. It is worthwhile to see how the five most significant solutions in procurement 4.0 can help in the assessment of partners.

6.3.1 IoT

IoT allows automatic collection of a range of information that can support evaluation of partners not only from an operational and management point of view but also when they are involved in providing services or goods supported by IoT. Thanks to IoT, an organization can record, for instance, arrival time, the duration of a service, solutions that do not meet acceptable quality, and so forth. The use of the IoT can thus yield many benefits for organizations. To realize the full benefits of IoT, the organizations need to be equipped to handle and interpret this data.[10]

6.3.2 Big Data

The IoT also collects a lot of data on partners and their products. Other electronic tools are available to gather data on supplies. An example is provided by the Service Desk. More and more organizations are using applications that enable the creation of a ticket to record incidents, problems, service and change requests, and knowledge management processes.

[10] Brous, P., Janssen, M., & Herder, P. (2018). Internet of Things adoption for reconfiguring decision-making processes in asset management. *Business Process Management Journal.*

Many of these tools can produce dashboards on compliance, with agreements on the levels of service. Thus, an organization can automatically record data on partner performance, compliance with contracts, and especially on trends. In this way, an organization can evaluate its partners and, if necessary, take action before a situation gets out of control.

All these data can be stored using big data technologies. Hence, it is now easy to access or produce statistical reports on performance.

6.3.3 AI

Big data also allows an organization to be connected through AI tools. These applications can provide operational and management level support. They can also be used to evaluate partners and support them in better delivery if they do not reach agreed performance targets.

6.3.4 Mobility

Where there is a need for a manual assessment of partner performance, organization personnel can use simple apps on their cell phones to collect data on partners' performance. In this case, the apps can also be used to remind employees of the need for assessment of partners, which requires only a few clicks.

6.3.5 Cloud Computing

Cloud computing is extending use of the tools mentioned above virtually to entire organizations, even when employees are very mobile, as in the case on ships, trains, or fleets of vehicles used by an organization.

6.4 Conclusions

Porter states that the source of competitive advantage in business is the skillful management of connections in the value network.[11] Other authors note that the complexity of offers increases along with the complexity of the partnerships necessary to deliver these offers.[12] The best offers involve

[11] Porter, M. E., & Heppelmann, J. E. (2014). How smart, connected products are transforming competition. *Harvard business review*, *92*(11), 64–88.

clients and partners in various combinations. As a result, strategic activities should be oriented to the reconfiguration of roles and relationships between partners, in order to create new forms of value for the customer. This observation is also very much applicable to value networks in which advanced solutions play a key role.[13] It is clear that the role of procurement 4.0 needs to change substantially.

Strong relationships with partners are essential for the success of procurement 4.0. It is important not to refer anymore to the supply chain but rather to the value network.[14] The operations of an organization are increasingly made up of a network in which different paths allow advanced customization of the product. The objective of procurement 4.0 is not simply to deliver products or services to add value to customers and the organization; in this new vision, procurement must work as a coordinator of the network of partners—the whole ecosystem must work as one team. With this in mind, assessment of partners is an important and essential aspect. The rationale here is that relationships with partners should be of mutual value and therefore must be assessed, in this context, so as to continuously improve or, at the extreme, to remediate or to close partnerships.

[12] Normann, R., & Ramirez, R. (1993). From value chain to value constellation: Designing interactive strategy. *Harvard business review*, *71*(4), 65–77.

[13] Wodecki, A. (2018). *Artificial intelligence in value creation: Improving competitive advantage*. Springer, Cham, Switzerland.

[14] Nicoletti, B. (2017), *Agile Procurement*. Volume I: Adding Value with Lean Processes, Springer International Publishing, London, UK. ISBN 978-3-319-61082-5.

CHAPTER 7

Future of Procurement 4.0

7.1 Introduction

This chapter deals with the future of procurement 4.0. It is worth mentioning that the great physicist Niels Bohr said: "It is very difficult to predict, especially the future."[1] Yet, for survival as human beings as well as organizations, it is important to try and predict the future. This observation holds more generally too, and even more so in the case of procurement because of its close links with the world outside of an organization. As usual, this interrelationship is even stronger in the case of procurement 4.0.

The simple answer to the future of procurement 4.0 will be procurement 5.0. This procurement 5.0 will be closely connected with industry 5.0, when it comes. Meanwhile, procurement will evolve in the short and medium term.

7.2 Scenario

To predict something it is necessary to define a possible scenario(s). This is simple for the short term. Slower growth and other difficulties around the world will make it difficult to resume the pre-financial crisis produc-

[1] Camussone, P. F. (2017). Digital for job: The future of work: technology. *Digital World*, 2: 1–15.

B. Nicoletti, *Procurement 4.0 and the Fourth Industrial Revolution*,
https://doi.org/10.1007/978-3-030-35979-9_7

tion levels of 2008. At the same time, globalization is now in crisis. The reasons for this are several. The acceleration on globalization was probably not the right way to go about things. The result has been a revival of localism and a surge in sovranism (a new term for nationalism, a term that evokes bad past times).

These changes will also be reflected in organizations and so in their procurement processes. To examine what could happen to procurement 4.0, it is useful to refer to the classic four Ps of the marketing mix: product, price, promotion, and place.

From the product point of view, dematerialization is prevailing. This pushes the services that start or expand from physical products in the direction of sharing economy, sharing of physical goods, for consumption, but also from the perspective of organizations. Outsourcing is the traditional mode of a sharing economy for organizations. The expectation here is that outsourcing will grow further.

From the price perspective, the trend will be to include in the economic balance of a product or service factors not strictly connected with the price but with the financial gains in general. It is to be expected that procurement will finance a major campaign to reduce costs and financial charges but also to facilitate trade and promote even the weaker partners.

In terms of promotion, it is interesting to note the start of diffusion in the procurement of organizations of some traditional forms of promotion to the consumers. An example is the consumerization of ICT for organizations. Another example is in transport, where there are special promotions for organizations.

The last P of these four aspects, the place, and thus the facilitation in delivery and development of logistics in support of trade, is increasingly visible.

7.3 The Four Ps of Procurement Management

At this point, an organization can try to identify how the future looks from the perspective of the four Ps listed above—in other words, how the future looks in terms of possible developments in platforms, processes, persons, and partnerships (Fig. 7.1).

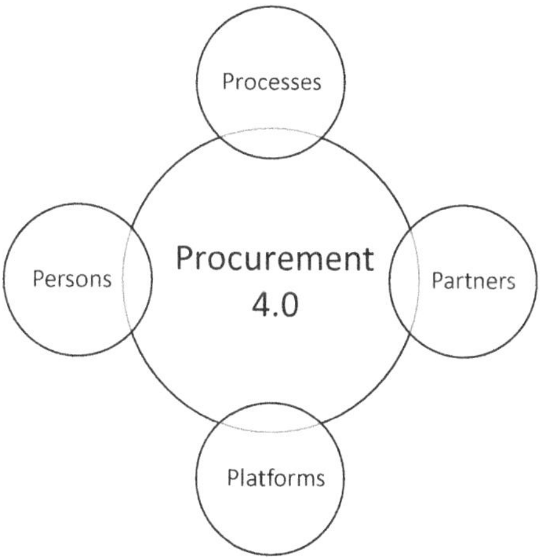

Fig. 7.1 Four Ps

7.3.1 *Platforms*

The most interesting aspect is constituted by the increasing diffusion of platforms as a business model. These are intended as telematics platforms that allow the matching of the other four Ps (Fig. 7.2):

- The Proprietor of the platform: those that have identified and funded this type of online information system;
- The Provider of the platform and, therefore, the one who provides the infrastructure, services, and software supporting that platform;
- The Producers, who provide the products, and especially services, made available on the platform;
- The Purchasers, who buy the products or the services available on the platform.

These roles can be exchanged. For example, Producers can become Purchasers and vice versa.

The platform usually exists in the cloud, to which all other applications will migrate over time. The most interesting solution made possible by cloud computing is the blockchain (a technological solution that was introduced in connection with cryptocurrency Bitcoin).[2] Within a short

[2] Nicoletti, B. (2017), *The Future of Fintech*, Springer International Publishing, Chem, Switzerland. ISBN 978-3-319-51414-7

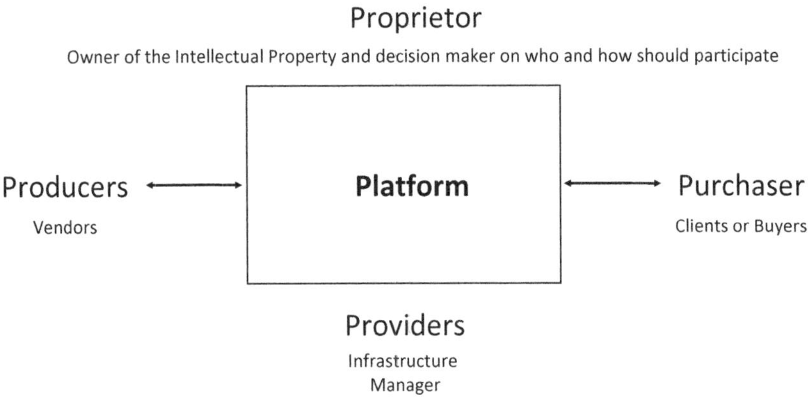

Fig. 7.2 Platform

time, this innovation has been appreciated for its capacity to substantially innovate work in groups. Procurement teams are one of the areas that can benefit the most. See further discussion on the uses and opportunities of the blockchain in Chap. 4.

7.3.2 Processes

Processes will become increasingly integrated as procurement 4.0 evolves into 5.0. For too long, the concept of lean-ness has been used to lighten up processes with organizational or logistic measures. The 'lean and digitize' methodology will be increasingly used as a way to make processes leaner and better integrated.[3]

In the future, with the spread of e-procurement functionality, an organization can connect all the applications mentioned in this book and employ management tools to support its procurement processes. One can imagine the automatic construction of black or gold lists of partners. Moreover, the information gathered can be shared in real time directly with partners in the value network.

In the future, the resilience of products and services received from partners should be a feature included in all orders and supply contracts. It is

[3] Nicoletti, B., (2012), *Lean and Digitize: An Integrated Approach to Process Improvement.* Gower Publishing, Farnham, UK. ISBN-10: 1409441946.

essential that resilience be an integral part of the assessment of potential products, services, and systems, and even more in the evaluation of potential partners.

Researchers are developing products with autonomic computing, the ability of a computer system in self-care or self-unlocking.[4] This means that products or services can autonomously detect and remedy failures and effect their own recovery. This can allow, for instance, large ICT systems, aimed at providing services 24/7, to meet their targets with little or no human intervention. Achieving self-care requires automated testing, possible with Jenkins continuous integration,[5] and the elicitation and maintenance of domain knowledge in the form of problem determination, diagnosis, and repair models.[6] Case-based reasoning (CBR) is a learning paradigm that reduces many of these types of bottleneck due to automatic knowledge acquisition.[7] Besides, the application of CBR for diagnosis and remediation in software systems looks promising. In this field, most mistakes are new occurrences of known issues. It is more difficult to develop an autonomic solution in the case of services due to the strong human presence in service provision. But it is not impossible. Most likely, the future holds some interesting developments in this area.

One other interesting element is the so-called shared-nothing architecture.[8] This is the architecture of distributed processing in which each node is independent and self-sufficient, and there is no point of contention in the entire system. More specifically, none of the nodes share memory or space on memory devices. The most appealing part of this system is the fact that there can be no single point of failure; the system is very scalable. This is a feature of great interest to partners, especially outsourcers.

[4] Montani, S., & Anglano, C. (2008). Achieving self-healing in service delivery systems software by means of case-based reasoning. *Applied Intelligence*, 28 (2), 139–152.

[5] Smart, J. F. (2011). *Jenkins: The Definitive Guide: Continuous Integration for the Masses.* O'Reilly Media, Inc., Sebastopol. CA:

[6] Yiran, W., Tongyang, Z., & Vidong, G. (2018). Design and implementation of continuous integration scheme based on Jenkins and Ansible. In *2018 International Conference on Artificial Intelligence and Big Data (ICAIBD).* IEEE, May: 245–249.

[7] Kolodner, J. (2014). *Case-based reasoning.* Morgan Kaufmann, Burlington, MA.

[8] Chaisuriya, S., Keretho, S., Sanguanpong, S., & Praneetpolgrang, P. (2018, January). A Security Architecture Framework for Critical Infrastructure with Ring-based Nested Network Zones. in *2018 10th International Conference on Knowledge and Smart Technology* (KST). IEEE: 248–253.

Digital resilience will be fully available in the more distant future. This is the ability to design customer applications, business processes, technology architectures, and related cybersecurity defenses with the protection of critical information and assets of the organization in mind.[9]

7.3.3 *Persons*

For persons, there is a very clear trend: There will simply be fewer persons engaged in procurement. They will work more as consultants for other functions of the organization rather than doing negotiation or behaving like old-fashioned buyers. It is possible that for specific purchases, procurement will be done by a third party or consortium entities. Yet, this will remain an exception. In the procurement office, there will also be more and more women—not only in line with their growing presence in the workplace in general, but also because of their innate abilities to purchase in particular. SAP Ariba conducted research which concluded that only 5% of respondent companies had highly automated processes in use, with 21% of respondents having mostly manual functions. Of respondents, 83% think the future digital transformation will have impacts on procurement, supply chains, and finance functions—with 63% already having automation on the roadmap for their companies.[10] Major roadblocks that were identified in this survey include talent management and inadequacy in talent strategy. Many organizations lack proper skills to shift their procurement to the next level.

7.3.4 *Partnerships*

From the perspective of partnerships, especially in the case of critical partners, future change will be strong. First of all, there will increasingly be a move from suppliers to partners. This will also push toward the consolidation of partners and their integration. The importance of partner location, and then the proximity of the partners to the organization, will be important.

[9] Kaplan JM, Bailey, T., O'Halloran, D., Marcus, A., & Rezek, C. (2015), *Beyond Cybersecurity: Protecting Your Digital Business*, John Wiley, Hoboken, NJ.

[10] SAP Ariba (2018). CPO Survey 2018 – What's the Next Big Thing in Procurement. https://www.ariba.com/resources/library/library-pages/cpo-survey-2018. Accessed August 1, 2019.

The digitization of contracts is evolving rapidly, too. Smart contracts will be used more and more.[11] These are computer-based protocols and telecommunications that facilitate, manage, or enforce the negotiation or execution of a contract. They allow data stores to be shared between virtual organization as parties of the contracts. It is necessary to guarantee the protection of data from their users, once the data are entered. This type of warranty comes from the use of blockchain.

Smart contracts usually also have an advanced user interface and often simulate the logic of standard contractual clauses. Proponents of smart contracts state that many types of contractual clauses can be made partially or fully automated, self-actuating, or both. Smart contracts are intended to ensure more security for existing contracts and to reduce the transaction costs associated with trading.

Open Manufacturing Platforms[12]

BMW's IoT platform currently connects over 3000 machines, robots, and autonomous transport systems. It is built on Microsoft's Azure cloud computing service. The two organizations are working together on an open manufacturing platform (OMP). This platform will create an open technology framework that will support the development of smart factory offerings. BMW and Microsoft are keen that other automotive organizations and manufacturers sign up too.

Each manufacturer's data can be hindered by proprietary systems that create data silos. Microsoft states that the idea of OMP is to offer a reference architecture with open source components based on open industry standards and an open data model, although it will all be built on Microsoft's Azure industry IoT cloud platform.

Utilizing industrial use cases and sample code, community members and other partners can develop services and solutions while maintaining control over their data.

(*continued*)

[11] Nicoletti, B., (2012), *Lean and Digitize: An Integrated Approach to Process Improvement*. Gower Publishing, Farnham, UK. ISBN-10: 1409441946.

[12] Ranger, S. (2019). Microsoft and BMW: We can help the organization build a smart factory with the cloud, robots, and IoT. https://www.zdnet.com/article/microsoft-and-bmw-we-can-help-you-build-a-smart-factory-with-the-cloud-robots-and-iot/. Accessed May 5, 2019.

(continued)

BMW provides examples, such as its use of IoT in its autonomous transport systems at its plant in Regensburg, Germany. These systems have allowed the organization to simplify logistics through central coordination of the transport system.

Other use cases—such as digital feedback loops, digital supply chain management, and predictive maintenance—are available within the OMP community. The OMP will be designed to address common industry challenges, such as machine connectivity and on-premises systems integration. This could make it easier to reuse software solutions among original equipment manufacturers and other partners, thus reducing implementation costs. A robotics standard for autonomous transport systems for production and logistics will be contributed by Microsoft to the OMP for everyone to use.

7.4 Sustainable Procurement

7.4.1 Procurement Sustainability

There are strong correlations between procurement 4.0 and sustainability.[13] An important component of sustainability in procurement is green procurement. Green procurement is the process by which an organization procures supplies in a manner that does not harm the environment.[14] There is a big push for green procurement in public administration for its social and community implications.[15] The European Commission defines

[13] Garcia-Muiña, FE; González-Sánchez, R. Ferrari, AM, & September-Blundo, D. (2018). The Paradigms of Industry 4.0 and Circular Economy as Enabling Drivers for the Competitiveness of Businesses and Territories: The Case of an Italian Ceramic Tiles Manufacturing Company. *Social Sciences*. MDPI, *Open Access Journal*, 7(12): 1–31, December.

[14] Nagel, M. H. (2000, May). Environmental supply-chain management versus green procurement in the scope of a business and leadership perspective. *Proceedings of the 2000 IEEE International Symposium on Electronics and the Environment (Cat. No. 00CH37082,)* 219–224. IEEE.

[15] Testa, F., Annunziata, E., Iraldo, F., & Frey, M. (2016). Drawbacks and opportunities of green public procurement: an effective tool for sustainable production. *Journal of Cleaner Production*, 112, 1893–1900.

green public procurement (GPP) as "[t]he approach whereby organizations integrate environmental criteria at all stages of the procurement process, encouraging the spread of environmental technologies and the development of viable products environmentally, through research and choosing outcomes and solutions that have the least possible impact on the environment throughout their entire life cycle."[16]

Green procurement is a voluntary environmental policy methodology that aims to encourage the development of a market for products and services with reduced environmental impacts through the lever of public demand. Public authorities that undertake GPP actions are committed both to rationalizing their sourcing and consumption and to increasing the environmental quality of their supplies and contracts.

Even private organizations should push for green procurement. There are several reasons:

- reduction of environmental impacts, and therefore of the related waste of energy and natural resources;
- improvement of competitiveness, as green procurement allows in many cases the reduction of costs (for example, through reduction in the use of electricity);
- stimulation of innovation;
- better-directed spending;
- reputation among customers and communities in which the organizations operate.

In addition to financial statements, some organizations publish an annual sustainability report. This is a voluntary commitment. This tool allows an organization to report to every stakeholder (carrier of interest) on its achievements in contributing to sustainable development, that is, its non-financial performance. Such a report is important since it includes discussion of positive impacts and actions to overcome possible negative impacts resulting from the organization's activities.

[16] European Commission. (2004). *Buying Green! A Handbook on Environmental Public Procurement*, European Union, Brussels, Belgium.

7.4.2 New Technologies for Sustainable Procurement

Many innovative solutions are available in support of sustainable procurement. The most interesting ones are as follows:

- cloud computing
- big data analytics
- mobility
- IoT
- AI.

Each of these can support sustainable procurement by making it more environmentally friendly, and at the same time improve implementation of procurement 4.0.

These solutions can help to effect so-called reverse logistics (Fig. 7.3). Reverse logistics (also called return logistics) is the process of planning, implementing, managing, and controlling the efficiency of semi-finished materials, finished products, and related information flows from the recovery point (or point of consumption) to the point of origin.[17]

Cloud Computing

Cloud computing refers to a method of supplying computing resources, such as storage, processing, or transmission of data, characterized by availability on demand, over the internet and from a set of existing resources, and in a way that is configurable. Thanks to the use of large computer rooms and new technologies, cloud computing allows for electricity savings. It also results in substantial savings of carbon dioxide dispersed into the atmosphere.

Big Data Analytics

Big data analytics is a new concept. It is the union of two concepts: big data and business analytics. Big data analytics refers to the exploitation of data, and possesses five V characteristics: volume, velocity, variety, and veracity, and being capable of adding value to the organization. Big data analytics can support green procurement. For example, it can be used to

[17] Dekker, R. Fleischmann, M., Inderfurth, K., & van Wassenhove, LN (Eds.). (2013). *Reverse logistics: quantitative models for closed-loop supply chains.* Springer Science & Business Media, Berlin, Germany.

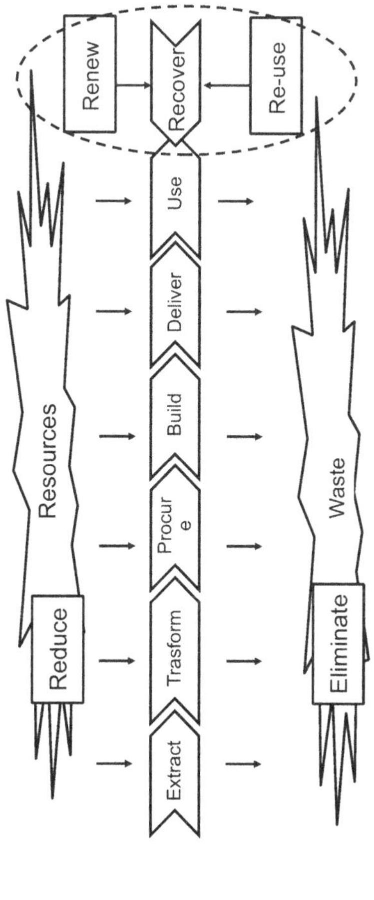

Fig. 7.3 Reverse logistics

collect, analyze, and integrate changes in the climate by comparing it with a network of 'green' data the value of products. The objective is to start a process of utilization of quantitative data to detect, monitor, and support the value network of the 'greenest partners.'

Mobility

Mobile computing refers generically to processing technology or data access (via the internet) with no constraints in terms of physical location or equipment involved. The use of mobile computing also reduces travel required to carry out certain operations in the case of procurement. Especially, it allows continuous working and without the use of paper. This reduces the handling and consumption of natural resources.

Internet of Things

The IoT refers to the extension of the internet to the world of objects and places. With the IoT, objects can interact with each other and with persons. This technology can achieve intelligent use of energy through several control devices. It allows the provision of an efficient model in the use of objects, whether they are industrial machinery or household devices, according to user needs. What unites these different technologies is not only their implications for environmental conservation; they can also deliver these efficiencies discreetly, and in a way that provides benefits to all who use them by respecting the environment and reducing the consumption of environmental resources.

Artificial Intelligence

Another important technology is AI, with particular reference to cognitive computing. Cognitive computing platforms are typically equipped with machine learning, reasoning skills, voice recognition capabilities, and natural language processing, as well as machine vision. They can perceive the environment through different sensory extensions similar to those of humans, process it through virtual agents, and suggest the best actions to implement in response to the context.

AI includes theory and techniques for the development of algorithms that allow machines (typically computers but also any object with a chip, such as a smartphones or tablet) to demonstrate an ability and/or intelligent activity, at least in specific domains.

The sustainability of software depends on the direct effects that result from programs that perform actions to reduce consumption of environmental resources, as well as the indirect effects that influence the sustainability of products incorporating this software. Indirect effects are caused, for example, by planned obsolescence when a manufacturer's device stops providing reliable performance, rendering it unusable.

To optimize the direct effects on green procurement, tools that provide methods for modeling energy usage and to analyze and optimize energy consumption are very useful. The indirect effects are more difficult to assess, since their optimization requires a change of economic incentives. However, they are important to optimize both types of effects in order to provide sustainable software, since the amount of energy consumed during the operation of a device is of the same order of magnitude as the energy used during its production.

7.5 Conclusions

The future is uncertain. Still, there are some forecasts, especially for the role of procurement. Organizations will most likely move more and more from a linear supply chain to value networks. The role of procurement will change from buyer to concentrator. In other words, the role of procurement will be to build and coordinate different value chains inside the value network with the collaboration of partners. It will not be an easy task, but it is a fundamental one.

The world, and therefore procurement, will continue to change. Because of the forecasts presented in this chapter, and the variability of the environment, any organization needs to plan carefully. It is, however, interesting to consider that 'plans are made to be changed.' So the secret for the success of an organization in terms of better procurement will be agility and thus flexibility to adapt to change.

The role of procurement will grow, increasingly moving out of buying/negotiation activity into being a creator of alliances with partners, and in the end also with customers. The latter will want to customize the products/services they buy. A key competence of partners will be in cognitive networks. They should create the environment and mobilize customers to generate value for themselves. Creating environments will be possible due to self-service platform solutions, systems enabling the creation and developing of AI solutions, and educational systems. Customers mobilization can be supported by reputation systems or financial incentive systems in the case of cryptocurrencies.

Due to the specificity of industry solutions and the need to adapt services to the specifics of customers' activities, partners will have to work out efficient mechanisms for creating preconfigured industry versions of their services. This will be supported by the ability to group customers into categories and identification of the version of a service optimal to a given customer category.[18]

According to the MECSPE Italian Observatory, as related to the second half of 2018, eight manufacturing organizations out of ten believe that their digital transformation has occurred in recent years and almost all (more than nine out of ten) believe they have a medium–high level of knowledge on the technology and digital opportunities in the market.[19] The future focus is on new enabling technologies, continuing in the direction of ICT security (74%), connectivity (60%), cloud computing (33%), and collaborative robotics (28%) that have already been introduced, and in research and innovation: 61% will invest up to 10% of their turnover, while 25% will dedicate between 10% and 20% thereof. Targeted advice (51%), knowledge transfer (42%), confrontation with competing organizations (39%), workshops (21%), and the tutorship from a university (15%) are considered useful tools for the development process.

Procurement should not be seen as a mere support function in organizations. It is a fundamental point of coordination with the ecosystem of the organization and provides primary support in adding value for customers and to the organization. Procurement has also been increasingly aligned with sustainability goals. Organizations can also gradually move toward the procurement 4.0 model to enhance resource conservation and recycling activities in support of circular economy efforts.[20] This study has demonstrated that organizations with a strong procurement strategy and effective procurement 4.0 review processes are most able to optimize their procurement processes and attain enhanced circular economy performance.[21]

[18] Wodecki, A. (2018). *Artificial intelligence in value creation: Improving competitive advantage*. Springer, Cham, Switzerland.

[19] https://www.mecspe.com/en/comunicati-stampa-en/osservatorio-mecspe-focus-nazionale/. Accessed 6 August 2019.

[20] Geissdoerfer, M., Savaget, P., Bocken, N. M., & Hultink, E. J. (2017). The Circular Economy–A new sustainability paradigm?. *Journal of cleaner production*, 143, 757–768.

[21] Bag, S., Wood, L. C., Mangla, S. K., & Luthra, S. (2020). Procurement 4.0 and its implications on business process performance in a circular economy. *Resources, Conservation and Recycling, 152*, 104–502.

Information processing capability, drawing on procurement 4.0 technologies, moderates the relationship between procurement 4.0 performance review and the intention to optimize. Organizations with a procurement 4.0 model are better able to leverage the performance review process and optimize their procurement processes. Procurement 4.0 applications can speed up procurement transactions by developing information processing capabilities to support organizational processing of information and data to support a more effective, efficient, and economical organization.

Procurement 4.0 provides an adaptive capability that helps companies adapt promptly through resource flexibility, whereas procurement 4.0's absorptive capability considers integrating external knowledge with internal knowledge for use in internal operations, and its innovative capability connects companies' inbuilt innovativeness to market-related gains.[22]

Organizations should now focus on four areas:

- Defining and implementing procurement 4.0 strategies for the development of procurement 4.0 capabilities. Organizations need to strengthen collaborative relationships, share technical knowhow with partners, adopt advanced processes and platforms and improve transparency/traceability over value networks. Procurement 4.0 strategies must be aligned with the strategic goals of the organization to reap more benefits and add value.
- Increasing procurement 4.0 awareness among employees and value network partners is necessary to improve their understanding of procurement 4.0's benefits and also its importance the in context of the circular economy. Increased awareness increases the intention to optimize procurement processes and platforms.
- Reviewing procurement 4.0 is key to assess the progress of its 4.0 deployment and to alter procurement 4.0 strategies accordingly. Organizations need to change the traditional system into a digital management system for better results in terms of optimization of resources and organizations' performance and results.

[22] Wang, C. L., Ahmed, P.K. (2007). Dynamic capabilities: a review and research agenda. *Int. J. Manage. Rev.*, 9 (1), 31–51.

- Measuring performance in the fields of sustainability such as resource outputs, energy outputs, consumption of energy and water, solid waste recycling rate, wastewater reuse rate in every stage of business processes can provide a real picture to the management. Organizations should gradually transform to procurement 4.0 by focusing on these parameters.[23]

To end with another quote, this time attributed to Charles Darwin: "It is not the strongest that survives, nor the most intelligent, but the most open to change."[24]

[23] Bag, S., Wood, L. C., Mangla, S. K., & Luthra, S. (2020). Procurement 4.0 and its implications on business process performance in a circular economy. *Resources, Conservation and Recycling*, *152*, 104–502.

[24] Girotto, V., Pievani, T., & Vallortigara, G. (2014). Supernatural beliefs: Adaptations for social life or by-products of cognitive adaptations?. *Behaviour*, *151*(2–3), 385–402.

CHAPTER 8

Conclusions

The future of procurement is filled with a multitude of questions and uncertainties. The Fourth Industrial Revolution will potentially take procurement to new heights, with the possibility of enabling a fully autonomous supply chain that harnesses the power of the IoT and other technological advances.

The future will certainly see a revolution in the management of procurement. Procurement 4.0 is an essential component to make this future real, as demonstrated throughout this book. The chapters have presented a model outlining the main components and solutions that can ensure effective, efficient, ethical, and economical procurement 4.0.

It is not easy to predict what the future will hold. But without doubt, procurement 4.0 is going to make a step-change when compared to e-procurement. Blockchain technology, such as digital trust mechanisms, and smart contracts, such as self-executing contracts, are just a couple of examples of future implementations in the field. These new solutions will definitely exceed imagination.

The case studies included in this book indicate that procurement 4.0 can bring many benefits, including supporting an organization's activities and daily administrative tasks to perform complex decision-making, facilitating better focus in strategic decisions and activities. The procurement process will increasingly become a strategic interface to support organizational efficiency, effectiveness, profitability, and the creation of new business models, products, and services.

B. Nicoletti, *Procurement 4.0 and the Fourth Industrial Revolution*,
https://doi.org/10.1007/978-3-030-35979-9_8

Yet, there are barriers to the digitalization of procurement processes. These obstacles are encountered in its procedures, processes, and existing capacity. This book has discussed several enabling technologies to support the digital transformation necessary and methods useful to overcome such challenges.

There are four leadership principles that must be taken into account when working in procurement 4.0:

- focus on solutions rather than technologies;
- empower organizations to master the new solutions and act to counter a fatalistic and deterministic view of progress;
- prioritize futures by design rather than by default;
- focus on key values as a feature of new solutions, rather than as a bug.[1]

Meanwhile, the waiting time before the emergence of the next industrial revolution decreases over time. In this view, procurement 5.0 will not be far in the future!

In the meantime, procurement 4.0 presents several challenges to organizations: large financial investments, implementation and operational risks, strict infrastructure requirements, new levels of education and skills of the personnel involved, and so on. At the same time, this concept is not fully defined because new technologies are continuously being developed and new solutions becoming available. Applying procurement 4.0 concepts within organizations is not a matter of choice but a matter of time. The question is simply, *when do we start*?

[1] Schwab, K. (2016). Four leadership principles for the Fourth Industrial Revolution. https://www.weforum.org/agenda/2016/10/four-leadership-principles-for-the-fourth-industrial-revolution. Accessed July 22, 2019.

Relevant Websites

www.3isite.com
www.aberdeen.comwww.aberdeen.com
www.agendadigitale.eu/cloudmate.com/about
www.altimate.ca
Appaltinnovativi.gov.it
www.asslogistica.it
www.assomoda.it
www.benetton.com
www.bernardonicoletti.com
www.bernardonicoletti.com
www.bershka.com
www.cameramoda.it
www.canon.it
www.chaseperformance.com
www.cloudmate.com
www.cnipa.it
www.consult.it
www.con-way.com
www.cscmp.org
www.cscmp.org
www.data.com
data.gov.uk
www.dcvelocity.com

B. Nicoletti, *Procurement 4.0 and the Fourth Industrial Revolution*,
https://doi.org/10.1007/978-3-030-35979-9

www.dylog.it
www.eccellere.com
www.esisinc.com
www.fraunhofer.de
www.freedomdefined.org/Definition
www.fujutsu.com
www.georgia-associates.com
www.gformula.com
www.hem.com
www.hp.it
www.i4punto0.it
www.ibm.it
www.idtech.it
www.ieee.com
www.iged.it
www.ilsole24ore.com
www.ilsole24ore.it
www.impind.de.unifi.it
www.impresaestesa.it
www.impresaprogetto.it
www.inditex.com
www.industriequattropuntozero.it
industry4.hu
www.industryweek.com
www.isixsigma.com
www.istitute-of-logistics.org.uk
www.iungo.it
www.laserfiche.com
www.leancenter.it
www.leancompany.it
www.leandigitize.com
www.lean-digitize.com
leanforum.se/boktorget.asp
leanforum.se/boktorget_anmalan.asp
www.leanmanufacturing.it
www.logility.com
www.ltdmgmt.com
www.managementstudyguide.com
www.massimodutti.com
www.mckinseyquarterly.com

www.microsoft.com
www.microsoft.it
www.novell.com
www.ohio-state.edu/index.php
www.opendefinition.org
openparliament.ca
www.openwork.it
www.optimialelectronics.com
www.organizzazioniaziendali.it/index.asp
www.oysho.com
www.panorama.it
www.pullandbear.com
www.qualityi.it
quattropuntozero.info
www.queoconsulting.it
www.qurius.it
www.reggiani.it
www.ryder.com
www.sas.com
www.sciencedirect.com
www.scmr.com
www.scodanibbio.com/site/access/homeaccess/65.html
searchmanufacturingerp.techtarget.com/news
searchstorage.techtarget.com/podcast/Understanding-stripped-down-hyperscale-storage-for-big-data-use-cases
www.sistemamodaitalia.it
www.skillprofiles.eu
www.stradivarius.com
www.supply-chain.org
www.theprocurement.it
www.toshiba.it
www.tso.it
www.unifi.it
www.unioncamere.it
www.unitec.it
www.uterque.es
www.xerox.it
www.zara.com
www.zara.com/no/no/dame-c390001.html
www.zarahome.com
www.zenshare.it

Glossary[1]

3D Printing Often used as a synonym for additive manufacturing; operates in a similar way to 2D inkjet printing: the three-dimensional object is constructed layer by layer, by jets of material or binder.[2] In common language, it refers to wire extrusion printers that use melt deposition modeling technology.

Account Payable A legally enforceable liability to a creditor recorded on the balance sheet. It usually arises from the purchases of goods and services on an open account basis and evidenced by a received invoice due to be paid within an agreed timeframe

Account Receivable A legally enforceable claim for payments held by an organization against a customer for goods or supplied or services rendered in execution of the customer's order, and recorded on the balance sheet. Such claims generally take the form of invoices raised by an organization and delivered to the customer for payment within an agreed timeframe.

Additive Manufacturing A process of making three-dimensional objects starting from a digital design, adding material layer by layer. It is commonly used as a synonym for 3D printing.

Agility A metric to measure how quickly a solution responds, as the customer's resource load scales, allocating additional resources to the activity.

Algorithms An essential part of modern advanced applications, these are used for a range of tasks from recommending books, movies, and music to automating the investments online. In stock markets, algorithms are

[1] This glossary is provided on the assumption that the reader may possibly need quick clarification. The definitions here are not necessarily accurate or complete. Please refer to the text for a full demonstration of the terms.

[2] https://blog.ansi.org/2016/11/3d-printing-additive-manufacturing-difference/#gref. Accessed August 12, 2019.

B. Nicoletti, *Procurement 4.0 and the Fourth Industrial Revolution*,
https://doi.org/10.1007/978-3-030-35979-9

connected directly into an electronic market and trading happens without any person's intervention. They suggest where the most money can be made, faster and more accurately than any human being, according to the BBC.[3] Pedro Domingos offers a simple definition: "An algorithm is a sequence of instructions telling a computer what to do."[4] He goes on to explain that algorithms are reducible to three logical operations—AND, OR, and NOT. While these operations can be chained together in complex ways, at the core, algorithms are built out of a simple rationale.

Anti-Money Laundering (AML) Anti-money laundering regulations are a set of procedures, laws, and regulations designed to stop the practice of generating income through illegal actions. In most cases, money launderers hide their actions through a series of steps that make it look like money coming from illegal or unethical sources was earned legitimately.

App Short for 'application.' This is a program or piece of software, especially as downloaded by a user into a mobile device.

Application A program that uses basic software, middleware, and network environments to achieve a specific function related to the purposes of an organization.

Application/App store The virtual locations for the distribution of digital applications; available on mobile devices.

Application Programming Interfaces (API) Specification for the interfaces used by software components to communicate with each other. These specifications include a set of requirements that define how two pieces of software can interact. It allows the moving of data between applications. An API may include specifications for routines, data structures, object classes, and variables. These are important because they enable other programmers to use components of existing software, allowing for faster and more reliable software development. This is a major component of the fintech movement.

Artificial Intelligence (AI) Any system that performs actions, reasoning, and behaviors that normally require a human being (visual perception, speech understanding, linguistic translation, organization, object management, decision-making ability). A chatbot is an example of AI

[3] http://www.bbc.com/news/technology-14841018. Accessed July 20, 2019.

[4] Domingos, P. (2015). *The master algorithm: How the quest for the ultimate learning machine will remake our world*. Basic Books. New York, NY.

applied to the customer services branch of a small or medium-sized organization.

Audit The process by which financial records, business processes, and information systems are independently verified by an internal or external auditor.

Augmented Reality (AR) Augmented reality is the solution that allows the enriching of the perception of reality by superimposing of information or virtual objects on real environments.

Authentication The verification of the identity of a user by a system or service.

Authorization The procedure to check whether a customer or another person inside or outside of an organization has the right to do a certain action—for instance, to transfer funds or access sensitive data.

Automation Automated handling of services or goods; also the percentage of requests to a partner handled without any human intervention.

Availability Metric that measures the percentage, usually computed on a period (such as a month) basis, and net of planned or unplanned service downtimes of service coverage.

Beacon Literally 'light signal,' technology, based on Bluetooth, through which beacons transmit and receive short messages within limited distances.

Benchmarking Comparison of processes and/or measures to other processes and/or measures implemented by well-organized entities or a large number of them.

Big Data Analytics An all-encompassing term for any collection of datasets so large and complex that it becomes difficult to process them using traditional data processing applications. Big data analytics possesses five V characteristics: volume, velocity, variety, veracity, and value.

Biometrics Process to detect and possibly record a person's unique physical and other traits, using an electronic device or system as a way of confirming identity.

Bitcoin A cryptocurrency, token of value exchanged between two parties.

Black Belt Term used to describe a certain high level of expertise. The black belt can help or direct a group that applies the Six Sigma method or other process improvement initiatives. A typical black belt must have completed several training courses and at least one major project. In some organizations, there is a process of official registration. It is a full-time position.

Black Swan Event Events that come as a surprise, have a major effect, and are often inappropriately rationalized after the fact with the benefit of hindsight.[5]

Block A record of transactions validated by a set of cryptographic keys. Once completed, it goes into the blockchain as a permanent database. A block makes transactions recordable and trackable, representing the source of truth for the included transactions.

Blockchain as a Service (BaaS) A new term, coined by William Mougayar of Virtual Capital Ventures in early 2015.[6] Equivalent terms include Ethereum blockchain-as-a-service (EthBaaS), or blockchain-as-a-platform (BaaP). Refers to the growing number of services, based on blockchain solutions, available in cloud computing. This platform allows organizations to begin working with blockchain solutions without having to make significant investments in hardware or base software.

Blockchain A distributed database where trust is established through mass collaboration. Each transaction is recorded continuously and sequentially on a public 'block,' creating a unique ongoing 'chain.' The blockchain is this technology, used for the first time by Bitcoin transactions.[7] It can record all sorts of cryptocurrency transactions and operates like a distributed public ledger where information, once entered, cannot be modified. Blockchain technology has several non-cryptocurrency potential solutions, including smart contracts and the recording of digital assets. It can record data—a digital ledger of transactions, agreements, contracts—in other words, anything that needs to be independently recorded and verified as having happened. The blockchain solutions run across several, hundreds, or even thousands of computers. Every time a new batch of transactions is encrypted, it is added to the ledger 'chain' as a 'block.' Its appeal stretches beyond fintech into government, trade, and other fields. The simplest definition is that the blockchain solution is a decentralized digital ledger. It records all digital transactions as a string of data stored on a global network of computers.

[5] http://mitpress.mit.edu/books/war-weather. Accessed June 20, 2019.

[6] http://www.slideshare.net/wmougayar/blockchain-2015-analyzing-the-blockchain-in-financial-services. Accessed July 30, 2016.

[7] Karajovic, M., Narula, H., Pandya, K., Patel, J., and Warring, I. (2017). *Blockchain: A Manager's Guide*, A Report for OMIS 3710 Schulich School of Business York University Toronto, Ontario.

Bluetooth A connection protocol and wireless communication between devices, with data exchange via radio waves.

Bluetooth Low Energy (BLE) Bluetooth feature for low-power applications, designed for wireless devices with a range of up to 50 meters; used for the IoT to borrow or rent assets owned by someone else.

Broad Network Access Facilitates network capabilities and their access through standard mechanisms. Heterogeneous thin or thick customer platforms promote use of the platform. Notebooks, tablet PCs, PDAs, smartphones, and so on are the devices that can access the network.

Business Continuity An ongoing process to ensure that the necessary steps are taken to identify impacts of potential losses and maintain viable recovery strategies, recovery plans, and continuity of services.[8]

Business Intelligence A broad category of applications and solutions for gathering, storing, analyzing, retrieving, and providing access to data to help users make better organization decisions. Business intelligence applications include activities such as decision support systems, querying and reporting, online analytical processing, statistical analysis, forecasting, and data mining. Analytics has generalized and extended business intelligence.

Business Model Canvas A strategic management and entrepreneurial tool. It allows describing, designing, challenging, inventing, and pivoting a business model. Introduced by Osterwalder and Pigneur.[9]

Business-to-Business (B2B) Refers to organizations that relate to other organizations, rather than customers.

Business-to-Consumer (B2C) Indicates solutions going from an organization to a consumer.

Buy-back Agreement or Guarantee Agreement between a buyer and a seller in which the seller agrees to repurchase goods or property from the buyer if a certain event occurs within a specified period. The buy-back price is usually set out in the agreement.

Buyer Credit Financing put in place by a buyer to purchase goods or services or provided for its benefit by a third party such as an Export

[8] NFPA 160. Accessed June 20, 2019.

[9] Osterwalder, A., & Pigneur, Y. (2010). *Business model generation: a handbook for visionaries, game changers, and challengers.* John Wiley & Sons.

Credit Agency (ECA). Contrast with a Partner credit. Buyer credits may be incorporated into supply chain finance (SCF) transactions.

Buyer In the context of SCF, a buyer is a corporate entity or person procuring goods and services, issuing orders and making payments to partners in its value network

Buyer-centric A description of an SCF transaction where the origination usually takes place through a relationship with a buyer, sometimes referred to as the anchor party.

Chatbot AI that simulates human conversations interactively, using preset sentences. Used for assistance services (customer care) or marketing, for example in social networks and instant messaging.

Circular Economy A circular economy aims to redefine growth, focusing on positive society-wide benefits.[10] It entails gradually decoupling economic activity from the consumption of finite resources, and designing waste out of the system. Underpinned by a transition to renewable energy sources, the circular model builds economic, natural, and social capital. Based on three principles:

- Design out waste and pollution
- Keep products and materials in use
- Regenerate natural systems

Client The customer. It could be either external or internal to the organization. In some cases, the word 'client' indicates an access device. In this latter meaning when used in this book, there is always a specification (such as a thin client). Legally, it is the contracting authority of the contract.

Cloud Computing Computing capability that provides convenient and on-demand network access to a shared pool of configurable computing resources.[11] These resources can be rapidly provisioned and released with minimal management effort or partner interaction. Cloud computing has six essential characteristics—pay-per-use, self-service, broad network access, resource pooling, rapid elasticity, and measured service. In general terms, cloud computing enables three possible modes:

[10] https://www.ellenmacarthurfoundation.org/circular-economy/concept. Accessed August 6, 2019.

[11] Liu, F., Tong, J., Mao, J., Bohn, R., Messina, J., Badger, L., & Leaf, D. (2011). NIST cloud computing reference architecture. *NIST special publication*, 500(2011), 1–28.

Infrastructure as a Service (IaaS), Platform as a Service (PaaS), Software as a Service (SaaS), and Business Process as a Service (BPaaS). It can be public, private, or hybrid.

Cloud A metaphor for a global network or synthetic for cloud computing. Initially, it referred to the telephone network. It now refers to the internet.

Collaboration Risks Risks arising from the legal structure of a joint venture. For example, while the finances of each partner in a joint venture might be robust, the joint venture vehicle itself may be poorly capitalized and carry real risk of insolvency.

Commercial Finance A 'super-category' or umbrella term used by finance providers to describe their business lines, organizational units, and activities. Commercial finance is usually used as a generic term for a range of asset-based finance services.

Commodity A raw material, for instance, foodstuff, metal ore or refined product, crude oil or oil product, for which there are normally liquid markets. Represents attractive collateral for the provision of finance.

Compliance Respect for the internal and external compulsory rules of an organization.

Consensus Mechanism A mechanism that allows computers to agree regularly on how to update the database, after which the modifications they have settled on are rendered unchangeable with the help of complex cryptography.

Consent The strategy of making a decision based on conviction and approval by all the members, who undertake to support the decision.

Continuous Improvement A structured methodology to improve the overall performance of the organization by using methods appropriate to its problems.[12] Its scope may be the quality or social responsibility of the organization. Continuous improvement is called *kaizen* in Japanese.

Corporate Performance Management (CPM) Information system for the management of key business metrics,

Crisis A situation formally declared as service interruption or the deterioration of one or more critical processes, or as systemically important because of incidents or disasters.

Critical Path Method (CPM) A network analysis technique used in complex project plans with a large number of activities. CPM diagrams

[12] Bessant, J., & Caffyn, S. (1997). High-involvement innovation through continuous improvement. *International Journal of Technology Management, 14*(1), 7–28.

all activities, the time required for their completion, and the interdependencies of each activity.[13] It is a tool for planning and control of projects through a reticular technique.

Crowdfunding The practice of funding a project or venture by raising money from a large number of persons. This takes place most often via online platforms. It can also happen through mail-order subscriptions, benefit events, and other methods. Equity crowdfunding is the process whereby persons (the 'crowd') invest, in an early stage, in unlisted organization or initiative in exchange for shares in that organization. A shareholder has partial ownership of an organization and stands to profit should that organization perform well. The opposite is also true, so if the organization fails, investors can lose some, or all, of their investment. Seedrs is an example of an equity-based crowdfunding platform in the UK.[14] Debt-based crowdfunding is when persons lend to an organization. The lenders earn a rate of return based on the interest charged on the loan. Typically, loans are secured against assets, which provide investors with some protection should the borrower fail to repay. Donation-based crowdfunding is when persons donate money to a project. In return, backers may receive token rewards that increase in prestige as the size of the donation increases; for small sums, the funder may receive nothing at all. There are two types of crowdfunding—rewards-based crowdfunding and equity-based crowdfunding. The first relates to platforms like Kickstarter or Indiegogo, where startups raise pledges and in return offer buy-in incentives for anything they produce. Equity crowdfunding is where pledgers are investors that receive a small share in the business in return for their contributions.

Customer Relationship Management (CRM) The information system for managing relationships with customers. It can manage the lifecycle of the customer, acquisition of new customers, and increase customer relationships and customer loyalty based on relationships with the organization. It lowers transaction costs between customers and the organization and integrates processes of customer management.

Customer Value Proposition The benefits a product or service holds for a customer. This is the reason a customer might buy that product or service.

[13] businessdictionary.com. Accessed June 20, 2019.

[14] https://www.seedr.cc/. Accessed April 22, 2019.

Customer The person who pays for the product, services, or activities; not necessarily the user of the product or the process or activity. Can be external or internal to the organization. In the latter case, unless there is a system of internal prices, the internal customer does not pay for the product, service, or activity but uses it. Customers should be seen as a reason for the existence of the process and not just because of the process of receptors.

Cybersecurity A set of solutions and services aimed at protecting computers, other connected devices, equipment, and ICT systems from attacks of several kinds (malware, viruses, trojans, ransomware, and so on), to prevent loss or compromise of data and information.

Cycle Time This term can be used in different situations. The cycle time provides the idea of the time it takes for a product/service to go from its beginning stage to final delivery. In the case of a manufacturing organization, the cycle time is the time that elapses between the arrival of raw materials and delivery of the finished product. If instead the cycle time is evaluated for the end customer, it can be defined as the total time that the customer must wait to receive a product/service after order.

Data Collection The process of collecting data to generate information that can be used to make decisions. In the case of a manual data collection, persons use 'sheets' check to collect information and facilitate their initial classification.

Data Governance and Compliance Defines who is responsible for what, and the policies and procedures that persons or groups need to follow. Data governance requires governing the organization's infrastructure and the infrastructure that the organization does not control. Data governance has two key components—understanding compliance and risk, and organization performance goals.

Data Source A database of personal information used by identity verification/identity proofing services to validate an identity. Examples of data sources include credit bureau records, government records, property files, customer marketing data, and telephone/utility records.

Dataset or Database It is a collection of data usually from a common source and assembled for a particular business or another purpose. The term is used generally to define data that could historically have been brought together in a document, but in an automated process is stored as a dataset.

Defects Lack of fulfillment of customer expectations by a process or service.

Define, Measure, Analyze, Develop, and Verify (DMADV) The Six Sigma method for drastic improvement of processes.

Define, Measure, Analyze, Improve, and Control (DMAIC) The Six Sigma method for continuous process improvement. This structured process eliminates non-productive steps, focusing on new measurements and applying solutions in order to improve.

Digital transformation The set of social, cultural, and technology transformations associated with the use of digital technologies.[15]

Disruptive Innovation An innovation that completely changes the way persons do something (for example, Amazon vs. in-store shopping). Describes innovations that improve products or services in unexpected ways and change both the way things are done and the market. The smartphone is an example of a disruptive solution, which has completely changed how users connect to ICT services.

Distributor Finance A defined procurement finance instrument wherein a finance provider provides financing for a distributor of a large manufacturer to cover the holding of goods for resale. Helps to bridge the liquidity gap until the receipt of funds from receivables following the sale of goods to a retailer or end-customer.

Distributor A person or entity that supplies goods on a wholesale basis to retail outlets or organizations. May be an organization entity, an arm of a manufacturing entity, or an independent entity. Can be physical or virtual.

Ecosystem The network of organizations, including partners, distributors, customers, competitors, government agencies, and so on, involved in the delivery of a specific product or service both through competition and cooperation.

Ecosystem Participants A set of organizations or individuals that can work together to gain synergies.

Electronic Data Interchange (EDI) Computer-to-computer exchange of documents in a standard format between partners.

Electronic Invoicing or e-Invoicing The exchange of an invoice document between a seller and a buyer wholly in an integrated format or dataset. Traditionally, invoicing, as with any heavily paper-based pro-

[15] Matt, C., Hess, T., & Benlian, A. (2015). Digital transformation strategies. *Business & Information Systems Engineering*, *57*(5), 339–343.

cess, is manually intensive and is prone to human error, resulting in increased costs and processing lifecycles for organizations.

Encryption The process of encoding messages or coding to protect the customer's information assets. Encryption is vital to organizations, to the blockchain, and anything else that needs to be secure. Documents or data, like names and numbers, are turned into code using algorithms (mathematical formulas). A key is required to turn that code back into readable useful data (decryption).

End-user The final user of an application.

Enterprise Content Management (ECM) The management of all content (data, unstructured documents, email, voice, video, and so on).

Enterprise Resource Planning The extension of manufacturing resource planning to the remaining functions in the organization, such as engineering, finance, and personnel administration and management. Consists of a software package with a single data model that facilitates the horizontal and vertical integration of all inter-organizational processes, improves process efficiency, and monitors processes through special KPIs according to quality, economic values, service levels, and timeliness. Some components of an ERP are accounting, industrial accounting, HR management, payrolls, sourcing, warehouse management, production, project control, sales, distribution, and facility maintenance

E-Procurement A tool for managing the cycle shop with the integration of partners B2B (business to business). Integrates the procurement process, reduces transaction costs for buyers, and simplifies the workflows for sellers with access to the market. E-procurement (electronic procurement) indicates that set of technologies, processes, operations, and organizational procedures for the acquisition of goods and services online through the opportunities offered by the development of the internet and electronic commerce's evolution and growth in the face of turbulent change.[16]

Extended Enterprise Resource Planning (EERP) An evolution of ERP, this adds tools for the control of connected partners (subsidiaries, sales channels, customers, partners, and so on).

[16]Community and Regional Resilience Institute (CARRI). Definitions of Community Resilience: An Analysis http://www.resilientus.org/wp-content/uploads/2013/08/definitions-ofcommunity-resilience.pdf, 2013. Accessed June 20, 2019.

Facilitator Someone who helps a group to achieve its full potential, through the identification and removal of barriers. He/she leads the group to achieve its mission.

Finance Provider A financial institution or other regulated or non-regulated provider of finance and related services, specifically here in the context of procurement finance.

Flow Progressive implementation of the operations from the beginning of the process until release of the result. One of the principles of Lean Thinking. In this method, the flow must proceed 'forward,' that is, toward the customer (internal or external) and proceed without interruption or rejects. It should be ensured that all activities create value without interruption from beginning to end, so that there are no waiting times, idle moments, or wastage during a step or between one phase and the next.

Flowchart A diagram or map of a process that uses symbols (for activities, for decision points, and other events) in a horizontal sequence to show what happens in a process or in the design of a new process.

Global Information Systems An organized collection of computer hardware, software, and geographic data designed to efficiently capture, store, update, process, analyze, and display all forms of geographically referenced information.[17]

Globalization The worldwide movement toward economic, financial, trade, and communications integration.[18]

Governance Refers to the controls and processes that ensure the effectiveness, efficiency, economics, and ethics of a sector. The sector might refer to the entire organization or an organization unit, process, or data.

Home Automation The set of technologies based on computer engineering and electronics, aimed at integrating devices capable of automating and simplifying the daily actions of a house or building. For using shared information, these technologies must be connected to a common computer network, usually the internet.

Identity verification The identification of individuals using their physiological and behavioral characteristics to establish a mapping from a person's online identity to their real-life identity.

[17] http://mitpress.mit.edu/books/war-weather. Accessed June 20, 2019.
[18] businessdictionary.com. Accessed June 20, 2019.

Incident An event that is not part of the standard operation of a service and that causes or may cause an interruption to, or a reduction in, the quality of that service.

Industrial Internet of Things Less known than the IoT, this is an application of it in the context of industry 4.0. The industrial internet of things (IIoT) is therefore linked to enterprise and is applied in the factory, in the context of industry 4.0. The aim is to optimize production processes through the connection between machines, whose health and functioning status is checked in advance. An IIoT object also allows operators and professionals to develop data for analysis and to control production times.

Industry 4.0 The model of production and work organization that brings automation to a form of digital integration of all components. The Fourth Industrial Revolution is based on the adoption of enabling technologies that connect physical and digital systems, analysis of information obtained from the network and more flexible management of the production cycle.

Information and Communication Technology (ICT) The combination of computers, storage, network, applications, and so on, that provides integrated computer-based services.

Input A resource introduced into the system or consumed in its operation which helps in getting a result or output.

Integration The process of combining components or systems into one integrated entity.

Internet of Everything The IoE goes beyond the interconnection of devices, involving everything: persons, objects, processes. It is the basis for a hyperconnected world that includes four categories: things, processes, data, and persons.

Internet of Humans Refers to direct or indirect interactions between devices and persons, generating a set of useful information to understand and improve the life and work of human beings.

Internet of Things The set of components and devices (for instance, sensors) embedded in objects and machinery to create an interface between the physical and digital world. Facilitates communication between objects over the internet, allowing information to be exchanged, behavior to be modified based on input received and instruction memory, and learning from interactions.

Internet Protocol The primary protocol for transmitting data or information over the internet.

Interoperability The ability of two or more systems, applications, networks, media, or components to exchange information and then use it. Applicable in different sectors.

Key Performance Indicators or Key Process Indicators KPIs are metrics (or measures) used within corporations to measure the performance of one department against another concerning revenue, sales lead conversion, costs, customer support, and so on.

Know Your Customer The process of an organization verifying the identity and standing of its customers and the character of the business or transactions they generate. Also used to refer to the legal regulations that govern these activities.

Lead Time Duration of time from the initiation to completion of an action or process. Apropos procurement, it is the amount of time from purchase order to receipt of the goods.

Lean and Digitize Method used to make processes simultaneously lean and automated, wherever it is useful to improve them.[19] The method discussed in this book is based on the review of processes to make them lean and then automated where necessary.

Lean Production An organizational and management model that achieves a structure in which the main objective is optimization of the production system, in terms of the speed of the process and eliminating waste. It is the application of improvements and standardization, and many other concepts and tools, to improve the quality, cost, or time of production. Many of the lessons learned in lean manufacturing can be applied to the operations of lean services.

Lean Six Sigma A complete, flexible, and highly structured method aimed at achieving, maintaining, and increasing customer value.[20]

Light Fidelity Technology that allows wireless communication between devices, using light to transmit high-speed data.

Loan Making available money to another party in exchange for future repayment of the principal amount plus interest or other finance charges. A loan may be for a specific, one-time amount or can be available as a variable credit line or overdraft up to a specified ceiling amount. It is also possible to make loans of actual real and financial assets.

[19] Nicoletti, B., (2012), *Lean and Digitize: An Integrated Approach to Process Improvement.* Gower Publishing, Farnham, UK. ISBN-10: 1409441946.

[20] Dahlgaard-Park, S. M., Andersson, R., Eriksson, H., & Torstensson, H. (2006). Similarities and differences between TQM, six sigma and lean. *The TQM magazine.*

Logical Security A set of processes and activities aimed at obtaining confidentiality, integrity, and availability of data and information through the adoption of measures—techniques (system for access control, anti-virus, firewalls, intrusion detection systems, and so on), organizational (definition of policies, safety standards, user profiling and related ratings, and so on), and procedural (process definition).

Management Process A method to optimize the organization as a system, determining what processes need improvement and/or control, defining priorities, and providing leadership to initiate and support efforts for improving processes. It is also the management of information obtained because of these processes.

Manufacturing Requirements Planning A computer application that automatically computes the timing and amount related to purchases and production. The outputs of these packages are obtained by analyzing the input data (cycle times, bill of materials, inventory status, and so on) from one or more databases.

Marketing The American Marketing Association defines this as the activity, set of institutions, and processes for creating, communicating, delivering, and exchanging offerings that have value for customers, partners, and society.[21]

Memorandum of Understanding A document that expresses mutual accord on an issue between two or more parties.[22]

Metrics An index of the performance of an organization that wants to show whether a goal is reached.

Mixed Reality Mixed reality overlaps physical, virtual, and augmented reality (AR) devices for an observation of the world that offers useful information (in AR) and allows interaction with virtual objects within it (in virtual reality (VR)).[23]

Mobile Device Includes smartphones, feature phones, and tablet computers. The term is also used interchangeably with 'mobile handset' or 'handset.'

MRP II The successor of manufacturing resource planning (MRP). MRP II adds to the base MRP a scheduler—module for calculation of the production capacity and the leveling of workloads.

[21] https://www.ama.org/the-definition-of-marketing/. Accessed June 22, 2019.

[22] businessdictionary.com. Accessed June 20, 2019.

[23] www.forbes.com/sites/quora/2018/02/02/the-difference-between-virtual-reality-augmented-reality-and-mixed-reality. Accessed August 12, 2019.

National Institute of Standards and Technology (NIST) A USA Department of Commerce agency which promotes the effective and secure use of cloud computing within organizations.

Near Field Communication Technology that allows the exchange of data and information without wires, between very close devices.

Node In this book, an element of the blockchain that receives/sends transactions.

Organization In this book, includes companies, public institutions, either central or local, a department, or a nonprofit organization.

Output The result of a product or system processes. Can be a product or a service and is the result produced by a system or process. The final output is normally a product, service, or initiative.

Outsourcing Defines an operation whereby an organization relies on an outside partner for the management of a specific process, sub-process, or activity already operational within the organization (usually non-core assets such as the purchase of indirect materials, administrative management, and so forth). Acquisition from an external partner of products or services that currently result from direct production activities and internal management organization.

Personal Productivity Software Software used for processing individual standards (for instance WinZip, Adobe, MS Office, Google Apps, MS Project, and so on).

Physical Value Network Describes the totality of organizations, systems, persons, activities, information, and resources involved in moving a product or service from a partner to a buyer

Platform Processing capability embedded in an ICT system and its surrounding management.

Policy In this book, a general term for an operating procedure.

Portability The ability to run applications, components, or systems running on one implementation and to deploy it on another, for instance that of another partner.

Problem The cause of an incident. Incidents that cannot be resolved due to the lack of an available solution, as well as repeated incidents related to a known issue ('known problem/error'), pass through the process of problem management. A workaround could remediate the problem, before finding the root causes and resolving them.

Process A set of interrelated activities that transform a set of inputs on one or more results. Sometimes the process is identified with a system. It would be correct to regard it as a component of a system.

Process Improvement A continuous effort to learn the causes and effects in a process to reduce complexity, variations, and the time required. The process gets better by removing incorrect causes. Through the redesign of the process, it is possible to reduce variations in common causes. Eliminating or reducing the effects of root causes improves processes.

Process Management Method used to optimize the organization as a system, determine which processes need to be improved and/or controlled, define priorities, and encourage leadership to initiate and sustain process improvement efforts. Manages the information obtained in these processes.

Procure to Pay Cycle or Process (P2P) Represents the process steps and time intervals between procurement, issue of a purchase order, delivery of goods and services, receipt of invoice, and payment to a partner.

Procurement Refers to the initiation, design, development, acquisition, logistics of goods and services for an organization. Procurement generalizes further the management of the value network, also including strategic aspects and outside the organization.

Procurement Finance This term generalizes the supply chain finance including all financial aspects of the entire procurement process, including trade finance, payments, and other instruments.[24]

Procurement Transaction A procurement transaction sets out descriptions, quantities, prices, discounts, payment terms, dates of performance or shipment, and other associated terms and conditions, and identifies a specific partner. It is used to control the sourcing of products and services from external partners. When accepted by the seller, it forms the basis of a contract which is binding for both parties.

Program A set of projects with similar objectives. An example is the set of projects for the improvement of systems installed at different subsidiaries of the same group.

Project Team A group consisting of persons from the same sector or, better, from different fields (and in some cases, from different organizations) working for a certain period to improve processes or implement an output.

[24] Nicoletti, B. (2018), *Procurement Finance*, Springer International Publishing, London, UK.

Purchase Order A buyer-generated document or dataset authorizing a purchase.

Quality A concept not easily defined, because there are several variants, at times specified by an adjective or specification added to the name. In general, one can say that quality is customer satisfaction expressed in a way that is profitable for the organization. There are many variations of the concept of quality, sometimes determined by an adjective or specifications.

Quality Checks The tools and operational activities undertaken to meet quality requirements.

Quality Plan A document or set of documents that describe standards, quality practices, resources, and activities.

Relationship Manager A dedicated customer service manager assigned to look after specific customers, usually high net worth customers.

Reporting Consists of supplying and updating representative data and indicators whose degree of detail tends to vary depending on the person or organization for whom or for which they are intended. For sustainable development, tools such as the GRI (Global Reporting Initiative) enable a standardized method to be agreed on at the international level.[25] In a certain number of countries, some laws require that all organizations beyond a certain size publish a corporate social responsibility or sustainability report.

Resilience The ability to anticipate risks, limit impacts, and bounce back rapidly through survival, adaptability, evolution, and growth in the face of turbulent change.[26]

Resilient Design Design that exceeds the level of robustness and/or redundancy of the life code such that impacts to facilities and associated systems from disruptive events are minimized.

Response Immediate and ongoing activities, tasks, programs, and systems to manage the effects of an incident that threatens life, property, operations, or the environment.[27]

[25] Willis, A. (2003). The role of the global reporting initiative's sustainability reporting guidelines in the social screening of investments. *Journal of Business Ethics*, 43(3), 233–237.

[26] Community and Regional Resilience Institute (CARRI) (2013). Definitions of Community Resilience: An Analysis http://www.resilientus.org/wp-content/uploads/2013/08/definitions-ofcommunity-resilience.pdf. Accessed July 30, 2019.

[27] www.nfpa.org/codes-and-standards. Accessed June 20, 2019.

Risk The effect of uncertainty on objectives, often expressed in terms of a combination of the consequences of an event and the associated likelihood.[28]

SaaS Software as a Service. One of the ways to use cloud computing, based on using the software as a service offered by a third party on their computers. It is a software distribution model in which applications are hosted by a partner or service partner and made available to customers over a network, typically the internet. Many fintech startups use this software distribution model. It refers to applications hosted by a partner on the cloud. Users can access them online for a subscription fee, as opposed to users buying the license of software outright in a hard or soft format like a tape or a CD.

Service Vendor An organization such as a bank, telecommunication organization, merchant, or such like that provides services to be integrated, for instance, with near field communication (NFC) mobile payments.

Sharing Economy An economic model based on sharing, swapping, trading, or renting products and services, enabling access or use over ownership.[29] It is reinventing not just what is consumed but how it is consumed.

Short Message Service A system of communicating by short messages over a mobile network. Can be rather secure if encrypted.

Sigma (σ) Eighteenth letter of the Greek alphabet. In statistical theory, it is connected with the variance. A metric based on the number of defects that occur per million opportunities.

Single Point of Failure It is an element or part of a system for which no backup exists and the failure of which will disable the entire system.[30]

Six Sigma A method and performance goal.[31] This method is a structured approach to continuous process improvement. The goal is a measure of the performance of a process defined as the number of defects per million opportunities. It is a philosophy, a performance objective, and a structured method for the continuous improvement of processes.

[28] www.iso.org/iso/catalogue_detail?csnumber=44651. Accessed June 20, 2019.

[29] Geissdoerfer, M., Savaget, P., Bocken, N. M., & Hultink, E. J. (2017). The Circular Economy–A new sustainability paradigm?. *Journal of cleaner production*, *143*, 757–768.

[30] businessdictionary.com. Accessed June 20, 2019.

[31] Schroeder, R. G., Linderman, K., Liedtke, C., & Choo, A. S. (2008). Six Sigma: Definition and underlying theory. *Journal of operations Management*, *26*(4), 536–554.

The objective is a measure of process performance defined in terms of defects, with 3.4 defective parts per million opportunities.

Smart Contracts A computer program that automatically executes a contract or part of a contract. These are automated and often blockchain-based contracts. They could save time and reduce costs in common transactions. Smart contracts are computer protocols that facilitate, verify, or enforce a digital contract. The idea is that these programs potentially replace notaries, lawyers, and financial institutions when handling common legal and financial transactions. Technically, it is a piece of code stored on a blockchain, triggered by blockchain transactions, and which reads and writes data in that blockchain database.

Sole Source Supplier A source that provides highly specialized services and from which all required design and construction services must be procured.

Sponsor A person in the organization, normally at a high level, who sponsors a project or initiative, having the necessary authority and power. Usually a member of the executive. An important success factor for a project.

Stakeholder An individual, group, or organization that is likely to be affected, directly or indirectly, by an activity, program, or particular arrangement of an organization. Stakeholders include all those groups that participate or are otherwise involved in its economic life (employees, customers, partners, shareholders), those who observe the organization (unions, nongovernmental organizations), and those that it affects either directly or indirectly (civil society, local authorities, and so on).

Standards Indications of voluntary or compulsory standardization.

Steering Committee A group that assembles periodically. It includes representatives of the executive, the project leader, and facilitators. Its main responsibilities are management of the efforts of the improvement process, assessment of the needs and overseeing support and training within its area of responsibility, communication of progress to all stakeholders and agreement on the direction of efforts.

Straight-Through Processing The implementation of a system that requires no personal intervention for the approval or processing of a customer application or transaction.

Supply Chain Finance (SCF) Use of financing and risk mitigation practices and techniques to optimize the management of working capital and liquidity invested in supply chain processes and transactions. SCF is typically applied to open account trade and is triggered by supply chain events. Visibility of underlying trade flows by the finance provider(s) is a necessary component of such financing arrangements, which can be enabled by a platform.

SWOT Analysis A structured planning method used to evaluate the strengths, weaknesses, opportunities, and threats involved in a project, initiative, or organization or a part of them.

System A network of interacting components that cooperate to achieve the objectives of the system.[32]

Tablet A general-purpose computer contained in a single panel, with a touchscreen as the input device.

Task Order A supplementary contractual and obligating document that usually includes a description of tasks.[33]

Telematics Denotes the synergy between telecommunications and informatics. In this book, it is included as part of ICT.

Threat A negative event that can cause a risk to become a loss. A threat may be a natural event such as an earthquake, flood, storm, or a human-made incident such as fire, power failure, sabotage, and so on.[34]

Throughput A metric on how quickly a service responds.

Time to Market In the process of development of new products, this is the time that elapses between the first phase of the concept of a new product and its launch on the market.

Total Cost Management (TCM) A business philosophy of managing the entire organization's resources and the activities that consume those resources. Managing costs in a TCM approach means focusing on activities and events, circumstances, or the conditions that cause or drive these cost-consuming activities.

Total Cost of Ownership A metric that takes into account the costs all along with the lifecycle of a solution. Typically includes procurement costs, installation, testing, maintenance, use, and disposal at the end of useful life.

Trade Finance A 'super-category' or umbrella term used by finance providers to describe their business lines, organizational units, and activities. Trade finance is usually used as a generic term for a range of traditional trade finance techniques and evolving procurement finance techniques.

[32] Deming, W.E. (1994). *The new economics for industry, government, education.* MIT Press; Boston, MA.

[33] businessdictionary.com. Accessed June 20, 2019.

[34] businessdictionary.com. Accessed June 20, 2019.

Transaction The action of executing a function or an application. An example of a transaction is the execution of a purchase at the point of sale and the processing of authorization and clearing messages.

Trust The ability for two parties to define a reliable relationship with a formal authentication of the two parties.

Validation A method to provide specific personal information to prove ownership of the identity for identity verification.

Value Chain Process used to deliver a good or service.

Value Engineering A systematic approach to reducing costs without reducing function.

Value Network Mapping The identification and subsequent graphical representation of all activities performed in the value network for a product/service or a family of products/services.

Value Network A set of activities required to design, order, manufacture, and supply (or provide in the case of a service) a given product or service. These activities cover the entire cycle of the product/service organization to the end customer. An objective analysis of the value network is to classify tasks into categories. The value network can be seen as the sequence of activities that bring value to the customer (and indirectly to the organization).

Value Value is defined by the end-user. Conceptually, it is the relationship between benefits and cost/damage of a product or service. It is expressed in terms of a product/service able to meet customer's needs at a given price and at a given time. It is also possible to talk about the value perceived by the customer as all the features of the product/service that the customer deems necessary and valuable. Any activity that consumes resources (including time) and does not create value is a waste (***muda*** in Japanese).

Variance In statistics, the average of the squared deviations. This is a dispersion index.

Variations Changes in the quantity or time value between cases caused by acts and not predictable.

Vendor Kanban Kanban handling/withdrawal. Used for the handling of material from the outside of the site/s of the organization for informing the partners. Indicates the cycle of the Kanban, in other words, the type of product to be supplied, the number and frequency of delivery.

Vendor A person or organization that provides goods or services for use by the process that is designed. In this book, the term denotes a partner.

Vendor-Managed Inventory A family of business models in which the buyer of a product (an organization) provides certain information to a partner of that product and the partner takes full responsibility for maintaining an agreed inventory of the material or components, usually at the buyer's consumption location (such as a store). Analogous to the holding of consignment stock.

Vertical and Horizontal Integration Vertical integration is the implementation of information and management systems capable of interacting and exchanging information between subjects in the production chain. Horizontal integration is the implementation of systems capable of interacting with organizations, distributors, and partners in the same value network.

Virtual Reality VR simulates reality, replacing it with a digital environment whose input is made possible by special accessories that allow an operator to interact within VR.

Vision The expression of what would represent success for an organization. The goal is to produce a mental image to strive toward so as to make sure that the organization produces and capitalizes on creative tensions between the current reality and the vision. For the value to be shared by the entire organization requires a lot of time, effort, and patience, and so having a mission is how the organization must make progress toward its vision. This is an expression of what would represent a success for the organization.

Voice of the Customer The customer's voice, or the voice of the citizen, in the case of public organizations.

Vulnerability Intrinsic properties of a system resulting in susceptibility to a hazard that can lead to an event.

Wearable technologies Solutions, developed based on the human body, which become natural support to make them work. These technologies detect and monitor the biological and emotional signals of the body, making it a valid solution for human needs.

Working Capital Financial resources invested by an organization in financing its current trading operations, usually expressed as the difference between current assets (receivables, inventory, and operating cash balances) and current liabilities (payables and short-term debt).

Zero-Notice Event An event that cannot be forecasted so that preparations can be made prior to its impact. An earthquake is an example of a zero-notice event.

References

‘- (2015, April), Cyber-Resilience in Supply Chains, *Technology Innovation Management Review*.

A.T. Kearney. (2015). *Digital supply chains: increasingly critical for competitive edge*. A.T. Kearney.

Abdi, F., Shavarini, S., & Hoseini, S. (2006), Glean lean: how to use lean approach in services industries?. *Journal of Services Research*, special issue, 6: 191–206.

Abeyratne, S. A., & Monfared, R. P. (2016), *Blockchain Ready Manufacturing Supply Chain Using Distributed Ledger*.

Accenture. (2014). *Global operations megatrend study: big data analytics in supply chain: hype or here to stay?* Canada. https://www.accenture.com/t20160106T194441__w__/fi-en/_acnmedia/Accenture/Conversion-Assets/DotCom/Documents/Global/PDF/Digital_1/Accenture-Global-Operations-Megatrends-Study-Big-Data-Analytics-v2.pdf [Accessed July 24, 2019].

Aggogeri, F. & Gentili, E. (2006), *Lean Six Sigma: la nuova frontiera per la qualità. La sinergia tra six sigma & lean production per un innovativo metodo di gestione & miglioramento dei processi industriali*, FrancoAngeli, Milan. Italy.

Agostini, L., Filippini, R. (2019). Organizational and managerial challenges in the path toward Industry 4.0. *European Journal of Innovation Management*. 22, 406–421.

Ahmed, E. et al. (2017), The role of big data analytics in Internet of Things, *Computer Network*,

Aisbett, J., Lasch, R., & Pires, G. (2005). A decision-making framework for adoption of e-procurement. *International Journal of Integrated Supply Management*, *1*(3), 278–293.

B. Nicoletti, *Procurement 4.0 and the Fourth Industrial Revolution*,
https://doi.org/10.1007/978-3-030-35979-9

Albrecht, C., Dean, D., & Hansen, J. (2005), Marketplace and technology standards for B2B e-commerce: progress, challenges, and the state of the art, *Information and Management*, 42.

Andriolo, A., Battini, D., Grubbström, R. W., Persona, A., & Sgarbossa, F. (2014). A century of evolution from Harris's basic lot size model: survey and research agenda. *International Journal of Production Economics*, *155*, 16–38.

Antony, J. (2006). Six Sigma for service processes. *Business Process Management Journal*. 12 (2): 234–248.

Antony, J., Kumar, M. & Byung, R. C. (2007). Six sigma in service organizations. Benefits, challenges & difficulties, common myths, empirical observations & success factors. *International Journal of Quality & Reliability Management*, 24 (3): 294–311.

Armbrust, M. et al. (2009), Above the Clouds: A Berkeley View of Cloud Computing, *Technical Report No. UCB/EECS-2009-28*.

Arnold, U. (1997). *Beschaffungsmanagement*. Stuttgart: Schäffer-Poeschel Verlag, Stuttgart, Germany.

Arnolds, H., Heege, F., Röh, C., & Tussing, W. (2013). *Materialwirtschaft und Einkauf* (12th ed.). Springer Gabler, Wiesbaden, Germany.

Ashton, K. (2009), That 'Internet of Things' Thing, *RFiD J*.

Atti, G. (2018). *La quarta rivoluzione industriale: verso la supply chain digitale. Il futuro degli acquisti pubblici & privati nell'era digitale*, FrancoAngeli, Milan, Italy.

Aymerich, F. M., Fenu, G., & Surcis, S. (2008, August). An approach to a cloud computing network. In *2008 First International Conference on the Applications of Digital Information and Web Technologies (ICADIWT)* IEEE, 113–118.

Baker, M. J., Nicoletti, B., et al. (1988). *L'impresa mondiale: Nuove strategie di produzione*, Franco Angeli, Milan, Italy

Bartezzaghi, E., & Ronchi, S. (2004), A portfolio approach in the e-purchasing of materials, *European Journal of Purchasing and Supply Management*, 10, 117–126.

Bartezzaghi, E., & Ronchi, S. (2005), E-sourcing in a buyer-operator-seller perspective: benefits and criticalities, *Production Planning and Control*, 16(4), 405–412.

Batran, A., Erben, A., & Spell, F. (2017). *Procurement 4.0*. University of Chicago Press Economics Books, Chicago, IL

Bauer, W., Schlund, S., Marrenbach, D., & Ganschar, O. (2014). *Industrie 4.0: Volkswirtschaftliches Potenzial für Deutschland*. Berlin: BITKOM.

Berman, B. (2012). 3-D printing: the new industrial revolution. *Business Horizons*, *55*(2), 155–162.

Bertelè, U., & Rangone, A. (2005), *eProcurement, eSupply Chain: una scelta tattica o strategica?*, School of Management – Politecnico di Milano, Milan, Italy.

Bertels T. (2003), *Rath & Strong's Six Sigma Leadership Handbook*, John Wiley & Sons, Hoboken, NJ.

Bienhaus, F., & Haddud, A. (2018). Procurement 4.0: factors influencing the digitisation of procurement and supply chains. *Business Process Management Journal, 24*(4), 965–984.

Blanchard, D. (2016). A Smarter Way to Run a Supply Chain, *IndustryWeek*, June 26.

Bodenstab, J. (2016). Ex Machina: AI and the Future of Supply Chain Planning, *ToolsGroup*, January 12.

Bokelberg, E., Doral, C., Feinzig, S., Guenole, N., Lesser, E., Mertens, J., & Steele, S. (2017). Extending expertise: How cognitive computing is transforming HR and the employee experience. https://www.ibm.com/downloads/cas/QVPR1K7D. Accessed June 30, 2019.

Booth, B; & Sharma, A. (2019). *Cognitive Procurement: Seizing the AI Opportunity.* IBM Institute for Business Value https://www.ibm.com/downloads/cas/MV6LX6R2, Accessed June 30, 2019.

Botthof, A. (2015). Zukunft der Arbeit im Kontext von Automatik und Industrie 4.0. In A. Botthof & E. A. Hartmann (Eds.), *Zukunft der arbeit in industrie 4.0,* 3–8. Springer, Berlin, Germany.

Bovaird, T. (2016), The ins & outs of outsourcing & in procurement: what have we learnt from the past 30 years?, *Public Money & Management*, 36:1, 67–74.

Brandon-Jones, A. & Kauppi, K. (2018). Examining the antecedents of the technology acceptance model within e-procurement, *International Journal of Operations & Production Management*, 38(1): 22–42.

Butner, K., Lubowe, D. & Ho, G. (2017). Welcome to the cognitive supply chain. IBM Institute for Business Value. www-935.ibm.com/services/us/gbs/thoughtleadership/cognitivesupplychain/. Accessed June 30, 2019.

Carvalho, H., Barroso, A. P., Machado, V. H., Azevedo, S., & Cruz-Machado, V. (2012), Supply chain redesign for resilience using simulation. *Computers & Industrial Engineering, 62*(1), 329–341.

Cecere, L. (2016). Go Horizontal. *Supply Chain Shaman*, June 21. http://www.supplychainshaman.com/demand/demanddriven/go-horizontal/. Accessed March 10, 2019.

Chopra, S., Dougan, D., & Taylor, G. (2001), B2B e-commerce opportunities, *Supply Chain Management Review*, May/June, 50–58.

Christopher, M. (2016). Want to Thrive in Disruptive Times? Start with an Agile Supply Chain. *Longitudes*, February 28.

Christopher, M., & Lee, H. (2004). Mitigating supply chain risk through improved confidence. *International journal of physical distribution & logistics management, 34*(5), 388–396.

Cimini, C., Pezzotta, G., Pinto, R., & Cavalieri, S. (2018, June). Industry 4.0 Technologies Impacts in the Manufacturing and Supply Chain Landscape: An

Overview. In *International Workshop on Service Orientation in Holonic and Multi-Agent Manufacturing* 109–120. Springer, Chem, Switzerland.

Clarke, I., & Flaherty, T. (2003), Web-based B2B portals, *Industrial Marketing Management*, 32.

Croom, S.R. (2000), The impact of web-based procurement on the management of operating resources supply, *The Journal of Supply Chain Management*, Winter.

Davenport, T. H., & Dyché, J. (2013). Big data in big companies. *International Institute for Analytics, 3.*

Davenport, T. H., & Harris, J. G. (2007). Competing on Analytics: The New Science of Winning. Harvard Business School Press, Cambridge, MA.

Davila, A., Gupta, M., & Palmer, R. (2003, February), Moving procurement systems to the internet: the adoption and use of e-procurement technology models, *European Management Journal*, 21(1).

Day, M. (2002), *Handbook of purchasing management*, Gower Publishing, Ltd, Farnham, UK.

Deloitte (2014), Industry 4.0: challenges and solutions for the digital transformation and use of exponential technologies. www2.deloitte.com. Accessed December 18, 2018.

Deloitte, (2017a), Digital Procurement New Capabilities form Disruptive Technologies, https://www2.deloitte.com/content/dam/Deloitte/us/Documents/process-and-operations/us-cons-digital-procurement.pdf. Accessed February 25, 2019.

Deloitte. (2017b). *Using autonomous robots to drive supply chain innovations.* https://www2.deloitte.com/content/dam/Deloitte/us/Documents/manufacturing/us-manufacturing-autonomous-robots-supply-chain-innovation.pdf. Accessed July 24, 2019.

Dobrin, C. (2014), Industry 4.0, M2m, Iot&S – All Equal?, *Acta Universitatis Cibiniensis. Technical Series*, v 64, n 1, 40–5, Nov. 2014; ISSN: 1583–7149; DOI: https://doi.org/10.2478/aucts-2014-0008; De Gruyter Open, Romania.

Donham, P. (2007), *Aligning IT to Business Processes: How BPM is Complementing ERP & Custom Applications*, Aberdeen Group, http://www.aberdeen.com/summary/report/benchmark/4097-RA-Align-Business.asp, Accessed January 20, 2019.

Doyle, P., Woodside, A. G., & Michell, P. (1979), Organizations buying in new task & rebuy situations, *Ind. Mark. Manag.*

Drath, R. (2014). Industrie 4.0. Eine Einführung. *Open Automation, 3*, 2–7.

Durgesh P., & Sharma M.K. (2009), Cloud Computing, *CSI Communication -2009*, 32(10), 10–13.

Eckerson, W. W. (2007). *Predictive analytics: extending the value of your data warehousing investment.* Renton: TDWI Research.

Eminente, G. & Nicoletti, B. (1985), *Strategia organizzazionele & sviluppo tecnologico*, Il Mulino, Bologna, Italy.

Eric W., & Sleigh, E. W, (2018), After GDPR, what's next for technology companies? *Thomson Reuters*, May 25.

European Commission (1997), European Initiative in Electronic Commerce, COM(97) 157, April, chapter 1. Also available at http://www.cordis.lu/esprit/src/ecomcom.htm. See also related publications at www.ispo.cec.be/ecommerce/.

European Commission (2004a), Communication to the Council, the European Parliament, the European Economic and Social Committee and the Committee of the Regions. *Action plan for the implementation of the legal framework for electronic public procurement.*

European Commission (2004b), On the coordination of procedures for the award of public works contracts, public supply contracts and public service contracts, *Directive 2004/18/EC of the European Parliament and of the Council*, March 31.

Fekete, N. (2016). What Can Artificial Intelligence Do for You? *Procurement Leaders*, June 20.

Fonseca, L.M. (2018). Industry 4.0 and the digital society: concepts, dimensions and envisioned benefits, *Sciendo*, 12(1), 386–397.

Fontana, F., Lacchini, M., & Nicoletti, B. (1966), *Casi di Management*, Giappichelli, Torino, Italy.

Forrester Research (1997), Sizing Intercompany Commerce, July 28. www.forrester.com. Accessed July 19, 2019.

Fostec. (2018). *Industrie 4.0.* https://www.fostec.com/de/kompetenzen/digitalisierungs-strategie/industrie-4-0/. Accessed July 19, 2019.

Foster, G., & Gupta, M. (1990). Manufacturing overhead cost driver analysis. *Journal of Accounting and Economics, 12*, 309–337.

Foster, M. (2019a). Expert Insights: The Cognitive Enterprise: Reinventing your company with AI- Seven keys to success, IBM Institute for Business Value https://www.ibm.com/events/in-en/think/skills-summit/assets/cog_enterprise_reinventing_your_company_research_insights_v2.pdf. Accessed July 19, 2019.

Foster, M. (2019b). *The Cognitive Enterprise: Part 1 – The journey to AI & the rise of platform-centric business architectures.* IBM Institute for Business Value. January. ibm.com/business/value/cogentpart1. Accessed June 30, 2019.

Francisco, K., & Swanson, D. (2018), The Supply Chain Has No Clothes: Technology Adoption of Blockchain for Supply Chain Transparency, *Logistics*, 2(1), 2.

G7-10 WG (1997), Electronic Commerce Better Practice, case study book of the G7 Global Marketplace for SMEs Pilot Project, first edition April. A Web version can be found at www.ispo.cec.be/ecommerce/bonn.html. Accessed July 19, 2019.

Garimella, K. K. (2006), *The Power of Process*, Meghan-Kiffer Press, Tampa, FL.

Gartner (2018), Dark Data. https://www.gartner.com/it-glossary/dark-data. Accessed January 19, 2019.

Gaudeul, A. and B. Jullien (2001): E-commerce: Quelques elements d'economie industrielle. *Revue Economique*, 52, 97–117.

Geissbauer, R., Weissbarth, R., & Wetzstein, J. (2016). *Procurement 4.0: are you ready for the digital revolution?* United States: Strategy&, PwC.

Glas, A. H., & Kleemann, F. C. (2016a). The impact of industry 4.0 on procurement and supply management: a conceptual and qualitative analysis. *International Journal of Business and Management Invention*, *6*(5), 55–66.

Glas, A. H., & Kleemann, F. C. (2016b). The impact of industry 4.0 on procurement and supply management: A conceptual and qualitative analysis. *International Journal of Business and Management Invention*, 5(6), 55–66.

Goldratt, E. M., & Jeff Cox, J. (2004), *The Goal: A Process of Ongoing Improvement*, 2nd. Ed., North River Publishing Corporation, Great Barrington, MA.

Gonzalez, R., Gasco, J., & Llopis, J. (2005), Information systems outsourcing risks: a study of large provider. *Industrial management & Data systems*, *105*(1), 45–62.

Grochla, E., & Schönbohm, P. (1980). *Beschaffung in der Unternehmung*. Stuttgart: Poeschel.

Grossman, R. L. (2009), The case of cloud computing, IEEE-2009, *Cloud Computing: First International Conference*, CloudCom 2009, Beijing, China.

Gulati, R. (2013), *Reorganize for resilience: Putting customers at the center of your business*. Harvard Business Review Press, Cambridge, MA.

Gyorffi, M. (2017). Digitising Industry (Industry 4.0 and Cybersecurity.) European Parliament. Industry, Research and Energy (ITRE). http://www.europarl.europa.eu/RegData/etudes/BRIE/2017/607361/IPOL_BRI(2017)607361_EN.pdf, Accessed August 7, 2019.

Hackius, N., & Petersen, M. (2017), Blockchain in Logistics & Supply Chain: Trick or Treat? Digit. Supply Chain Manag. Logist. in *Proceedings Hamburg International Conference on Logistics*, 3–18. https://tore.tuhh.de/bitstream/11420/1447/1/petersen_hackius_blockchain_in_scm_and_logistics_hicl_2017.pdf, Accessed May 16, 2019.

Halaburda, H., (2018). Blockchain Revolution Without the Blockchain. Bank of Canada Staff Analytical Note 2018–5. https://ssrn.com/abstract=3133313 or https://doi.org/10.2139/ssrn.3133313. Accessed February 26, 2019.

Hartley, J, Lane, L, & Hong, Y (2004, May), An exploration of the adoption of e-auctions in supply management, *IEEE Transactions on Engineering management*, 51(2).

Heek, R. (2006), *Implementing and Managing E-Government*, Vistaar Publication, New Delhi, India

Hofmann, E., & Rilsch, M. (2017). Industry 4.0 and the current status as well as future prospects on logistics, *Computers in Industry*, 89, 23–34.

Hofmann, E., & Rüsch, M. (2017). Industry 4.0 and the current status as well as future prospects on logistics. *Computers in Industry*, 89, 23–34.

Hofmann, M.,.Neukart, F., & Bäck, T. (2017), Artificial Intelligence & Data Science in the Automotive Industry, *Data Sci. Blog*, 489: 484–489.

Howells, R. (2016). Top 3 Drivers of Supply Chain Transformation, *Digitalist Magazine by SAP*, January 20.

Hütter, S.H. (2007). *Beschaffungskosten und eProcurement.* Lohmar: Josef Eul Verlag, Siegburg, Germany.

Iansiti, M., & Lakhani, K. R. (2017), The truth about blockchain, *Harvard Business Review.*

Janssen, M, Cresswell, A (2005), Enterprise Architecture Integration in E-Government, *Proceedings of the 38th Annual Hawaii International Conference on System Sciences*, January 3.

Jeske, M., Grilner, M., & Weig, F. (2013). Big Data in Logistics. www.dhl.com. Accessed July 19, 2019.

Jeston, J., & Nelis, J. (2006), *Business Process Management*, Elsevier Science B.V., Amsterdam, Netherlands.

Johannsen, F. & Leist, S. (2009). A Six Sigma approach for integrated solutions. *Managing Service Quality*, 19 (5): 558–80.

Jones, D. T., & Womack, J. P. (2006), *Lean thinking. Come creare valore & bandire gli sprechi*, Guerini, Milan. Italy.

Jost, J. (2019), Im Wandel der Digitalisierung, *Thesis Hochschule Furtwangen, Germany.*

Jullien, B (2005): Two-Sided Markets and Electronic Intermediaries *CESifo Economic Studies*, 51 (2–3): 235–262

Jullien, B (2006): Pricing and other business strategies for e-Procurement platforms, in Dimitri, N., Piga, G. and Spagnolo, G. (eds), *Handbook of Procurement*, Cambridge University Press, Cambridge, UK

Kagermann, H. (2015). Change through digitization: value creation in the age of industry 4.0. In Albach, H., Meffert, A. Pinkwart, H. & Reichwald, R. (Eds.) (2015), *Management of permanent change*, 23–45. Wiesbaden: Springer Gabler.

Kagermann, H., Wahlster, W., & Helbig, J. (2012). *Umsetzungsempfehlung für das Zukunftsprojekt Industrie 4.0: Abschluss des Arbeitskreises Industrie 4.0.* Berlin: Acatech.

Kalakota, R (2000), Next-generation B2B solutions, *Supply Chain Management Review*, July/August

Kamble, S. S., Gunasekaran, A., & Gawankar, S. A. (2018). Sustainable Industry 4.0 framework: A systematic literature review identifying the current trends and future perspectives. *Process Safety and Environmental Protection*, 117, 408–425.

Kaplan, J. M., Bailey, T., ÒHalloran, D., Marcus, A., & Rezek, C. (2015), *Beyond Cybersecurity: Protecting Your Digital Business*, John Wiley, Hoboken, NJ.

Kaplan, S, & Sawhney, M (2000), E-hubs: the new B2B marketplaces, *Harvard Business Review*, May–June, 97–103

Kastner, P. S., (2006). The Business Process Management Benchmark Report, Aberdeen Group, http://www.aberdeen.com/summary/report/benchmark/RA_BPM_PK_3385.asp, Accessed February 26, 2019.

Kaufman, J. & Sato, Y. (2005), Value Analysis Tear-Down: A New Process for Product Development & Innovation, Industrial Press Inc., New York, NY.

Kayikci, Y. (2018). Sustainability impact of digitization in logistics, Procedia Manufacturing, 21, 782–789.

Keen, P., & McDonald, M. (2000), *The eProcess Edge: Creating Customer Value & Business in the Internet Era.*, Osborn/McGraw-Hill, New York, NY.

Kenneth F. C., Gupta, A., & Sommer, D. (2015). *Maverick Research: Surviving the Rise of 'Smart Machines,' the Loss of 'Dream Jobs' & '90% Unemployment,'* Gartner Maverick Research. September 23, 2013, refreshed January 6, 2015.

Kerkhoff, G., Schäfer, D. et al (2017). *Procurement 4.0: Digitales Management von Variantenvielfalt zur kontinuierlichen Best-Preis-Sicherung – Erfolgreiche Praxisbeispiele.* Wiley VCH Verlag GmbH, Weinhaim, Germany.

Khuan, L. S., & Swee, M. F. S. H. (2018). Technologies for Procurement: Current Trends & Emerging Trends. *Emerging Technologies for Supply Chain Management*, Chapter 4; 45–61

Kiel, D., Arnold, C., & Voigt, K.-I. (2017). The influence of the industrial internet of things in business models of established manufacturing companies: a business level perspective. *Technovation, 68*, 4–19.

Kim, J, & Shunk, D (2004), Matching indirect procurement process with different B2B e-procurement systems, *Computers in Industry*, 53

Kimberley, J., & Minvielle, E., (2000). *The Quality imperative. Measurement & management of Quality in healthcare*, 1st reprint, Imperial College press, London, UK,

Kleemann, F.C. & Glas, A. H. (2017). *Einkauf 4.0: Digitale Transformation Der Beschaffung*, Springer Gabler, Wiesbaden, Germany.

Kleindorfer, P.R., & Saad, G. H. (2005). Managing disruption risks in supply chains. *Production & operations management, 14*(1), 53–68.

Kloppenborg, T.J., & Petrick, J.A., (2002). *Managing Project Quality, Management Concepts*, Vienna, VA.

Klünder, T., Dörseln, J. N., & Steven, M. (2019). Procurement 4.0: How the digital disruption supports cost-reduction in Procurement. *Production, 29.*

Koehler, P., Six, B., & Michels, J. S. (2015). Industrie 4.0: Ein Überblick. In C. Koehler-Schute (Ed.), *Industrie 4.0: Ein praxisorientierter Ansatz*, 17–39. KS-Energy, Berlin, Germany.

Kolodner, J. (2014). *Case-based reasoning.* Morgan Kaufmann, Burlington, MA.

Kotler, P. (2002). *Marketing Management*. Prentice Hall, Upper Saddle River, NJ.

Krampf, P. (2014). *Beschaffungsmanagement* (2nd ed.). München: Vahlen.

Kummer, S., Grün, O., & Jammernegg, W. (2013). *Grundzüge der Beschaffung, Produktion und Logistik* (3rd ed.). München: Pearson.

Kunreuther, H. & Heal, G. (2004), Interdependent security: the case of identical agents, *Journal of Risk & Uncertainty*, 23 (2): 103–20

Kwak, Y.H. & Anbari, F.T. (2006). Benefits, obstacles, & future of six sigma approach, *Technovation*, 26 (1): 708–15.

Larsen, T, Kotzab, H, Grieger, M (2003), Electronic marketplaces and supply chain relationships, *Industrial Marketing Management*, 32

Lasi, H., Fettke, P., Feld, T., & Hoffmann, M. (2014a). Industry 4.0. *Business & Information Systems Engineering*, *4*, 239–242.

Lasi, K., Kemper, H.-G., Fettke, P., Feld T, & Hoffmann, M. (2014b). Industry 4.0, *BISE Journal.*

Lee, H., Padmanabhan, V., & Whang, S. (1997). The bullwhip effect in supply chains. *Sloan Management Review*, *38*(3), 93–102.

Lezzi, M., Lazoi, M. & Corallo, A. (2018). Cybersecurity for industry 4.0 in the current literature: a reference framework. *Computers in Industry*,103, 97–110.

Liang, X., Shetty, S., Tosh, D., Ji, Y., & Li, D. (2018). Towards a Reliable & Accountable Cyber Supply Chain in Energy Delivery System Using Blockchain. In *International Conference on Security & Privacy in Communication Systems,* 43–62. Springer, Cham, Switzerland.

Liker, J. (2004): *The Toyota Way 14 Management Principles from the World's Greatest Manufacturer*, McGraw-Hill, New York, NY.

Liker, J., et al. (2008), *Toyota Culture: The Heart & Soul of the Toyota Way*, McGraw-Hill, New York, NY.

Liker, J.K., & Meier, D. (2006), *The Toyota Way Fieldbook*, McGraw-Hill, New York, NY.

Lima, T., Santos, B. (2018). Indústria 4.0: Desafios e Oportunidades. *Revista Produção e Desenvolvimento*, V. 4, n° 1, 111–124.

Linderman, K., Schroeder, R.G., Zaheer, S. & Choo, A.S. (2003). Six Sigma: A goal-theoretic perspective. *Journal of Operations Management*, 21 (1): 536–54.

Lombardi, R. (2019). Knowledge transfer & organizational performance & business process: past, present & future researches. *Business Process Management Journal*, *25*(1), 2–9.

Loucks, J., Davenport, T. & Schatsky, D, (2018). State of AI in the enterprise: 2nd Edition: Early adopters combine bullish enthusiasm with strategic investments, *Deloitte Insights.*

Lucking-Reiley, D. & Spulber, D. F. (2001): Business-to-Business Electronic Commerce, *Journal of Economic Perspectives*, 15 (1), pp 55–68

Lupi, C. (2007), Una intervista a Bernardo Nicoletti: Lean Six Sigma: un percorso di successo, *Sistemi & Impresa*, N. 4, May.

Luthra, S., & Mangla, S. K. (2018). Evaluating challenges to Industry 4.0 initiatives for supply chain sustainability in emerging economies. *Process Safety and Environmental Protection*, 117, 168–179.

Marawar, T, Kale, S, & Araspure, K (2010), e-Governance, *International Conference on Data Storage and Data Engineering*, Bangalore, India, February 9–10.

Martin, J.W. (2007), *Lean Six Sigma for supply chain management*, McGraw-Hill. New York, NY.

McKinsey Global Institute, (2013), Disruptive technologies: advances that will transform life, business, & the global economy. https://www.mckinsey.com/business-functions/digital-mckinsey/our-insights/disruptive-technologies, Accessed February 18, 2019.

McPhee, C., & Khan, O. (2015). Editorial: Cyber-Resilience in Supply Chains. *Technology Innovation Management Review*, *5*(4), 3–5.

Mela, F. (2019). Appalti Smart, Decolla il sito Agid per l'e.Procurement 4.0, https://www.corrierecomunicazioni.it/pa-digitale/appalti-smart-debutta-il-sito-agid-per-le-procurement-4-0/. Accessed March 3, 2019.

Melzer-Ridinger, R. (2008). *Materialwirtschaft und Einkauf* (5th ed.). München: Oldenbourg.

Mithas, S and J L Jones (2007): Do Auction Parameters Affect Buyer Surplus in E-Auctions for Procurement?, *Production and Operations Management*, 16 (4), pp 455–470

Mogre, R., Lindgreen, A., & Hingley, M. (2017). Tracing the evolution of purchasing research: future trends and directions for purchasing practices. *Journal of Business & Industrial Marketing*, 32(2), 251–257.

Mohamed, M. (2018). Challenges and benefits of Industry 4.0: an overview. *International Journal of Supply and Operations Management*. 5, 256–265.

Möllering, G., Behar, B., & Sommer, F. (2005). Strategische Beschaffung in hybriden Organisationsformen. *WiSt. Wirtschaftswissenschaftliches Studium*, *34*(6), 315–320.

Moon, M J (2005): E-procurement Management in State Governments: Diffusion of E-procurement Practices and its Determinants *Journal of Public Procurement*, 5 (1), 54–72

Mougayar, W. (2016), *The Business Blockchain*, John Wiley, Hoboken, NJ.

Muhuri, P., Shukla, A. & Abraham, A. (2019). Industry 4.0: A bibliometric analysis and detailed overview. *Engineering Applications of Artificial Intelligence*. 78. 218–235. https://doi.org/10.1016/j.engappai.2018.11.007.

Muñoz-Garcia, C., & Vila, J. (2018). Value creation in the international public procurement market: In search of springbok firms. *Journal of Business Research*.

Nakamoto, S. (2008), Bitcoin: A Peer-to-Peer Electronic Cash System | Satoshi Nakamoto Institute, 2008-10-31, http://nakamotoinstitute.org/bitcoin/, Accessed February 27, 2019.

Neef, D (2001), *E-procurement: From Strategy to Implementation* Prentice Hall, Upper Saddle River, NJ, USA

Nicoletti, B. (1986), *I circoli di qualità*, FrancoAngeli, Milan, Italy.

Nicoletti, B. (1987), *La gestione della qualità*, FrancoAngeli, Milan, Italy.

Nicoletti, B. (1994), *Management per l'edilizia*, DEI Tipografia del Genio Civile, Rome, Italy.

Nicoletti, B. (1999), *La Calidad Total y su Gestión en la Pequeña y Mediana Empresa*, Universidad Nacional de Mar del Plata, Mar del Plata, Argentina.

Nicoletti, B. (2012a), *The Methodology of Lean & Digitize*, Gower, London, UK.

Nicoletti, B. (2017a), *Agile Procurement. Volume I: Adding Value with Lean Processes*, Springer International Publishing, London, UK. ISBN 978-3-319-61082-5

Nicoletti, B. (2017b), *Agile Procurement. Volume II: Designing & Implementing a Digital Transformation*, Springer International Publishing, London, UK, ISBN 978-3-319-61085-6.

Nicoletti, B. (2018). Fintech & Procurement Finance 4.0. In *Procurement Finance*, 155–248. Palgrave Macmillan, Cham.

Nicoletti, B. (2012b), Rebalancing global procurement risk, *Procurement Leaders*, May–Jun.: 38.

Nicoletti, B. (2017c) The Future: Procurement 4.0, in, *Agile Procurement*, Palgrave Macmillan, London, UK.

Nicoletti, B. (2008). Project Management 2.0, *IPMA Congress*, Rome, Italy, Oct.: 10–13.

Normann, R. (2002), *Service Management: Strategy & Leadership in Service Business*, 3rd Edition, John Wiley & Sons, Chichester, UK.

Nowosel, K., Terrill, A., & Timmermann, K. (2015). Procurement next Frontier–The Future Will Give Rise to an Organization of One. *Accenture Strategy.*

Oakland, J. S. (2003), *TQM: Text with Cases,* Elsevier, Oxford, UK.

Olegków-Szlapka J., Stachowiak A. (2019). The Framework of Logistics 4.0 Maturity Model. In: Intelligent Systems in Production Engineering and Maintenance. ISPEM 2018. Advances in Intelligent Systems and Computing, 835. Springer, Cham, Switzerland

Osei-Bryson, K. M., & Ngwenyama, O. K. (2006). Managing risks in information systems outsourcing: An approach to analyzing outsourcing risks & structuring incentive contracts. *European Journal of Operational Research, 174*(1), 245–264.

Osmonbekov, T., & Johnston, W. J. (2018), Adoption of the Internet of Things technologies in business procurement: impact on organizational buying behavior, *J. Bus. Ind. Mark.*

Panda, P, & Sahu, G. P. (2012), E-Procurement Implementation: Critical Analysis of Success Factors' Impact on project Outcome, *Working Paper*

Pause, D., & Blum, M. (2018, August). Conceptual Design of a Digital Shadow for the Procurement of Stocked Products. In *IFIP International Conference on*

Advances in Production Management Systems, 288–295. Springer, Cham, Switzerland.

Pereira, R. C., Christopher, M., & Lago Da Silva, A. (2014). Achieving supply chain resilience: the role of procurement. *Supply Chain Management: An International Journal*, *19*(5/6), 626–642.

Pereira, T. Barreto, L. & Amaral, A. (2017). Network and information security challenges within industry 4.0 paradigm. *Procedia Manufacturing*, 13, 1253–1260.

Piercy, N., & Rich, N. V. (2008). Lean transformation in the pure service environment: the case of the call service centre. *International Journal of Operations & Production Management*, 29(1): 54–76

Plaster, G.A., & Alderman, J.D. (2006), *Beyond Six Sigma: Profitable Growth Through Customer Value Creation*, John Wiley & Sons, Hoboken, NJ.

Pokharel, M. & Park S. S. (2009), Cloud computing: future solution for e-governance, *Proceeding of the 3rd international conference on Theory and practice of electronic governance*, 409–410

PricewaterhouseCoopers – PwC. (2014). *Industrie 4.0: Chancen und Herausforderungen der vierten industriellen Revolution*. Munich: GRIN Verlag.

Prier, E, Csáki, C, McCue, C (2012), The efficacy of applying maturity models to public e- procurement and e-Government, *Proceedings of the 5th National Conference*, Seattle, USA, August 17–19.

Prieto, B, Plumbee, J. & Vaughn, D (2015a), Resilience: An Engineering & Construction Perspective; https://s3.amazonaws.com/academia.edu.documents/38644143/Resilience_Managing_the_Risk_of_Natural_Disaster.pdf?response-content-disposition=inline%3B%20filename%3DRESILIENCE_Managing_the_Risk_of_Natural.pdf&X-Amz-Algorithm=AWS4-HMAC-SHA256&X-Amz-Credential=AKIAIWOWYYGZ2Y53UL3A%2F20190606%2Fus-east-1%2Fs3%2Faws4_request&X-Amz-Date=20190606T210701Z&X-Amz-Expires=3600&X-Amz-SignedHeaders=host&X-Amz-Signature=fc3ced97e772d858a626802ee7674c81f9f84b183bfeceea9ef1ad46d03ffc6b. Accessed December 29, 2018.

Prieto, B, Plumbee, J., Vaughn, D. & Vaughn, J. (2015b), Resilience: Managing the Risk of Natural Disaster, *Fluor*, *Proceedings of the 3rd International Conference on Theory and Practice of Electronic Governance*, Bogota, Colombia, November 10–13, 409–410.

Pyzdek, T. (2003), *The Six Sigma handbook*, McGraw-Hill, New York, NY.

Radivojević, G., Bjelić, N., & Popović, D. (2017). Internet of Thing in Logistics, *Proceedings of the 3rd Logistics International Conference – LOGIC 2017*, 185–190, Belgrade, Serbia.

Rainie, L. (2018), Americans' complicated feelings about social media in an era of privacy concerns, *Pew Research*, March 27.

Rajput, S., Singh, S.P. (2018). Identifying Industry 4.0 IoT enablers by integrated PCA-ISM-DEMATEL approach. *Management Decisions*.

Rejeb, A. (2018), Blockchain Potential in Tilapia Supply Chain in Ghana, *Acta Tech. Jaurinensis Ser. Logist.*, 11: 15.

Rejeb, A., Sűle, E., & Keogh, J. G. (2018), Exploring new technologies in procurement. *Transport & Logistics: The International Journal*, 18(45), December, ISSN 2406-1069

Riva, A. (2018). The impact of Industry 4.0 on procurement & supply management: a multinational food company case. *Tesi Politecnico di Milano*, Milan, Italy.

Robinson, P. J., Faris, C. W., & Wind, Y. (1967). *Industrial buying & creative marketing*. Allyn & Bacon, Boston, MA.

Röck, D. & Hofmann, E. (2019). *Distributed ledger technology in supply chains: An information processing view. Annual Nordic Logistics Research Network Conference (NOFOMA)*, Oslo, Norway.

Roden, S., Nucciarelli, A., Li, F., & Graham, G. (2017), Big data & the transformation of operations models: A framework & a new research agenda, *Prod. Plan. Control.*

Rother, M., & Harris, R. (2006), *Creating Continuous Flow: una guida all'azione per manager, ingegneri & direttori di produzione*, The Lean Enterprise Institute, Milan, Italy.

Rother, M., & Shook, J. (2003), *Learning to See, la mappatura del flusso del valore per creare valore & eliminare i muda*, The Lean Enterprise Institute, Milan. Italy

Rübmann, M., Lorenz, M., Gerbert, P., Waldner, M., Justus, J., Engel, P., & Harnisch, M. (2015). Industry 4.0, the future of productivity and growth in manufacturing industries. BCG, The Boston Consulting Group.http://image-src.bcg.com/Images_Industry_40_Future_of_Productivity_April_2015_tcm9-61694.pdf, Accessed August 7, 2019.

Sanders, N. R., (2014). *Big Data Driven Supply Chain Management: A Framework for Implementing Analytics & Turning Information into Intelligence*. Pearson Education, 131–147.

Santos, C., Mehrsai, A., Barros, A.C., Araujo, M., &Ares, E. (2017). Towards Industry 4.0: An Overview of European Strategic Roadmaps, Procedia Manufacturing, 13, 972–979.

Schawb, K. (2017). *A Quarta Revolução Industrial*. Edição: Levoir, Marketing e Conteúdos Multimédia, S.A., Lisbon, Portugal.

Schelechtendal, J., Keinert, M., Kretschmer, F., Lechler, A. & Verl, A. (2015). Making existing production system Industry 4.0-ready In *Production Engineering Research and Development*, 9, 143–148, Springer, Cham, Switzerland.

Schlick, J., Stephan, P., Loskyll, M., & Lappe, D. (2014). Industrie 4.0 in der praktischen Anwendung. In T. Bauernhansl, M. ten Hompel & B. Vogel-Heuser (Eds.), *Industrie 4.0 in Produktion, Automatisierung und Logistik: Anwendung, Technologien, Migration*. 57–84. Springer, Wiesbaden, Germany.

Schmidt, R., Möhring, M., Härtling, R. C., Reichstein, C., Neimaier, P., & Jozinovic, P. (2015). Potentials for creating smart products: empirical research results. In W. Abramowicz (Ed.), *Business information systems*, 16–27. Springer, Cham: Switzerland.

Schoenherr, T. (2018). *The Evolution of Electronic Procurement: Transforming Business as Usual.* Springer. Cham, Switzerland.

Schoenherr, T., & Speier-Pero, C. (2015). Data science, predictive analytics, and big data in supply chain management: current state and future potential. *Journal of Business Logistics*, *36*(1), 120–132.

Schroeder, R. G., Linderman, K., Liedtke, C. & Choo, A.S. (2008). Six Sigma: Definition & underlying theory. *Journal of Operations Management*, 26 (4): 536–554.

Schrauf, S. & Berttram, P. (2016), Industry 4.0: how digitization makes the supply chain more efficient, agile, and customer-focused., www.strategyand.pwc.com/reports/industry4.0. Accessed December 21, 2018.

Seville. E. (2016), *Resilient Organizations: How to Survive, Thrive and Create Opportunities Through Crisis henkeand Change.* Kogan Page Publishers, London, UK.

Shurter, S., & Towers, S., (2002), *Customer Expectation Management & Successful Customer Outcomes*, Meghan Kiffer Press, Tampa, FL.

Silverstein, D., Samuel, P., & DeCarlo, N. (2009), *The Innovator's Toolkit*, John Wiley, Hoboken, NJ.

Simpson, M and A J Docherty (2004): E-commerce adoption support and advice for UK SMEs, *Journal of Small Business and Enterprise Development*, 11 (3), pp 315–328

Sinha, M. N. (2018). Selected papers from 9th Canadian Quality Congress. *Business Process Management Journal*, *24*(6), 1286–1288.

Skalle, Ramachandran S., Schuster M., Szaloky V., & Antoun S. (2009), *Aligning Business Process Management, Service-Oriented Architecture, & Lean Six Sigma for Real Business Results*, IBM Redbooks, Armonk, NY.

Slowik, M. (2013). World Procurement Congress: Looking into Procurement's Crystal Ball, *Procurement Leaders Global Intelligence Network*, May 21.

Slusarczyk, B. (2018). Industry 4.0 – Are we ready? *Pol. J. Manag. Stud.* 17, 232–248.

Smalley A. (2004), *Creating Level Pull, A lean production-system improvement guide for production-control, operations, & engineering professionals*, The Lean Enterprise Institute, Cambridge, MA.

Smit, J., Kreutzer, S., Moeller, C., & Carlberg, M. (2016). Industry 4.0. European Parliament. Study for the ITRE Committee. http://www.europarl.europa.eu/RegData/etudes/STUD/2016/570007/IPOL_STU(2016)570007_EN.pdfv, Accessed August 7, 2019.

Smith, H., Fingar, P. (2003a), *Business Process Management, The Third Wave*, Meghan-Kiffer, Tampa, FL.

Smith, H., Fingar, P. (2003b). *IT Doesn't matter – Business Processes Do*, Meghan-Kiffer, Tampa, FL.

Smock, D., Rudzki, R. A., A., & Rogers, S. C. (2007), *On-demand supply management: world class strategies, practices, & technology*, J. Ross Publishing, Plantation, FL.

Snee, R. D., Hoerl R. W. (2003), *Leading Six Sigma. A step-by-step Guide Based on Experience with GE & Other Six Sigma Companies*, Pearson Education, Upper Saddle River, NJ.

Snyder, N. (2016). Improving Competitive Advantage with an Intelligent Supply Chain, *IndustryWeek*, March 24.

Somasundaram, R (2004), Diffusion of e-Procurement in the Public Sector: Revisiting Centralized vs Decentralized Debates As a Twist in the Tale, *Proceedings of the 13th European Conference on Information Systems*

Somasundaram, R, Galih, S (2012), Cloud computing scheme for lower IT cost in Indonesian government's e–procurement system, *International Journal of Information and Communication Technology*, Vol 4, No 2–4, pp 187–197

Somasundaram, R, J Damsgaard (2005), Policy Recommendations for Electronic Public Procurement, *Electronic Journal of e-Government*, 3 (3), 147–156

Sousa, R. & Voss, C. (2002). Quality management re-visited: A reflective review & agenda for future research. *Journal of Operations Management*, 20 (1): 91–109.

Spekman, R. (1979), Influence & information: An exploratory investigation of the boundary role person's basis of power, *Academy of Management Journal* 22:1, 104–117.

SrinSoft, (2018), IoT (Internet of Things) Solutions & Services, [Online]. Available: https://www.srinsofttech.com/iot-solutions-internet-of-things.html. Accessed December 19.

Stamison CM, Campbell, A, Winkler, M (2011), Beyond EDI: An Agent's Role in the Cloud *Proceedings of the Charleston Library Conference*

Stephens, J., & Valverde, R. (2013), Security of E-Procurement Transactions in Supply Chain Reengineering, *Comput. Inf. Sci.*

Steven, M. (2013). *Einführung in die Produktionswirtschaft.* Kohlhammer, Stuttgart, Germany.

Steven, M., & Klünder, T. (2018). Nachhaltigkeit schlanker Industrie 4.0-Netzwerke. In A. Khare, D. Kessler & J. Wirsam (Eds.), *Marktorientiertes Produkt- und Produktionsmanagement in digitalen Umwelten*, 201–221. Springer Gabler. Wiesbaden, Germany.

Stevens, E. & Dimitriadis, S. (2004). New service development through the lens of organisational learning: evidence from longitudinal case studies. *Journal of Business Research*, 57 (10): 1074–84.

Ströhnisch, F. (2019). Development of a Maturity-and Quadrant Model to Assess and Classify E-purchasing solutions. Master's thesis, University of Twente. Twente., Netherlands.

Subramaniam, C and M J Shaw (2004): The effects of process characteristics on the value of B2B e-procurement, *Information, Technology and Management*, 5 (1–2), 161–180

Sullivan, W. E., & Ngwenyama, O. K. (2005), How are public sector organizations managing IS outsourcing risks? An analysis of outsourcing guidelines from three jurisdictions. *Journal of Computer Information Systems*, 45(3), 73–87.

Szozda, N. (2017). Industry 4.0 and its impact on the functioning of supply chains. *Logforum*, 13.

Telukdarie, A., Buhulaiga, E., Bag, S., Gupta, S., & Luo, Z. (2018). Industry 4.0 implementation for multinationals. *Process Safety and Environmental Protection*, 118, 316–329.

ten Hompel, M., & Kerner, S. (2015). Logistics 4.0: The vision of the Internet of Autonomous Things, *Informatik-Spektrum*, 38(3), 176–182.

Tessarini, G., & Saltorato, P. (2018). Impactos da indústria 4.0 na organização do trabalho: uma revisão sistemática da literatura. *Revista Produção Online*, 18(2), 743–769.

Theisen, P. (1974). Beschaffung und Beschaffungslehre. In E. Grochla & W. Wittmann (Eds.), *Handwörterbuch der Betriebswirtschaft*, 494–503. Springer, Stuttgart, Germany.

Tierney, K. & Bruneau, M. (2007), Conceptualizing & Measuring Resilience: A Key to Disaster Loss Reduction, *TR News*, May–Jun., No. 250: 14–16.

Timm, I. J., & Lorig, F. (2015), Logistics 4.0: A challenge for simulation, *2015 Winter Simulation Conference (WSC). Proceedings*, 3118–19.

Timmers, P (1998), Business Models for Electronic Markets, *CommerceNet Research Report*, September 9.

Tjahjono, B., Esplugues, C., Ares, E., & Pelaez, G. (2017). What does industry 4.0 mean to supply chain? *Procedia Manufacturing*, 13, 1175–1182.

Torn, I. A. R. (2017). The future of purchasing and industry 4.0: how purchasing can progress and benefit the fourth industrial revolution. *Master's thesis, University of Twente*, Twente, Netherlands.

Townsend, A. (2014). *Re-programming mobility*. New York: NY

Turban, E., (2008), *Information Technology for Management: Transforming Organizations in the Digital Economy*, 6th ed., John Wiley & Sons, Hoboken, NJ.

Uday, M.A., Chon, G. (2004), Applying lean manufacturing principles to information intensive services. *International Journal of Services Technology & Management*, 5(5–6): 488–506.

Ulrich, D., Kerr, S., & Ashkenas, R. (2002), *The GE Work-Out: How to Implement GÈ's Revolutionary Method for Busting Bureaucracy & Attacking Organizational Problems — Fast!*, McGraw-Hill, New York, NY.

Vaidya, S., Ambad, P., & Bhosle, S. (2018). Industry 4.0 – A Glimpse, *Procedia Manufacturing*, 20, 233–238.

Various Authors (2007), *Rath & Strong's Integrated Lean Six Sigma Pocket Guide*, Rath & Strong.

Vollmer, M. & Murphy, B. (2017). The Road to Intelligent Procurement Enabling the journey to value, file:///C:/Users/18HW010075/Downloads/The%20 Road%20to%20Intelligent%20Procurement.pdf. Accessed June 30, 2019.

Voss, C., Tsikriktsis, N. & Frohlich, M. (2002). Case Research in Operations Management. International *Journal of Operations & Production Management*, (2): 195–219.

Wagner, U. Tribis, Y., El Bouchti, A., & Bouayad, H. (2018). Supply Chain Management based on Blockchain: A Systematic Mapping Study. In *MATEC Web of Conferences* (Vol. 200, p. 00020). EDP Sciences.

Waller, M. A., & Fawcett, S. (2013). Data science, predictive analytics, and big data: a revolution that will transform supply chain design and management. *Journal of Business Logistics*, *34*(2), 77–84.

Wang, K. (2016), Logistics 4.0 Solution New Challenges and Opportunities, *Proceedings of the 6th International Workshop of Advanced Manufacturing and Automation – IWAMA 2016*, 68–74, Manchester, UK, November 10–11.

Ward, A. C. (2007), *Lean Product & Process Development*, Lean Enterprise Institute, Cambridge, MA.

Waters, D. (2011), *Supply chain risk management: vulnerability & resilience in logistics*, Kogan Page Publishers, London, UK.

West, D. M., & Allen, J. R. (2018). How artificial intelligence is transforming the world. *Brookings Institution, Washington DC.*

Wilkinson, A., Dainty, A. &, Neely, A. (2009). Changing times & changing tim-escales: the servitization of manufacturing. *International Journal of Operations & Production Management.* 29 (5): 425–30.

Williams, R (2006): Generalized ordered logit/partial proportional odds models for ordinal dependent variables *The Stata Journal*, 6 (1), 58–82

Wüllenweber, K., & Weitzel, T. (2007). An empirical exploration of h240c-240cow process standardization reduces outsourcing risks. *System Sciences*, IEEE, January: 240–250.

Yin, R. K. (2003). *Case study research: Design & methods.* 3rd Edition, in *Applied Social Research Methods Series*, Sage Publications, Beverly Hills (CA), 3rd ed.

Youseff, L, Butrico, M, & DaSilva, D (2008), Towards a Unified Ontology of Cloud Computing *Grid Computing Environments Workshop*, GCE08, 1–10

Zhang, S, Zhang, S, Chen, X, & Huo, X (2010), Cloud Computing Research and Development Trend, *2010 Second International Conference on Future Networks*

Zhou, L, Zhu, Y, Lin, Y, & Bentley, Y (2012), Cloud Supply Chain: A Conceptual Model, *The 17th International Working Seminar on Production Economics*, February 20–24, Innsbruck, Austria.

Zillmann, M. & Appel, B. (2016). *Keine Industrie 4.0 ohne Digitalisierung der Supply Chain.* Lünendonk, Mindelheim, Germany.

The manufacturer's authorised representative in the EU is Springer Nature Customer Service Centre GmbH, Europaplatz 3, 69115 Heidelberg, Germany. If you have any concerns regarding our products, please contact ProductSafety@springernature.com

Printed and bound by CPI Group (UK) Ltd, Croydon, CR0 4YY

30/09/2026

02225461-0010